Muhammad's Body

Islamic Civilization and Muslim Networks

CARL W. ERNST AND BRUCE B. LAWRENCE, EDITORS

Highlighting themes with historical as well as contemporary significance, Islamic Civilization and Muslim Networks features works that explore Islamic societies and Muslim peoples from a fresh perspective, drawing on new interpretive frameworks or theoretical strategies in a variety of disciplines. Special emphasis is given to systems of exchange that have promoted the creation and development of Islamic identities—cultural, religious, or geopolitical. The series spans all periods and regions of Islamic civilization.

A complete list of titles published in this series appears at the end of the book.

Muhammad's Body

Baraka Networks and the Prophetic Assemblage

Michael Muhammad Knight

The University of North Carolina Press
Chapel Hill

Set in Cycles with Arepo display
by Tseng Information Systems, Inc.
Manufactured in the United States of America

The University of North Carolina Press has been a member
of the Green Press Initiative since 2003.

Cover illustration: *Footmark of the Prophet*, © iStock.com/Yamko

Library of Congress Cataloging-in-Publication Data
Names: Knight, Michael Muhammad, author.
Title: Muhammad's body : baraka networks and the prophetic assemblage /
Michael Muhammad Knight.
Other titles: Islamic civilization & Muslim networks.
Description: Chapel Hill : The University of North Carolina Press, 2020. |
Series: Islamic civilization and Muslim networks | Includes bibliographical
references and index.
Identifiers: LCCN 2020004298 | ISBN 9781469658902 (cloth: alk. paper) |
ISBN 9781469658919 (pbk.: alk. paper) | ISBN 9781469658926 (ebook)
Subjects: LCSH: Muḥammad, Prophet, -632. | Barakah. | Hadith. | Human body—
Social aspects—Islamic countries. | Human body—Religious aspects—Islam.
Classification: LCC BP135.8.M85 K565 2020 | DDC 297.6/3—dc23
LC record available at https://lccn.loc.gov/2020004298

For Jibreel, from Azreal

Contents

Acknowledgments

I could not write about the Prophet as an assemblage of encounters and connections but then imagine myself as a singular intellect working in pure isolation. My work has been informed and transformed over the years by more relationships than I can name here.

First, Sadaf Knight, who makes the world in which my work is possible, and my mother, Susan Knight, who always encouraged my love of books even when I made that very, very hard.

Juliane Hammer has been a guiding light for this project at every stage. I cannot say enough for her significance to this work, her mentorship more generally, and the value of her friendship.

Laury Silvers opened so many doors for me, both in human social and professional worlds and inside my own head, and brought me to my first American Academy of Religion conference that basically started my new life.

Omid Safi has been a mentor and friend since my preacademic writing days, and I owe him so much for everything that he has given to my development.

Carl Ernst's encouragement and guidance have meant the world to me, and I am grateful to Bruce Lawrence for his continued support and generosity. Writing this in September 2019, as forces of bigotry and fear have specifically targeted the legacies of UNC-Duke collaboration in Islamic studies and Middle East studies, I become even more acutely aware of my debt to Carl and Bruce and proud to represent North Carolina's academic triangle in this field.

This project was strengthened by the insights of brilliant scholars giving me the benefit of their close reads, namely Jessica Boon sharing her expertise in mysticism and theories of the body and Scott C. Lucas sharing his expertise in these specific sources and their adjacent literatures. I am also thankful for Cemil Aydin sharing his insights and observations as this project took shape, and for our many conversations in which he made intellectual life seem like a joyful and energizing thing. Mohsen Kadivar was a treasure during my course work in North Carolina. Additionally, this book benefited immeasurably from the insights of two anonymous readers on behalf of the publisher. I thank Elaine Maisner and the University of North Carolina Press for their support to make this project materialize.

It requires a particular strength to remain optimistic about the heart of the matter while also maintaining our intellectual integrity and courage to speak the truth without flinching. No one embodies that strength like amina wadud.

Kecia Ali has been exceedingly generous to my growth, and I have also witnessed her as a model of mentorship with an entire field of rising junior scholars.

My heartfelt thanks to Scott Kugle for the ways that his scholarship has expanded our possibilities of the thinkable, and also for what he brings into the room as a human being who emanates compassion and spiritually engaged intellect.

Some things in this book were hard to say, and while I have sought to define my work in part through a willingness to say difficult things, I might have felt inclined toward caution during my first steps in a new arena. At such moments, I found inspiration and strength in the intellectual courage of Aysha Hidayatullah. I am thankful for our conversations, her work, and even her book's presence as an artifact on my desk as I wrote.

So much respect to Shehnaz Haqqani, a living template for making our own lanes in academia and thriving while remaining truly ourselves. My appreciation for the FITNA group for the conversation space that it created and maintains, and for the chance to grow through listening.

Gratitude for the scholars whom I have encountered whether strictly in their scholarship or as people in "real life" who make our field better and have enriched my own work: Sa'diyya Shaikh, Amanullah De Sondy, Edward E. Curtis IV, Ash Geissinger, Marion Katz, Kristian Petersen, Sarah Eltantawi, Shabana Mir, Kayla Wheeler.

I am thankful for my colleagues at the University of North Carolina at Chapel Hill, both within and beyond the Department of Religious Studies: Andrew Aghapour, Rose Aslan, Zahra Ayubi, Samah Choudhury, Matt Dougherty, Bo Eberle, Isaiah Ellis, Kathy Foody, Ilyse Morgenstein Fuerst, Megan Goodwin, Matt Hotham, Micah Hughes, Atiya Husain, G. A. Lipton, Matt Lynch, Kate Merriman, Candace Mixon, Shaily Patel, Travis Proctor, Shannon Schorey, Tim Smith, David Supp-Montgomerie, Jenna Supp-Montgomerie, Tehseen Thaver, and Armond Towns. On the Duke side, I am grateful for Zaid Adhami and Saadia Yacoob. Of the friends who enriched our time in North Carolina, I offer gratitude to Emmie Aghapour, Sarah Ireland, Casey Proctor, Sara Biondi Smith, and especially Leyla and Mehtap.

Respect to the undergrad-led activism that made Chapel Hill a better place before, during, and after my time there.

Before coming to North Carolina, I spent a wonderful and fruitful two years at Harvard Divinity School, where Ali Asani became my unofficial adviser and a dear friend who helped me find a way for myself into this line of work. I remember later visiting Boston and having a conversation with Arafat Razzaque that turned to connections with the Prophet via milk kinship, and walking away from it completely tripped out. That afternoon left a mark on this project. Peace to Shahab Ahmed, whose Ibn ʿArabi seminar was a transformative experience.

Appreciation for my UCF colleagues for their warm welcome and generous collaborative spirit, especially Ann Gleig, Shelley Park, Claudia Schippert, Jeanine Viau, and Cyrus Zargar.

My deep personal gratitude for the Muslim Alliance for Sexual and Gender Diversity (MASGD), which invited me to an ally workshop shortly after my arrival in Orlando. My gratitude for every time that I'm invited to a Muslim space. Thank you to every reader who took the time to reach out after already giving time to my words.

Note on Transliteration

For the most part, diacritical marks appear only in the notes and bibliography, as these marks are neither necessary for specialists nor helpful for readers unfamiliar with Arabic. Additionally, terms such as "hadith" and "isnad" are given anglicized plurals, becoming "hadiths" and "isnads" rather than plurals in adherence to Arabic grammatical forms.

Muhammad's Body

Introduction

What Can a Prophetic Body Do?

> We know nothing about a body until we know what it can do, in other words, what its affects are, how they can or cannot enter into composition with other affects, with the affects of another body . . . to destroy that body or to be destroyed by it . . . to exchange actions and passions with it or to join with it in composing a more powerful body.
>
> —GILLES DELEUZE AND FÉLIX GUATTARI

While working as a medical doctor at the Islamic University of Medina's hospital in the 1960s, Muhsin Khan was transformed by a dream encounter with the Prophet Muhammad. In the dream, Khan observed Muhammad perspiring and realized that the best way for him to help the Prophet was to swallow his sweat. Informed by his understanding that if someone saw Muhammad in a dream, it was *really* Muhammad, Khan later sought to understand the Prophet's visit. He reported the dream to renowned Salafi scholar Shaykh ʿAbd al-Aziz bin Baz, who interpreted Khan's drinking of prophetic sweat to signify that Khan would "do service to the Sunna." As a fluent English speaker living among esteemed religious scholars in the city of the Prophet, Khan decided that he would translate the Qur'an and hadith literature into English.[1] Khan's translation of the Qur'an with Muhammad Taqi-ud-Din al-Hilali ultimately came to supplant Yusuf Ali's translation as the preferred text for Saudi-networked English media, and Khan also provided these networks with a translation of the most prestigious Sunni hadith collection, Bukhari's *Sahih*.[2]

Relating Khan's dream to an AlMaghrib Institute class in Calgary, Yasir Qadhi paused and addressed a palpable tension in the room: "Of course," he explained, gesturing to his own arm and signifying the flow of fluids from bodies, "this is *baraka*, to drink the Prophet's sweat."[3] Baraka, discussed in greater detail later in this introduction, popularly (and perhaps problematically) appears in English translation as "blessings."[4] While some students in Qadhi's class might have felt discomfort at the notion of a medical doctor such as Khan desiring the ostensibly irrational and perhaps disturbing or even soteriologically dangerous act of drinking sweat from another man's body—even the body of the Prophet—Qadhi bypassed Bin Baz's metaphorical interpretation to focus on the sweat itself as a site at which baraka could be accessed. The dream functioned not only as a text to interpret but also as a flow of baraka from Muhammad's pores into Khan's stomach.

Though Khan's consumption of Muhammad's sweat occurred within a dream, the event was conceivably "real" due to Muhammad's promise, recorded in archives with the utmost canonical privilege, that his appearances in dreams are genuine. Moreover, the dream's imagery related to a popular theme in textual representations of Muhammad's life: the association of his body and its by-products with baraka, and the desire of the first Muslim community, his Companions, to acquire and even consume materials that had been produced by or within his body, including his sweat. In a canonically privileged tradition, Umm Sulaym bottled Muhammad's sweat for both its pleasing scent and the baraka that it contained. Such connections become modes by which Muhammad achieves an extended body, transcending his corporeal boundaries and seemingly merging his body with others to form a greater composite body. This expanded body can be envisioned as a power grid composed of the bodies through which baraka-suffused Muhammadi ontology circulates. On this power grid, connections with divine and angelic bodies transform Muhammad's body into a conduit of baraka, through which the force flows into other human bodies. These bodies in turn link other bodies to the grid, those in the post-Companion classes of the Followers (*al-tabiʿiun*) and Followers of the Followers (*tabi al-tabiʿin*). Beyond these three privileged generations, the prophetic body continues to expand its reach through the thousands of traditionists reporting his sayings and actions, their narrations contributing to a cumulative representation of Muhammad, crystallized via an immense literary corpus, or written body. This textual representation opens portals by which believers such as Muhsin Khan can achieve their own intercorporeal links with Muhammad and thus enter into the power grid of his extended body.

In the study that follows, I examine the textual constructions of Muhammad's body that emerge within the genres of *sira/maghazi* and

Sunni hadith literature from the earliest sources through the eleventh century CE. Focusing on Muhammad's corporeal boundaries and limits, asking where Muhammad's body begins and ends, I track change in regard to the prophetic body's representation. I argue that changes across the sources express a growing investment in his power to achieve intercorporeal linkage with other bodies, through which Muhammad's body reaches beyond the expected boundaries of his own flesh. Muhammad's Companions, transformed by these connections, become authorized in the literature not only as eyewitness reporters of his sayings and actions but also as intensely embodied traces of his corporeality. I also demonstrate that while Muhammad's body grows in its capacity for intercorporeal connection, this movement does not evidence an absolute transformation or sweeping erasure of past narratives. Rather, as narrations of Muhammad's bodily powers intensify through the developing literature, early and later traditions often coexist, producing an unstable imaginary of prophetic corporeality. Muhammad's body does not emerge in this literary corpus with clearly drawn boundaries but grows increasingly unpredictable in terms of its limits and powers. The incoherence of Muhammad's body reflects diverse methodological commitments among his reporters. It also highlights the heterogeneity of voices that participate in the textual making of his body, which presents significantly divergent imaginaries between two Companions such as Anas and A'isha.

This project participates in a shift within hadith studies away from the "authenticity question," the problem of whether premodern methods of vetting hadiths and their transmitters—either independently or supplemented by modern methods of source criticism—have made it possible to reliably access the historical Muhammad or even the generation that knew him.[5] I do not presuppose a singularly authentic or "original" account of Muhammad that later tradition either preserves or distorts, nor am I attempting to recover the "real" Muhammad from this material. While examining change over time, I recognize Harald Motzki's caution against assuming that traditions found in the oldest collections are *always* the oldest traditions.[6]

In hadith studies, narrations of the prophetic body surface incidentally. M. J. Kister has produced helpful articles that survey reports of Muhammad having eaten meat that had been dedicated to pre-Islamic goddesses prior to his prophethood,[7] as well as the question of whether Muhammad was born circumcised.[8] In the former, Kister points to exercises in editorial sovereignty on the part of the stories' reporters, arguing for an intensified concern with establishing Muhammad's protection from sin. Kister's student Uri Rubin has similarly provided useful studies of Muhammad's textual representation, arguing for changes in Muhammad's biographical details as expressions of shifting priorities and anxieties on the part of Muhammad's reporters. These details include narrations of Muhammad's body, such as the marking of his prophethood with a material signifier on his back (the *khatam* or "seal"), though the body itself does not receive attention in these works as a focus of theoretical consideration.[9] In the case of Muhammad and the "bag of meat" tradition, the problem of Muhammad possibly eating meat that had been slaughtered in a false deity's name can be examined not only in relation to prophetic moral infallibility and protection from sin but also for the *material* dangers to his body from consuming polytheists' sacrifices. In other words, the meat matters because when the meat enters Muhammad's stomach, it *becomes Muhammad*. Apart from the question of Muhammad's capacity for sin, moral error, or misguided belief, can the meat impose changes from within Muhammad's digestive tract that render his body somehow less Muhammad-like? If so, what does it mean to have a Muhammad-like body in the first place?

Rather than perform forensic dissections of oral transmission histories to expose forgeries and chase after pure origins, I join a number of scholars who are asking different questions of the sources. In particular, my exploration of the prophetic body draws hadith studies, and Islamic studies more generally, into conversations between theories of the body and religious studies. In attending to the gendering of Muhammad's body, my discussion also contributes to the nascent study of Muslim masculinities.

Baraka Networks

The hadith corpus and its related genre of sira/maghazi abound with reports of direct physical contact with Muhammad's body producing change in the bodies of his Companions. One tradition, for example, presents Muhammad rubbing the chest of a boy possessed by a demon. Through his touch and prayer, Muhammad causes a creature resembling a black puppy to come crawling out of the boy's mouth.[10] Muhammad's touch even contributes to his successful preservation by a future body, a literary corpus: Muhammad rubs Abu Hurayra's cloak, which then endows Abu Hurayra with a flawless capacity for remembering and narrating hadiths.[11] Narrating this hadith himself, Abu Hurayra thus establishes his own authority through an account of his transformation by the prophetic body. Prophetic skin, as the boundary separating the interior of Muhammad's body from the outside world, operates as an interface at which his Companions can engage the powerful energies that flow through Muhammad's body, the site upon which the Qur'an descends in revelation.

Muhammad's skin does not preserve an absolute separation between inside and outside. Like all bodies, the surface of Muhammad's body includes points at which leakages cross the border and spill out to the world. These leakages include not only the typical fluids and disjecta from human bodies, such as saliva, sweat, blood, urine, feces, sexual discharge, and discarded hair and fingernail trimmings, but also exceptional ejections such as the water that miraculously flows from his hands to answer the needs of his Companions. Things not only come out of Muhammad's body, however; they also go into him. Just as Muhammad exceeds his corporeal boundaries when he penetrates other bodies, he also links to new bodies by undergoing penetration, as in the tradition of angels cutting open Muhammad's chest to wash his heart, as well as accounts of God personally injecting knowledge into Muhammad's body through physical touch. The revelation of the Qur'an, as an event that produced observable effects on his body, also appears as a penetration of divine forces into his flesh and organs. My treatment of Muhammad's body focuses on points at which the distinction between Muhammad's inside and outside becomes unclear and permeable. Through these penetrations and transformations, Muhammad's body mediates between human and extrahuman forces, and between physical and metaphysical worlds.

I ground this discussion of Muhammad's corporeal border crossings in the notion of baraka. In the Qur'an, the *b-r-k* root appears chiefly in verb form, signifying an action performed by God and directed upon objects that include human beings, spatial designations such as lands and cities, natural phenomena such as trees and the rain that God causes to fall to Earth, and divinely revealed discourses that descend to humankind from the heavens.[12] The Qur'an also describes God himself (and in fact exclusively God) as *tabaraka*: "*Tabaraka* is he in whose hand is dominion, and he has power over everything" (67:1). In its references to the bestowal of baraka upon material objects (such as living things or human cultural constructions such as cities) or units of time (such as the Qur'an's revelation during a *laylatin mubarakatin*, a "baraka-laden night"),[13] God's opening of baraka between the heavens and Earth,[14] and of course the Qur'an's self-identification as *mubarak*,[15] the text of the Qur'an opens a variety of possibilities for considering baraka's relation to space and time.

Hadith sources expand these possibilities, identifying high concentrations of baraka in particular locations, such as sheep's bodies or the foreheads of horses.[16] Baraka also appears capable of movement, undergoing transferals from one location to another. Muhammad reportedly instructed his Companions to eat food from its edges rather than its center, because baraka descends into the center; to delay consumption of the center ostensibly enables a greater accumulation of baraka for the consumers to ingest into their bodies.[17] Muhammad recommends using olive oil for eating and for treating the skin, since it comes from a *shajaratin mubarakatin*, a tree with baraka.[18] Baraka exists within designated material objects and become accessible through one's proximity to them. Traditions depict objects infused with baraka, including human bodies, as capable of transmitting their baraka through physical contact.

While typically translated as "blessings," baraka has been more precisely defined by G. S. Colin as a "beneficent force, of divine origin, which causes superabundance in the physical sphere and happiness in the psychic order."[19] Edmond Doutte describes baraka as a "force impregnating, radiating, which transmits itself to anything that it touches and to anything that it surrounds."[20] Mohammad Ali Amir-Moezzi articulates baraka as "a kind of mysterious and beneficial flow, an energy or spiritual influx transmitted by contact."[21] Academic treatments of baraka as a force transmission between bodies often focus on the powers of advanced friends of God or "saints" (*awliya'*) in Sufi traditions and expressions of "popular" or "folk" religion. Baraka thus appears in academic literature as significant chiefly for mystical elites and shrines at which the bodily remains of saints and prophets or material traces of their presence (worn sandals and cloaks, preserved hair, etc.) are treated as loci of its flows. In particular, a growing body of anthropological literature has touched upon baraka's popular conception as an "active energy" that can heal and protect, as well as its significance in material culture and the demarcation of physical spaces as sites at which transcendent forces can be accessed.[22]

Ahmet T. Karamustafa conceptualizes baraka as "the holy power inherent in a saintly figure that set him/her apart from everyone else; it was normally conceived as a fluid force that emanated from the saint, alive or dead, and permeated the places, persons and objects around him, and its ultimate proof was the saintly miracle, karama."[23] Josef Meri describes baraka as an "innate" and "emotive" force that emanates from saintly bodies and can remain accessible even after their deaths through pilgrimage to their tombs and material relics associated with them (including clothing, hair, and fingernails). While noting that in premodern sources, baraka does not receive the same scholarly attention and theorization as sainthood (*walaya*), Meri identifies a tension between different conceptualizations of baraka. For thinkers such as Damascene jurist Ibn Taymiyya (d. 1328), baraka operates primarily not as a force to be accessed through physical encounters with baraka-emitting objects but rather as something closer to a point system in which God awards credits for religious knowledge and obedience to divine command.[24] The questions of where believers can locate baraka and how one should go about accessing it become meaningful for locating authentic Muslim practice and the tradition's center of gravity.

Omid Safi has examined baraka's social consequences as a bargaining chip in relations between rulers and the saintly figures whose bodies, operating as baraka's material conduits, can convey baraka and thus political credibility. Safi warns against conceptualizing baraka as simply an abstract "'spiritual' blessing bereft of any earthly ramifications." Rather, Safi argues, "Baraka is, as much as anything else, about power: the spiritual power of the saint, the power of the saints to interact with mighty rulers, and the power to lend them legitimacy."[25] If special bodies, living or dead, function as sites at which baraka becomes accessible, relationships to those bodies can also mark privilege and map power relations between a variety of other bodies. Baraka thus becomes an authorizing cement in the hadith corpus. Muhammad, whom Joseph Chelhod terms "la personnification par excellence de la *baraka*,"[26] connects with his Companions' bodies in no small part through baraka flows and from these connections authorizes the scholarly assemblage that transmits his words and actions. This study's exploration of prophetic corporeality through the Deleuzo-Guattarian question, "What can a body do?" demonstrates "baraka" to be an acceptable short answer: Baraka is what the prophetic body does.

Muhammad's body perhaps most famously operates as a conduit of baraka in its capacity as the mode through which God reveals the Qur'an to humankind. Multiple traditions attest to Muhammad's reception of divine revelation producing observable effects on his body, such as profuse sweat or a dramatic increase in his weight. Baraka often appears as something akin to a contagion within Muhammad's body that he transmits to other bodies in the same modes as more typical contagions: baraka can pass from Muhammad's body into another via touch, breath, or contact with Muhammad's bodily fluids. Various reports describe Muhammad or Companions mentioning baraka in reference to Muhammad's corporeal traces, such as his saliva, sweat, the water that pours forth from between his fingers, or water that he had used for ritual ablutions. In less popular traditions, even Muhammad's blood and urine function as material traces of his baraka, defined not by their status as objectionable or even polluting substances but rather by their origins within his privileged body. The Companions' acquisitions of these materials enable transmissions of baraka from Muhammad's body into their own. Having been transformed into extensions of Muhammad's body, the Companions likewise become carriers of his bodily baraka to later generations. They provide links to Muhammad not only for their positions in hadith reports' chains of transmission as his eyewitness reporters but also for the transformation of their own bodies by heightened exposure to his baraka.

In this attempted start of a prophetic corporeography, I speak to a developing theoretical interest in the body within Islamic studies and an underexamined dimension within the sira/maghazi and hadith literature. As with baraka, the most salient discussions of the body in Islamic studies for this project have focused on Sufi traditions. Scott Kugle's *Sufis & Saints' Bodies* (2007) examines imaginaries of the body within Sufi traditions, particularly saintly hagiographies, analyzing representations of saints' bodies as "symbolic resources for generating religious meaning, communal solidarity, and experience of the sacred."[27] In particular, Kugle's fourth chapter, "Body Enraptured: The Lips of Shah Hussayn," discusses the motif in Sufi hagiographical traditions of initiation through intercorporeal exchange (in this case, a kiss between master and disciple) and the power of bodily fluids such as saliva to transmit knowledge and metaphysical grace.[28] Shahzad Bashir's *Sufi Bodies* (2011) looks to the significance of corporeal themes in literature and paintings as a window into what he calls "the Persianate social and religious world" from the fourteenth to sixteenth centuries CE.[29] Bashir introduces his project with a reference to prophetic corporeality, discussing the tradition in which Muhammad promises intercession not only for the man who shakes his hand but for also the man who shakes that man's hand, and the man who shakes *his* hand, and so on, up to seven degrees of separation from the touch of Muhammad's hand.[30]

The Prophetic Assemblage

Gilles Deleuze and Félix Guattari, as Elizabeth Grosz observes, have not produced their own systematic theory of the body.[31] Joe Hughes similarly notes in his introduction to the edited essay collection *Deleuze and the Body* (2011), "It is not clear what kind of work the concept [of the body] is supposed to do within Deleuze's corpus, and it is not immediately clear what we can do with it."[32] Nonetheless, a growing literature around Deleuze (and Guattari) recognizes the significance of bodies to his (their) thought (and frequently cites Grosz as a thinker drawing from their treatments of the body).[33] Grosz engages Deleuze and Guattari for their complex significance to gender studies and provides a helpful interlocution with figures such as Julia Kristeva and Judith Butler.[34] Ian Buchanan treats the question that drove this book, "What can a body do?," as "the basis of their whole thought on the body," which centers on the body's capacity for producing relations. In the Deleuzo-Guattarian project, Buchanan explains, a body is "the capacity to form new relations," illustrated by something as straightforward as the ingesting and digesting of food.[35]

My use of Deleuze and Guattari also draws inspiration from Alexander G. Weheliye's "methodological breather" in *Habeas Viscus: Racializing Assemblages, Biopolitics, and Black Feminist Theories of the Human* (2014), in which Weheliye cites Grosz among thinkers such as Jasbir Puar, Manuel DeLanda, and others who have creatively engaged and appropriated Deleuze and Guattari for their own projects. Such scholars, while evading "the quagmire of orthodox Deleuzianism," create "novel assemblages and insights that only become possible when these ideas are put to work in milieus (e.g., racialized minority discourse or queer theory) beyond the snowy masculinist precincts of European philosophy." In Weheliye's analysis, such appropriation remains faithful to Deleuze and Guattari, who extend an "invitation to plunder their ideas in the service of producing new concepts and assemblages."[36] Like critical race studies or queer theory, Islamic studies constitutes a milieu outside Deleuze and Guattari's expertise or meaningful investment. Deleuze and Guattari make only rare references to Islam or Muslims, and these mentions amount to little more than repetitions of Orientalist tropes and racial essentialism.[37] My project selectively appropriates from Deleuze and Guattari for the questions they ask of bodies without requiring faithfulness to an "orthodox Deleuzianism" or a clearly defined Deleuzo-Guattarian system of the body or, for that matter, searching for any significant insight specifically on Islam or Muslims in their work.

Engaging Baruch Spinoza and Friedrich Nietzsche, Deleuze and Guattari envision bodies as assemblages characterized by internal multiplicities of forces in changing relations rather than as fixed entities and unitary wholes; in their unstable relations to each other, these forces continually construct and reconstruct the body as an ongoing process.[38] For Deleuze and Guattari, the principal question to ask of a body concerns its capacity for affecting other composite bodies, extending its powers by entering into relations that in turn produce greater composites.[39] This interest in the body as multiplicity serves as a launch pad for my thinking about Muhammad's body and the connections it forges with other bodies. The prophetic assemblage expresses its internal multiplicities and heterogeneities as Muhammad's bodily powers and boundaries alternately expand or constrict through his relations to other bodies, whether human, angelic, or divine. The borders between these bodies remain permeable.

To call Muhammad's extended corporeality an "assemblage" in Deleuzo-Guattarian terms means more than simply saying that it is made of parts or that these parts relate to each other in messy ways. The assemblage requires some consideration of the forces that collect, arrange, order, and name the multiplicities that form this extended corporeality, producing the conditions by which such a phenomenon becomes possible. This means that the assemblage calls attention to power. Deleuze and Guattari envision this process taking place on a horizontal axis between "machinic" and "collective" assemblages. The machinic assemblage consists of the material bodies as they relate to and connect with one another. The first elements in this machinic assemblage are the bodies of Muhammad and his community, and also the extrahuman forces (such as the angel Gabriel, who in various accounts becomes visible to Muhammad, squeezes his body, performs heart surgery on him, escorts him into the heavens, and interacts with members of his community) that act upon them. This machinic assemblage expands beyond Muhammad's personal reach and continues to operate after his death, as those bodies that had connected to him in space and time become modes of connection for others that did not have access to him. These face-to-face linkages continue to extend past the generation that had known Muhammad, producing a vast network of interconnected bodies. This machinic assemblage of bodies and relations becomes discursively transformed by the collective assemblage, the assemblage of enunciation, which arranges the bodies through concepts and words and names their connections. The assemblage of enunciation inscribes categories upon this mingling of bodies, starting with *Companion* for those who had personally met Muhammad, accepted his prophethood during his lifetime, and died as Muslims. *Companion* becomes an order-word, an incorporeal modification of bodies and striation over what had been a smooth space. With this category comes the theorization of a privileged class possessing universal probity as transmitters of Muhammad's sayings and actions. Preceding the creation and crystallization of *Companions* as an organizing principle, the Companions' voices could not have been gathered and ordered in this way during their own lifetimes. By all appearances, the surviving members of Muhammad's movement continued to talk about him after his death, but their acts of remembrance did not take place in a context more formal or structured than seniors telling stories to their juniors. There was not yet a system, blueprint, or centralizing hierarchy to govern this process or regulate participation within it. The Companions themselves did not share a universal or "common sense" definition of what it meant to be a Companion. Even if hadiths depicted the Prophet as praising his Companions, statements attributed to the Companions themselves illustrate that they defined this identity in different ways, with some definitions more expansive than others. Nor can it be suggested that the Companions ever shared a united social or political alignment or set of interests, let alone a mutually affirmed custodianship over the prophetic memory. The figures who would later be grouped together as Companions disagreed with each other on important questions, challenged each other regarding the integrity of their narrations (which included, in rare cases such as A'isha's accusation against Ibn ʿUmar, calling each other liars),[40] and even fought each other on the physical battlefield.

Just as the "Companions" came into existence through inscriptions of the collective assemblage upon the machinic assemblage, the generation of their students—retroactively labeled the "Followers"—did not gather itself as a united class engaged in a universalizing project. Rather, this label for their relationship to the Prophet was inscribed upon them. As Followers reported the sayings of those Companions to whom they had access, each Companion-centered network takes a distinct and local character: Anas, for example, taught in Basra, while Ibn Mas'ud was the local sage of Kufa, and A'isha maintained an influential circle of students in Medina. Though these networks did have overlaps, they remained distinct. At the level of Companion-Successor transmissions, the Companions' personal networks have not yet become parts of a larger collectivity. The Followers in turn transmitted their narrations to the generation after them, which becomes constructed as its own distinct class, the "Followers of the Followers." While cities such as Basra, Kufa, and Medina had developed their own molecular bodies of knowledge with unique legal, ritual, and theological positions, travel between cities enabled local scholarly lineages to become increasingly interpenetrative, even merging into what might be called a more "global" (or "molar" in Deleuzo-Guattarian terms) constellation for its time and molarizing the molecular into a territory of *ahl al-sunna wa-l-jamaʿa*, Sunni Islam. While *al-jamaʿa* in this context usually is translated as "the congregation" or "the community," the *j-m-ʿa* root signifies broader meanings of gathering, combining, and assembling. One could render *ahl al-sunna wa-l-jamaʿa* as "People of the Sunna and the Assemblage."

As the collective/enunciative assemblage organizes the machinic assemblage through concepts and language, the resultant changes can either open the prophetic assemblage to greater multiplicity and malleability or enforce a more rigid and stabilized order upon its bodies. This is where the machinic-enunciative horizontal axis intersects a vertical axis, of which one end represents "reterritorialization" and the other "deterritorialization." As bodies and discourses move along this axis, an assemblage enhances or suppresses its potential for variability and change. Among the first generations of Muslims, hadith transmission was significantly deterritorialized. They produced not an authoritative literary canon or elite coterie of governing experts but rather a multiplicity of loose assemblages formed between local elders and their teaching circles, occupying in Deleuzo-Guattarian terms a smooth space that had not yet been subjected to rigid striation. Reterritorialization emerged as these networks grew interconnected and developed concepts to further organize and order their bodies, as with categories of "Companions," "Followers," and "Followers of Followers." The supreme agent of reterritorialization was the *isnad*, the chain of transmission that could track a hadith's textual history in this growing network. Isnad-based hadith evaluation served to stabilize the circulation of hadiths and govern a chaotic field. From the isnad's development emerged new methodologies and literatures: formal grading systems by which isnads and their transmitters could be ranked, exhaustive biographical dictionaries of the thousands of bodies that together comprised this professional field, and polemics against methods and ideologies that fell outside the new assemblage. As they reterritorialized hadith dissemination networks, master scholars consolidated local and molecular entities into a molar mass with greater powers of self-regulation. Scott C. Lucas argues that this molar mass of hadith scholars, cemented by three foundational values—the collective valorization of the Companions as a class, the rise of isnad-based hadith evaluation, and a shared historical consciousness—provided a nucleus for the emergence of Sunni Islam.[41] Lucas focuses his attention on the generation of Ibn Sa'd, Ibn Ma'in, and Ibn Hanbal in the first half of the third Islamic century, "eve of the compilation of the six canonical Sunni hadith books" and an era in which hadith scholarship was centered in Iraq (foremost the capital of Baghdad, followed by Basra and Kufa), with support from Iran and Central Asia.[42] Though this also happens to have been the age of the Mihna, during which hadith masters such as Ibn Hanbal were persecuted by the caliphate for their theological positions, Lucas and other scholars have argued that Orientalist scholarship overstates the Mihna's significance in this process.[43]

For tracking reterritorialization in the hadith corpus, the isnad remains an amazing resource. The transmitters who appear in an isnad, having been associated with specific cities and regions, can tell us where a particular narrative or position was popular and how it traveled; looking at levels across the chains can illustrate the rise and fall of a hadith hub such as the Umayyad capital of Damascus, supplanted by eastward movement toward hadith networks centered in Iraq. As examined in a handful of projects that utilize isnads and their supplementary literatures to track patterns in hadith transmission, the chains bear witness to multiple reterritorializings in this period. John Nawas collects geographic backgrounds and ethnic identities of hadith transmitters, finding that while Arabs were predictably dominant at the earliest levels of isnads (that is, the generations closest to the Prophet), *mawali* (non-Arab convert) transmitters overtook Arab transmitters in the third century of Islam as primary agents of hadith scholarship.[44] Christopher Melchert searches chains for reporters who had been accused of advocating unacceptable doctrines or associated with sectarian minorities, demonstrating their intensified marginalization from hadith networks around the early third century.[45] Asma Sayeed investigates the presence or absence of women reporters, finding that between the generation of the Followers and the Six Books' compilation (from the end of the first Islamic century to the early fourth century), women virtually disappeared from the chains.[46] Finally, Lyall R. Armstrong's scholarship on popular preachers and storytellers (*qussas*) in early Islam, drawing from hadith masters' evaluations of transmitters, suggests that an isnad-based study of the qussas would likely chart their declining reputation in hadith networks between the end of the Umayyad period in the early second Islamic century (when, as Armstrong demonstrates, the qussas were overwhelmingly treated as reliable hadith transmitters) and hadith scholars' professional sophistication in the late third century (as marked by Muslim declaring in his *Sahih*'s introduction, "Do not seek the company of the qussas!"),[47] as the qussas grew collectively despised for their perceived lack of scholarly rigor.[48] As hadith masters began to articulate a doctrine of the Companions' collective integrity as a class, systematized their methodologies for measuring and vetting connections to that class, catalogued and ranked their colleagues, and defended their field's border against the outside, achieving the appearance of unity that Deleuze and Guattari would attribute to a "power takeover in the multiplicity,"[49] the isnad left traces of their reterritorialization across ethnic, sectarian, gendered, and methodological lines.

The other end of the vertical axis represents deterritorialization. Despite its movements toward stasis and control, the prophetic assemblage retains what Deleuze and Guattari call "lines of flight," destabilizing resources within an arborescent system that can undermine its artificial unity. The isnad represents what Deleuze and Guattari would term arborescent thought, producing ordered genealogies and naming centers and margins. But as much as the chains construct tree-like authority, they can also deconstruct, revealing the internal diversity among these generations of networked transmitters and the Companions themselves prior to their molarization. A Deleuzo-Guattarian hadith analysis would point to the ways that this appearance of a tree obscures the potential for an open, rootless, limitless rhizome.

The classical hadith masters' methods for vetting transmitters and evaluating a transmission's authenticity, as I referenced with the earlier anecdote of Muhsin Khan drinking Muhammad's sweat, include application of a tradition that the Prophet can make genuine appearances in dreams and convey meaningful information. Premodern hadith criticism thus abounds with scholars reporting what they had learned about specific hadiths, transmitters, and chains in their dream encounters with the Prophet and other Muslim luminaries, potentially complicating their claims to epistemological supremacy.[50] The isnad can also shift between reterritorialization and deterritorialization by reversing the direction of its flows, starting with an ostensibly monolithic "hadith corpus" and going backward to witness its formation from local networks centered around specific Companions and their immediate teaching circles. Depending on which Companions we read, we'd arrive at different possibilities on matters such as Muhammad's vision of God, his continued sentience and bodily integrity in his grave, and even his physical appearance. The canonical sources' *musannaf* style of arrangement (organizing hadith traditions by topic) serves a particular reterritorialization, since it presents the Companions as a coherent whole. Reverting to the earlier *musnad* format, which organizes traditions by the Companion to whom they are attributed, could lead to deterritorialization (or an alternative reterritorialization) by preserving Companions as distinct individuals with their own subjectivities and enabling a seeker to prioritize one Companion's corpus of reports and ignore another.

One might perceive two "prophetic assemblages" here. First: the material body of Muhammad, which enters into relations with entities such as God, angels, and the Companions. Second: the scholarly assemblage, connected to the Prophet by chains of teacher-student relationships, that reterritorializes hadith transmission as a field with its own epistemology, methods, canon of authorizing discourse, and even sectarian affiliation. These two arrangements come together as one greater assemblage of prophetic corporeality. Master scholars such as Bukhari did not perform their work only as archivists of transmitted discourse; instead, they claimed a degree of intercorporeal merger with the Companions, who themselves were bodies transformed by their intercorporeality with the Prophet. The literary corpus formed from these thousands of intergenerational encounters presents itself as an extension of Muhammad's physical presence.

Gender Justice and Hadith

Referring to amina wadud's immeasurable contribution to gender-progressive readings of the Qur'an, a dear mentor and lover of the Prophet had once told me with regret, "There's no amina wadud for hadith." For a number of reasons, Muslim feminist scholarship has prioritized the Qur'an and its exegetical literature (*tafsir*) over the hadith corpus as the natural sites for rethinkings and reconstructions of Islamic tradition.[51] As Aysha Hidayatullah explains in *Feminist Edges of the Qur'an* (2014), Muslim feminist scholarship tends to treat hadith materials with ambivalence and skepticism, and thus has not produced feminist hadith commentary with anything close to the sizeable and growing archive of feminist Qur'an commentary. As an exception, Hidayatullah refers to Sa'diyya Shaikh, who has examined select narrations from Bukhari's *Sahih* through a lens of feminist hermeneutics in part to challenge their ostensibly sexist consequences and offer alternative readings as "counter-narratives."[52]

Asma Sayeed and Denise Spellberg offer important engagements of prophetic traditions independently of the "authenticity question" with their respective monographs *Women and the Transmission of Religious Knowledge in Islam* (2013)[53] and *Politics, Gender, and the Islamic Past: The Legacy of 'A'isha Bint Abi Bakr* (1994).[54] As mentioned above, Sayeed examines hadiths' chains of transmission in canonical Sunni collections with an eye for the inclusion or marginalization of women as reporters. Sayeed explains that her analysis does not depend on the transmissions actually coming from the reporters to whom they are attributed: "Even if they are wholesale forgeries, they are still valuable because they reveal the perceptions that Muslims had of the early female narrators as dependable transmitters."[55] Spellberg likewise exempts her project from the problem of recovering A'isha's "real life" in the sources, instead examining A'isha's significance for those who made historical claims upon her.[56] Ash Geissinger has investigated A'isha's exegetical traditions and employed gender studies as an analytical lens for engaging the early sources.[57] Geissinger's *Gender and Muslim Constructions of Exegetical Authority* (2015), while prioritizing tafsir, necessarily discusses hadith sources for their treatments of gender without requiring a verdict on the authenticity question.[58] In my examination of A'isha traditions, I engage A'isha not only as a historical individual but just as meaningfully a transmission network or "brand," a complex assemblage in her own right.

Despite a substantive body of scholarship on questions of gender in Muslim traditions, the study of Muslim masculinities remains critically neglected. Amanullah De Sondy initiates an academic conversation in his *The Crisis of Islamic Masculinities* (2014). In resonance with Muslim feminist focus on the Qur'an, De Sondy identifies the Qur'an, rather than hadith literature, as the intuitive starting point for discussing Muslim masculinities.[59] Zahra Ayubi's *Gendered Morality* (2019) powerfully demonstrates the ways Muslim ethical literature (*akhlaq*) developed within (and continued to uphold) a masculinized cosmology that privileged men as its default ethical subjects.[60] The developing study of Muslim masculinities has not yet attempted a sustained focus on the hadith corpus or the Prophet's significance as a gendered body. This work thus aims to address a gap at the meeting of hadith studies and gender studies.

Muslim feminist scholarship is my personal and professional genealogy. To Juliane Hammer I owe an increased mindfulness of the ways scholarship is activism and, as the personal remains political, my work is inseparable from my own positionality.[61] To name gender as a priority in this project and to self-position as Muslim and feminist calls me to confront my own relationship to the questions that I ask, particularly concerning the sacred sources' possible relationships to patriarchy and liberation. A substantive body of gender-progressive Muslim scholarship upholds the sacred sources themselves (primarily the Qur'an, with a more complicated treatment of hadith literature) as innocent of sexism and even innately egalitarian, with the sources' sexist consequences treated as only a product of flawed interpretations that developed in patriarchal historical contexts. In this framework, our sense of gender justice becomes reinscribed as a timeless value of Islam, and it becomes the task of Muslim feminist scholarship to liberate our sources from their misreadings and recover the sources' presumed "essence" of revolutionary gender equality. For some of us, a palpable tension grows when this approach becomes incompatible with what our eyes show us on the page. As Hidayatullah discusses in *Feminist Edges of the Qur'an,* the stakes at this tension can include faith in the sources' transcendence and the possible incommensurability of that faith with a feminist ethic.[62] I acknowledge that when approaching the sources as a man, I remain, to borrow Shaikh's phrasing, advantaged as "the normative addressee of the text," not "the 'Other' within the house of Islam" and therefore do not face the same stakes as women whose engagements of the sources have produced a necessary tradition of Muslim feminist scriptural exegesis.[63] While acknowledging the urgency and strategic import of prescriptively reconstructing the texts' meanings and values, I also find myself at what Hidayatullah, quoting Judith Plaskow, names "the edge of a deep abyss" where we consider that the sources might not be on our side.[64] At points during this research, I found my analysis contesting popular tropes of gender-progressive Muslim thought, including arguments for which I am personally sympathetic. While I have written on an Islamic divine feminine and its personal significance for me in confessional writings, for example, I cannot assert that I find the Qur'an and hadith corpus self-evidently articulating the possibility of a divine feminine or even a god that transcends gender.[65] I struggle with the idea that my scholarship might take something away from people who need it, but I also recognize that prescriptive textual foundationalism is not an approach that fulfills everyone's needs either. It is not my position that writing with a feminist lens requires us to exonerate our sacred texts, speak for an essence hidden behind their words, mine them for secret points of resistance, or wrestle them into speaking for us. In short, there's more than one way to do Muslim feminist scholarship. Nourished by Hidayatullah's reflection on the consequences of her project, I hope that my own work builds rather than destroys.

I would add that, as Ayesha S. Chaudhry demonstrates in her scholarship on the Qur'an's "wife-beating verse" (4:34), asking what a source "says" and what it ultimately "means" remain two distinct questions. Chaudhry's work reveals that whether the Qur'an advocates patriarchy or gender egalitarianism is not reducible to a plain-sense reading of its bare verses but instead manifests through the various patriarchal or egalitarian "idealized cosmologies" that guide communities as they interpret those verses. As readers' ideas about the Qur'an and Islam precede their acts of interpretation, Chaudhry tells us, "the actual words of the Qur'anic text are less important . . . than the specific set of expectations that believers bring to this text."[66] As Hammer reveals in her ethnographic study of American Muslims who work against domestic violence, antiabuse ethical commitments "do not begin with scriptural sources" but the other way around: antiabuse activists come to their scriptural sources already with an experientially grounded "ethic of non-abuse, a deep-seated sense," in hand.[67]

The sources are never "just the sources." Whatever they might say, they cannot stand alone in producing meaning. As readers come to a sacred source bringing their own expectations for what it will say, they also bring their own tools for working with its challenges. I ask difficult questions of the sources but do not prescribe a particular formulation of texts and authorities that can intervene and answer those questions on behalf of what someone might perceive as the Qur'an's true essence, the historically verifiable Muhammad, or "true Islam." The specific arrangement of materials to constitute "true Islam" that a reader chooses, of course, impacts the consequences of my work. First, it must be acknowledged that not all Muslims—not even all Sunni Muslims—maintain the same investment in Sunni hadith canon (which is neither universally defined in itself nor even the only "hadith canon" out there), so these sources are not weighted the same for everyone. Second, Muslims read these sources through lenses informed by their own supplementary archives. As Sa'diyya Shaikh's masterful engagement of Ibn al-'Arabi demonstrates, the sources' gendered theologies can become more complicated if a reader looks to Ibn al-'Arabi's thought as a resource for understanding them—and that reader is open to Shaikh's scholarship and analytical frameworks as resources for understanding Ibn al-'Arabi.[68] Meanwhile, as illustrated in Wesley Muhammad's scholarship on the Qur'an and hadith literature, the potential problem of a corporeally anthropomorphic god in the Prophet's vision would not be a problem at all for followers of the Honorable Elijah Muhammad, who taught that God is literally a man with a body.[69] Like the flesh-and-blood body at the center of my project, the literary corpus reflects an unstable assemblage conditioned by the bodies with which it achieves connection. Textual meaning is a question not merely of what the words can say but also of what forces can interact with the words.

The Sources

Charting shifts in imaginaries of Muhammad across the first centuries of Islam, I start with the Qur'an. Fred Donner has convincingly argued for an "early Qur'an" that can be located at least within the generation following the Prophet. Donner makes his case in part by demonstrating that the Qur'an and canonical hadith collections, which emerged in the third/ninth century, depart from one another so severely in vocabulary and content that it seems untenable to locate their productions within the same historical setting.[70] I follow Donner in privileging the Qur'an as the source most reliably connected to the earliest Muslim community.[71]

Early sources on Muhammad also include sira/maghazi literatures, which are distinguished from other genres of hadith literatures in terms of methodology, organization, and the positionality of their producers. What would be the oldest surviving sira/maghazi work, Wahb ibn Munabbih's (d. ca. 730) *Maghazi Rasul Allah*, comes from the century after Muhammad but has been preserved only in fragments.[72] The *Maghazi* of Ibn Ishaq (d. 767 CE), typically considered the earliest extant biography of Muhammad, is accessible through the recensions of later scholars such as Ibn Hisham (d. 833) and Yunus ibn Bukayr (d. 814). The *Kitab al-Maghazi* of Muhammad ibn 'Umar al-Waqidi (d. 823) follows that of Ibn Ishaq by decades, but al-Waqidi's work appears as a contemporary to the Ibn Hisham and Ibn Bukayr recensions.[73] These works represent a stage of prophetic biography prior to the development of hadith scholarship as a formalized specialization with unique tools, methodologies, and normative expectations (evidenced by inconsistent attention to the report's isnad, or chain of transmitters).[74] The *Kitab al-Maghazi* of Ma'mar ibn al-Rashid (d. 770), which bears the strongest connection to the Medinan scholarly networks that scorned Ibn Ishaq, survives through its inclusion in the hadith collection of his student 'Abd al-Razzaq al-San'an'i (d. 826).[75]

Rather than the work of a singular author, the typical sira/maghazi text reflects an assemblage of teacher-student chains and scholarly networks. Ma'mar's *Maghazi*, for example, can be reimagined as an assemblage formed by his teachers (most prominently the traditionist Shihab al-Zuhri [d. 741]), his teachers' teachers (such as al-Zuhri's teacher and one of the "seven jurists of Medina," 'Urwa ibn al-Zubayr), *their* teachers (such as 'Urwa's aunt, A'isha), and his student, 'Abd al-Razzaq.[76] Rethinking these works as assemblages rather than monographs highlights overlaps and intersections that challenge the border between sira/maghazi and hadith collection genres. Of course, sira/maghazi works are also hadith collections, and the producers of sira/maghazi were hadith experts in their own right. Teacher-student relationships additionally bring the worlds of sira/maghazi writers and traditionists together. While Ibn Ishaq and Ma'mar ibn al-Rashid differed in their methodological orientations, they shared a mentor in al-Zuhri, who himself was alleged to have compiled a maghazi work.[77] Nonetheless, the genre of sira/maghazi was largely disdained by hadith partisans such as Ibn Hanbal for its scholars' apparent lack of rigor, as betrayed by inconsistent commitments to the chains of transmission and nascent modes of vetting reporters, as well as a willingness to combine variant reports into coherent narratives.[78]

Sira/maghazi works vary among themselves in their representations of Muhammad's body. In comparison to Ibn Ishaq and the *Maghazi* of al-Waqidi, Ma'mar's *Maghazi* is decidedly the most conservative in regards to the boundaries of Muhammad's body. It also bears noting that diverse imaginaries of the prophetic body emerge even between sources within a specific scholar's collection. While Ma'mar's *Maghazi* imagines a relatively mundane prophetic body, his *Kitab al-Jami'*, also found in the *Musannaf* of his student 'Abd al-Razzaq, offers an intensified investment. The text's *bab al-nubuwwa* section, for example, reports the tradition of Muhammad ejecting miraculous water from his hands, as well as a Companion's attestation to having seen the distinctive mark between Muhammad's shoulders.[79]

Ibn Ishaq (and his editors) and al-Waqidi expand upon the special properties of the prophetic body, its powers and transcendent perfection. Despite frequent overlap in the writers' scholarly interlocutors, these departures point to heterogeneity in the discourses on Muhammad's body between various epistemological and geographic distinctions. Muhammad's body emerges from these sources as an assemblage constructed by jurists and historians, hadith transmitters and folklorists, and Medinan and Iraqi networks, working in both competition and collaboration.

Moving from Ma'mar's era to the generation of his students, I examine the collections attributed to hadith masters in the first half of the ninth century CE, corresponding roughly to the early third century AH. These sources are organized in the subgenres of musnad and musannaf; the former providing hadiths arranged by the Companions to whom they are attributed, the latter arranging hadiths by topic. In different ways, these subgenres and their internal structures express and further contribute to the Companions' collective authorization as trustworthy reporters. Lucas argues that the acceptance of Companions as hadith narrators regardless of their positions in intra-Companion conflicts—as evidenced powerfully in Ibn Hanbal's massive *Musnad*—contributed forcefully to resolution of intra-Companion conflict as an epistemological crisis.[80] The musannaf collections, organized by topic rather than narrator, operate on the assumption of the Companions' collective probity and similarly contribute to its acceptance. The *Musannaf* of Ibn Abi Shayba includes a section devoted to the virtues (*fada'il*) of various prophets and Companions, similar to those found in the later collections of Bukhari and Muslim. Lucas explains that the fada'il chapters, praising Companions who had actively opposed each other in the power struggles of the early community, serve to smooth over intra-Companion conflicts and construct the "Companions" as a united category in which all members possess authority as reporters.[81]

In addition to these hadith sources, I include the earliest extant biographical dictionary, the *Tabaqat al-Kubra* of Ibn Sa'd (d. 845). Organized as a chronological and geographically arranged compilation of traditionists and other prominent historical figures, the *Tabaqat* begins with a two-volume collection of hadiths concerning Muhammad. The traditions are organized by topic; those pertaining to specific historical events are arranged chronologically, presenting Muhammad's life in a sir-styled narrative. The *Tabaqat*'s treatment of Muhammad could therefore be regarded as a liminal text between the genres of sira/maghazi and hadith collection and also between the networks that produced them. Ibn Sa'd's intellectual genealogy places him as an heir to the writers of sira/maghazi (his primary teacher was al-Waqidi), though he was also a hadith partisan, and his immense biographical dictionary serves the ideological and scholarly interests of hadith transmitter networks in delineating generations and cataloguing reporters. Along with the use of the Companions' as hadith transmitters and the devotion of chapters to extolling their merits, Lucas regards the biographical collection, exemplified in Ibn Sa'd's *Tabaqat*, as a significant means by which hadith scholars reconciled their methodological investments in Companions.[82]

Ibn Sa'd's *Tabaqat* also appears as a liminal artifact for its particular constructions of Muhammad's body. The *Tabaqat*'s treatment offers a prophetic body that is simultaneously more transcendent and more abjected than what is found in the sira/maghazi works. Hovering between Ma'mar's depictions of Muhammad and those in the hadith collections, Ibn Sa'd's liminal text produces not only a prophetic body that surpasses the Muhammad of other sources in its capacity to transmit baraka and extend his corporeality into and through other bodies but also one that remains more vulnerable to becoming undesirable through typical human experiences of filth and decay. The *Tabaqat* could stand between the genres of sira/maghazi and hadith collection in its representations of the prophetic body and its potential for producing or overcoming abjection. Muhammad's body, as assembled by a multiplicity of voices in the *Tabaqat* and these sources at large, remains significantly unstable in its powers and limits.

The ongoing formation of the hadith corpus over the course of the ninth century CE is marked by an increasing trend toward using only the most rigorously evidenced hadiths, whether by evaluation of a report's chain of transmitters or by widespread scholarly acceptance.[83] In contrast to Ibn Hanbal and the master critics of his generation, whose massive collections included numerous reports that satisfied varying standards of evidence, scholars in their students' generation produced collections with boasts that they had only included the most rigorously authenticated reports and discarded weaker narrations. These collections, comprising the sahih and sunan genres, are regarded as expressions of a "Sahih/Sunan movement" that in many ways departed profoundly from the preexisting culture of hadith transmission.[84] Six of the collections from this phenomenon enjoy widespread canonical authorization as the "Six Books" (*Kutub Sitta*); These are the *Sahih* collections of Bukhari (810–70) and Muslim (815–75), the *Sunan* works of Nasa'i (829–915), Abu Dawud (817–89), and Ibn Maja (824–87), and the *Jami'* of Tirmidhi (824–92). The "Two *Sahihs*" (*al-Sahihayn*) of Bukhari and Muslim achieved particular prestige in the tenth and eleventh centuries CE, when they were established as the foundation for a canonical roster that would come to include the other collections.[85] With the exception of Ibn Maja, the compilers of these works shared in a deeply interconnected network of hadith scholars centered around hubs such as Ibn Hanbal, as demonstrated in their considerable overlap of reported traditions and sources.[86] Within the construct of the Six Books, Ibn Maja's *Sunan* stands as a significant outlier. James Robson describes Ibn Maja's collection as having a "somewhat checquered career" and mixed critical reception prior to its inclusion in the Six Books.[87] Jonathan Brown argues that Ibn Maja's *Sunan* was gradually admitted into this six-collection canon precisely because Ibn Maja existed outside the scholarly network that linked the other collectors, which meant that his archive included numerous traditions that could not be found in their collections. They therefore expanded the corpus of canonical reports.[88]

While the collections of Bukhari, Muslim, Nasa'i, Abu Dawud, Tirmidhi, and Ibn Maja would gradually come to form a canonical roster as the Six Books, this canonization developed over time as a historical process rather than emerging instantly as a self-evident fact from the moment of their production. Treating the Six Books as a natural or inevitable canon projects later judgments upon them, falsely assuming an innate unity and coherence among the sources as well as consensus in their reception. This particular arrangement of sources was by no means the only option, as traditions of Sunni hadith scholarship offer multiple possibilities for imagining the canon. Some scholars' lists of preferred sources, for example, shunned Ibn Maja's *Sunan* in favor of collections such as Malik ibn Anas's *Muwatta*.[89] Moreover, that there would be a roster of six canonical works was not a given; some scholars favored shorter or longer lists of authorized collections. Ibn Khaldun refers to a five-book canon and presumes a six-book canon to represent the opinion of eastern Muslims,[90] while Ibn Hajar's ranking of the ten most trustworthy sources after the Six Books could present a sixteen-book canon.[91] Although I refer to the hadith collections of Bukhari, Muslim, Nasa'i, Abu Dawud, Tirmidhi, and Ibn Maja as the collective Six Books, I do this with a significant caution against overstating the discursive unity of these texts or imagining a shared project among their compilers.

In addition to his *Jami'*, Tirmidhi also produced a collection with special salience for a discussion of the prophetic body: his *Kitab al-Shama'il*, dedicated to describing qualities of Muhammad's physical appearance, possessions, and habits. The *Shama'il* appears to be modeled after organizational elements of Ibn Sa'd's treatment of Muhammad in his *Tabaqat*.[92] In the case of Nasa'i's *Sunan*, I examine two collections, his "greater" and "lesser" versions. Nasa'i's *Sunan al-Sughra*, a refined version of his immense *Sunan al-Kubra* boasting heightened rigor for authentication, provides the *Sunan* included in the Six Books. Beyond the scholars of this period whose works would come to be privileged under the Six Books rubric, I also include significant collections from the later ninth century CE by scholars such as ʿAbd Allah al-Darimi (d. 869), whose *Sunan* is regarded by some traditionists as more authentic and worthy of the canon than the *Sunan* of Ibn Maja.[93]

While intensified attention to transmitter-based criticism certainly produces consequences for the texts (and even if these critics who prioritized the transmission history [*isnad*] were more open to assessing reports by textual content [*matn*] than they were often willing to admit),[94] I suggest that observable patterns within these works do not amount to a discursive unity or a sweeping and absolute transformation in the corpus's treatment of Muhammad's body. Some narratives do appear to be empowered or marginalized within the Six Books and their contemporaries; specific possibilities for Muhammad's body are privileged, erased, or appear in completely new traditions without observable precedents in previous collections; and broad trends regarding imaginaries of Muhammad's body and its capabilities can be observed. Despite significant developments in the corpus during this period, however, Muhammad's body resists a uniform construction across the literature. While these sources, particularly the collections that would become the Six Books, may appear to give the prophetic body increased structure or "skeletization," the prophetic body remains significantly fluid and capable of change from one report to another.

While the *Sahih* works of Bukhari and Muslim began to circulate and achieve some degree of canonical authority from the tenth century onward,[95] the corpus was not closed; hadith scholars continued to produce their own collections. Collections emerging from the tenth and eleventh centuries broaden the literary genre of the hadith collection increasingly beyond the proto-Hanbali domain, as compilers such as al-Tabarani (d. 971), Ibn Khuzayma (d. 923), Daraqutni (d. 995), al-Hakim Naysaburi (d. 1012), his prolific student Bayhaqi (d. 1066), and Abu Nu'aym al-Isfahani (d. 1038) reflect an ascendant nexus of Ash'ari theology and Shafi'i jurisprudence that would become dominant in the eleventh century CE.[96] These Shafi'i scholars varied in their relationships to the earlier hadith partisan networks, the major collections produced within those networks, and later Hanabila. For example, Ibn Khuzayma, compiler of his own *Sahih* collection, had studied directly under Bukhari and Muslim.[97] Al-Khatib al-Baghdadi (d. 1071), considered one of the most significant systematizers of Sunni hadith methodologies, started his career in the Hanbali school and converted to Shafi'i affiliation later, falling into acrimonious and polemical engagements with the Hanbali scholars of his day.[98] Historian Muhammad ibn Jarir al-Tabari (d. 923), the "imam of hadith historiography"[99] and eponym for his own Jariri legal school who died before finishing his hadith collection, became the target of vehement Hanbali antagonism.[100] Despite the Hanbali condemnation of al-Tabari, however, the roster of teachers in al-Tabari's genealogy nonetheless overlaps significantly with that of Ibn Hanbal's son and chief transmitter, 'Abd Allah.[101] In short, the proliferation of proto-Sunni hadith scholarship, along with its contribution to the ongoing crystallization of collective Sunni identity, meant that the Sunni hadith transmission universe could not be pinned down to the domain of a singular network, elite scholarly coterie, or theological orientation.

The continuing expansion of hadith transmitter networks is paralleled by the growth of the material. While the ninth-century Sahih/Sunan movement attempted to regulate what had already been a chaotic sea of narrators and their reports by imposing more stringent standards for acceptance, later sources challenged those texts' attempts at closure, offered competing claims, and significantly deregulated the corpus. The result constitutes a discursive explosion of Muhammad's corporeal possibilities. Later collections include numerous traditions that present the prophetic body as more powerful than ever in terms of the materially facilitated baraka transmissions through which it can form connections with other bodies. However, as narratives of Muhammad's special prophetic ontology neither simply erase traditions that could emphasize his mundane humanity nor deny such connections, these sources also preserve and even intensify the relative instability of the prophetic body found in earlier sources. Traditions in which Muhammad's urine becomes an entirely deabjected and efficacious transmitter of baraka coexist alongside traditions demonstrating Muhammad's need to wash traces of his urine from his own body. Muhammad's semen continues to appear in narrations concerned with praxis as mere waste to be scratched out of his garments with a fingernail, while alternative reports present Muhammad's semen that he had ejaculated immediately after his ascension to paradise—formed from fruit that he had eaten from a tree in that alterior world—as containing material traces of paradise that would manifest in his daughter Fatima. The prophetic body, as defined in this growing archive of stories from Companions whose bodies entered into varying relations and encounters with it, does not appear as a rigorously bounded body with clear limits. Rather, as the literary corpus expands, the prophetic body grows increasingly unpredictable in both its borders and powers. Muhammad's body, examined here for what it can do, emerges as an unstable construction subject to its relations. Through these relations, Muhammad's bodily baraka spreads to other bodies, though the modes of baraka's transmission remain inconsistent and lacking systematization.

With the collections that followed and elaborated upon the Sahih/Sunan movement, the hadith collection as a literary genre is popularly believed to have reached its conclusion: the complete transferal of existing prophetic traditions from oral transmission to a textual archive.[102] While scholars of subsequent generations continued to assemble their own hadith collections, Bayhaqi's massive *Sunan al-Kubra* was widely perceived as representing the end of "original" hadith compilation,[103] and Bayhaqi himself declared that all trustworthy hadiths had been collected.[104] Compared to the collections of Bukhari and his contemporaries, which had sought to restrict the corpus to a stringently evidenced canon, Bayhaqi's *Sunan al-Kubra* reflects an aim at comprehensiveness more akin to Ibn Hanbal's archive. Similarly, the *Mu'jam al-Kabir* (Great lexicon) of Tabarani, containing at least 30,000 reports, rivals the combined number of narrations in the entire Six Books roster.[105] However, the era also produced smaller Sahih works via compilers such as Ibn Hibban and Ibn Khuzayma, and Tabarani's corpus includes less daunting Mu'jam collections, his logically titled *Mu'jam al-Awsat* (Medium lexicon) and *Mu'jam al-Saghir* (Small lexicon). Among these later sources, I also consider *dala'il al-nubuwwa* (proofs of prophethood) works, principally those of Bayhaqi and Abu Nu'aym, for the ways these explicitly named projects endeavor to mark the truth of Muhammad's station on and in his body. Bayhaqi's significant theological project, his *Al-Asma' wa l-Sifat*, additionally provides a prophetological resource for considerations of God's interactions with Muhammad's body.

Following the ostensible conclusion of original hadith compilations, hadith scholarship shifted from efforts to record previously unwritten hadiths toward a proliferation of commentaries on past collections. In these works, scholars often employed transmitter-based assessment to reconsider the judgments of master critics such as Bukhari and Muslim. The *mustadrak* genre of hadith collections emerged as an effort to broaden the hadith field that the Sahih/Sunan movement had narrowed, arguing for inclusion of traditions that Bukhari and his most rigorous contemporaries had excluded.[106] An important example, al-Hakim's *Al-Mustadrak ʿala al-Sahihayn*, illustrates a scholarly effort to argue against Bukhari and Muslim's exclusions and thus reopen the corpus.

Later biographical dictionaries also reflect an expanding corpus, most prominently in al-Khatib al-Baghdadi's enormous *Tarikh Madinat al-Salam* (History of the city of peace, or History of baghdad), which includes numerous rare traditions. In addition to Khatib's *Tarikh*, I examine Abu Nu'aym's *Hilya al-Awliya' wa-Tabaqat al-Asfiya'*, a biographical dictionary covering roughly the first four Muslim centuries. In the *Hilya*, as observed by Meis al-Kaisi, Abu Nu'aym constructs a vision of Sufi asceticism and piety as entirely "orthodox" through carefully curated representations of Muhammad's Companions and Followers.[107]

Arrangement

Within thematically arranged chapters, this book follows changes and multiplicities across the sources. The first chapter, "Reading the Prophetic Body: Genealogy, Physiognomy, and Witness," introduces Muhammad's body in terms of his ancestral genealogy and physical appearance as reported by numerous Companions, both of which spoke to the perfection of his prophetic corporeality. This chapter highlights the significance of Muhammad's body as formed from the best lineage and observably a reflection of his superior character, demonstrating that Muhammad's body is part of what qualifies him as a prophet. In this chapter, I place descriptions of Muhammad's body in conversation with discourses of physiognomy that circulated throughout the broader Mediterranean milieu (and beyond) in late antiquity, arguing that these ostensibly innocent reports of Muhammad's physical data can in fact be considered as ideologically loaded texts that seek to prove his prophethood through visibly observable facts of his body. Further examining the significance of Muhammad's body as a readable text, this chapter examines its impact on the body's viewer/reader. To see the prophetic body is to be transformed by it; the eyes of a believer not only are granted probity through their witness of Muhammad's body but become material entry points through which the witness's body becomes infused with baraka. The witness's body, according to prophetic traditions, can in turn transmit this baraka to the bodies that similarly enjoy ocular witness of it.

While the first chapter examines the prophetic body as one that is idealized for its superior ancestry and physical appearance, chapter 2, "Muhammad's Heart: The Modified Body," discusses traditions in which Muhammad's body requires various interventions by transcendent entities, including angels and even God. These entities upgrade Muhammad's body for its special vocation. In particular, this chapter focuses on Muhammad's heart as the site of supernatural modification. To become the Prophet, Muhammad's heart must not only receive discursive content from the unseen but also the injection of faith and wisdom as apparently material substances.

Chapter 3, "Bottling Muhammad: Corporeal Traces," considers Muhammad's bodily by-products, such as hair, fingernails, saliva, sweat, blood, and digestive waste. These materials provoke the question of Muhammad's capacity for bodily abjection and a significant tension with his body's relationship to flows of baraka. Are bodily fluids that would be considered offensive or disgusting when ejected or leaked from typical bodies received differently when they come from a prophetic body? Is a baraka-transmitting body's waste to be engaged simply as filthy and polluting "waste" or as a possible conduit of baraka? Can a prophetic body, subject to normal bodily processes, possibly elicit feelings of revulsion from its eyewitnesses? The sources' treatments of these materials highlights the various instabilities of the literary corpus: the changes in imaginaries of Muhammad's body over time, hierarchies of bodily products that cause some substances to be more thinkable as baraka transmitters than others, and profound differences in the ways that specific Companions (and/or the reporter networks that circulated these Companions' traditions) thought about Muhammad's body and their own relations to it.

Chapter 4, "The Sex of Revelation: Prophethood and Gendered Bodies," examines the ways that Muhammad's body and its capacity to forge connections with other bodies become characterized by gendered powers and limits. While previous chapters consider Muhammad's body as a conduit of baraka transmission between bodies, this chapter calls attention to the significance of gender in determining who can access this special body, and under what terms. This chapter argues that the sources effectively gender prophetic and angelic bodies—and even a divine body—as masculine, while also considering narratives in the sources that locate the truth of Muhammad's prophetic station in his gendered embodiment.

The concluding chapter, "Secreting Baraka: Muhammad's Body after Muhammad," briefly examines two modes by which Muhammad's body continued to operate as a potential facilitator of baraka flows and connecting node between bodies after his death: his material postmortem remains and the body of his daughter Fatima. Following this discussion, I bring together the arguments of preceding chapters to consider the instability of Muhammad's bodily powers and its reporters, reflecting on openings and closings in the prophetic assemblage.

CHAPTER ONE

Reading the Prophetic Body

Genealogy, Physiognomy, and Witness

Before asking what Muhammad's body can do, this chapter asks how that body came into the world and became observably special to the bodies with which it would interact. I first consider the forces that come together to make this body possible. What kinds of bodies precede Muhammad and contribute to the making and organizing of his parts? What claims become confirmed in the naming of his ancestors? When these bodies forge connections and produce a new body that's physically appropriate for the reception of the Qur'an, what observable symptoms can reveal the condition of such a form—and how does the body enact meaningful change upon those who see it?

The first mode through which Muhammad links to other bodies reflects a rather conventional detail of what it means to be human: simply put, Muhammad had parents. His body came from bodies that in turn connected him to the bodies from which *they* came, and so on, connecting him biologically to a chain of distant prophetic ancestors such as Abraham and his son Ishmael. In Muhammad's most immediate context, his birth automatically located him within organizations of bodies, namely families, clans, and tribes. In turn, Muhammad's body, producing descendants through his daughter Fatima, also enabled future chains of bodies that could authorize themselves via their biological credentials from him. In numerous contexts throughout Muslim-majority societies—ranging from the Imamate to numerous ruling dynasties to Sufi orders to scholars and even beggars on the street—claiming sayyid or sharif status as a descendent of Muhammad staked a claim to certain privileges of respect, consideration, and power.[1] Descent from Muhammad is meaningful because he was the best of God's creation, but Muhammad did not materialize from nothing;

his special status becomes established in part through narratives about the family tree that produced him. His body, to borrow from a 1990s advertising slogan, was "made from the best stuff on earth"; Muhammad was better because his body came from better ingredients.

How does this body prove itself? Descriptions of Muhammad's appearance, attributed to its eyewitnesses, circulate as mundane checklists of ostensibly neutral data such as the amount of hair on his torso and the manner of his stride. When it comes to the prophetic body, however, there are no neutral facts. The transmission networks that disseminated reports of his body's details inhabited a world in which facts of the body were regarded as keys to understanding facts of the soul. Even without a singular, shared ur-logic or unified theory of bodies that informed all hadith transmitters, people talked about Muhammad's body because his body contained readable signs: his body could tell stories.

This chapter begins our discussions of Muhammad's body by first investigating its origins and appearance: Where did this body come from, what did it look like, and how do the sources' answers to these questions express particular assumptions about bodies? After examining the processes through which Muhammad's body appeared in the world and the ways this special body became manifested as such to its observers, I consider the eyes and hands that could access this body and the ways that such encounters can transform the witness.

Prophetic Genealogies

The Qur'an's historical setting of late Mediterranean antiquity places it in potential encounter with diverse theories of human reproduction, including both a "one-seed" model, in which a fetus develops exclusively from the father's sperm, and a "two-seed" model, in which both parents contribute materially to the formation of their child. Kathryn Kueny has argued that the Qur'an and hadith corpus favor a Hippocratic two-seed model, and that the two-seed model was embraced by most medieval Muslim physicians and jurists.[2] The Qur'an's precise construction of each parent's role is not immediately self-evident. Though one reference describes the semen (*nutfa*) that produces a fetus in the womb as "mixed," suggesting a two-seed model, the text of the Qur'an also presents human reproduction as derived singularly from a man's deposit in the womb, which God then molds through various stages.[3]

In a well-circulated and canonical tradition regarding ritual purity laws,

Muhammad tells Umm Salama (or A'isha, depending on the version) that women have nocturnal emissions like men, and cites as evidence the fact that children can resemble their mothers.[4] In a more detailed version attributed to Anas (often as Anas narrating an exchange between Muhammad and Anas's mother, Umm Sulaym), the Prophet explains that men's "water" is white and thick, while women's water is yellow and thin, and the child will resemble whichever parent's water dominates.[5] In shorter versions, Muhammad simply gives his prescriptive ruling on ritual ablutions and does not approach the topic of heredity. Such versions appear throughout the Six Books as well as the *Muwatta* of Malik ibn Anas, who had rejected the Hippocratic position and held that only fathers contribute materially to their offspring's form.[6] Kueny also notes that the popular embrace of a two-seed model did not result in egalitarian views of reproduction, and that patriarchal assumptions about heredity still flourished in Muslim medical and juristic literatures.[7] Though both father and mother were recognized as material contributors to the fetal body, Muslim thinkers such as Avicenna also followed Aristotle in attributing the soul entirely to the father's semen.[8]

The Qur'an does not give a "family tree" for Muhammad; it does not name Muhammad's parents or grandparents, clan, or tribal lineage. The Qur'an does mention a construct called Quraysh, which historical tradition has identified as Muhammad's tribe, though the text itself does not self-evidently designate Quraysh as a tribe. As Daniel Martin Vorisco points out, "The term Quraysh is itself problematic[,] . . . a nickname" rather than a conventional tribal name (that is, the name of a founding ancestor), and it is not clear when Quraysh came to be understood as a tribal unit.[9] When examining the Qur'an for the significance of Muhammad's ancestry, I read largely for silences.

Vorisco observes, "Even if the genealogy of the Prophet is assumed to be largely a myth, the important point is how and why genealogists constructed it"; prophetic genealogy operates as an authorizing discourse, establishing Muhammad's biological line to Abraham and Ishmael and producing a context for his prophethood.[10] The *Sira* invests powerful meanings in Muhammad's ancestry, starting the prophetic biography with an extensive patrilineal genealogy that traces all the way back to Adam, and devotes special attention to the descendants of Ishmael.[11] Later discussing the marriage of Muhammad's parents, Ibn Ishaq also documents the patrilineal descent of Muhammad's mother, establishing that his parents share a patrilineal grandfather in Abdu' Manaf, and traces her matrilineal descent to demonstrate a further connection with the same line.[12] These are the bodies through which Muhammad's body was produced, legitimizing Muhammad as a physical descendent of Abraham.

Hadith traditions would amplify Muhammad's genealogical elitism. Ibn Sa'd reports Muhammad stating that when God intends to appoint a prophet, he identifies the best tribe and then appoints its best man.[13] In a tradition appearing in the *Tabaqat*, Ibn Abi Shayba's *Musannaf*, and Ibn Hanbal's *Musnad*, Muhammad explains that he has descended from the best son of every best son, asserting that from the sons of Abraham, God chose Ishmael; from the sons of Ishmael, God chose Kinana; from the sons of Kinana, God chose the tribe of Quraysh, and from the Quraysh, God chose the clan of Banu Hashim. From the Banu Hashim, God chose Muhammad.[14] Another tradition presents Muhammad explaining that he came from the best family, from the best tribe, from the best group; in one variant, he issues this statement in response to unnamed critics' slights upon his ancestry.[15] Ibn Abi Shayba reports this tradition from a pro-'Alid narrator, Muhammad ibn Fudayl. Both Ibn Abi Shayba and Ibn Hanbal trace the transmission to pro-'Alid narrator Yazid ibn Abi Ziyad, who attributes the narration to 'Abd Allah ibn al-Harith ibn Nawful (who happens to be the Prophet's first cousin once removed, tracing his patrilineal descent to al-Harith ibn 'Abd al-Muttalib, son of Muhammad's grandfather). Varying chains in turn locate the original source for 'Abd Allah's narration either as Muhammad's uncle 'Abbas or 'Abd al-Muttalib ibn Rabi'a, grandson of al-Harith ibn 'Abd al-Muttalib and thereby 'Abd Allah's first cousin once removed.[16] Narrations of Muhammad's genealogical privilege serve a double authorization: while locating Muhammad atop a biological pyramid, they also privilege their reporters who share his roots.

Ibn Sa'd preserves three variations of the tradition in which Muhammad describes himself as the chosen individual from a chosen clan, from a chosen tribe, and so on, which departs from the above "chosen" tradition in describing God's selection with the verb *akhtara* rather than *astafa*. The akhtara versions additionally include Arabs as one of the chosen categories. Two of these trace the report to Muhammad al-Baqir, the fifth Shi'i Imam (and Muhammad's great-great-grandson). In an extended version, presented in the isnad as a transmission from al-Baqir to his son, the sixth Imam, Ja'far as-Sadiq, the Prophet expands God's process of choosing at both ends: "God divided the earth into two halves and made me from the best of them. Then he divided the half into thirds and I was from the best third. Then he preferred the Arabs from humanity. Then he preferred Quraysh from the Arabs. Then he preferred Bani Hashim from Quraysh. Then he preferred Bani ʿAbd al-Muttalib from Bani Hashim. Then he preferred me from Bani ʿAbd al-Muttalib."[17]

The inclusion of ʿAbd al-Muttalib's progeny among the privileged categories grants an increased share in Muhammad's prestige to his paternal cousins ʿAli and Ibn ʿAbbas. The tradition also appears in the canonical collections of Tirmidhi and Muslim with a shortened version, leaving out ʿAbd al-Muttalib.[18]

The high esteem with which the sources treat Muhammad's ancestors reads in tension with another theme of the prophetic biography and early Muslim historiography: depictions of pre-Islamic Arabia as lost in depraved ignorance (*jahiliyya*). A number of traditions address the problem. Muhammad declares, "I came from marriage; I do not come from fornication. From the time of Adam, the fornication of jahiliyya never touched me." Versions of the tradition appear with chains that include the Prophet's descendants, the fifth and sixth Imams, as transmitters. Ibn Sa'd also includes a shorter version ("I came from marriage, not fornication") attributed to A'isha.[19] Insofar as Muhammad's moral integrity relates to the integrity of his lineage, he remains protected in every generation that precedes him.

Muhammad apparently existed within these bodies prior to his own formation. Rubin's discussions of Qur'an exegesis reveal openings in the text for consideration of Muhammad as preexisting his conception as "part of the spermatic substance of his ancestors."[20] Rubin observes early Muslim sources imagining Muhammad as an "integral prophetic entity" that existed throughout the generations, leading to this entity's "visible manifestation on earth, through the corporeal Muhammad."[21] Citing pre-Islamic poetry, Rubin points out that this "notion of a primordial spermatic substance wandering through pure forefathers" expressed ideas about bodies that were already established in Muhammad's setting.[22]

Though Muhammad's preexistence does not find explicit articulation in the sira/maghazi sources, Ibn Ishaq's *Sira* provides an account in which Muhammad's father, ʿAbd Allah, becomes marked by a shining light on his forehead (described in one account as "a blaze like the blaze of a horse"). A woman (whose own genealogy is provided in the *Sira*, establishing her as a legitimate candidate) offers herself to ʿAbd Allah, but he declines, marries Amina, and consummates their marriage. When ʿAbd Allah sees the woman again, he asks her why she does not repeat her earlier offer, to which she answers that the light had vanished. The woman adds that she had heard from her Christian brother Waraqa that a prophet would soon appear. ʿAbd

Allah apparently lost the blazing light with the ejection of his prophetic semen; the light next manifests from Amina after she becomes pregnant.[23]

In the *Musnad* and *Tabaqat*, Abu Hurayra reports Muhammad stating, "I was sent from the best generations of Bani Adam, generation after generation, until I was sent from the generation that I am in."[24] Ibn Sa'd presents a tradition in which Ibn 'Abbas explains the statement of the Qur'an "And your movement among those who prostrate"[25] as signifying that Muhammad had passed through generations of his pious forefathers. According to Ibn 'Abbas, this verse amounts to God telling Muhammad, "From prophet to prophet, and from prophet to prophet, until I brought you out as a prophet."[26] A popular tradition identifies Muhammad as a prophet prior to the formation of Adam; an interlocutor asks Muhammad about the beginning of his prophethood, to which Muhammad answers, "When Adam was between spirit and body."[27] Slight variations in wording produce meaningful differences for the prophetic ontology; some versions represent the inquirer asking Muhammad how long he had been a prophet (*matta kunta nabiyan?*), while others depict the inquirer asking when Muhammad was appointed (*ju'ilta*) or written (*kutibta*) as a prophet. In the latter reading, Muhammad was only a prophet prior to Adam in the sense that God had decreed his prophethood in advance, as with all things. A Kufan transmission attributed to 'Amir al-Sha'bi reports an unnamed man asking Muhammad, "When did you become a prophet?" (*mata astunbi'ta?*) to which Muhammad gives an extended answer: "When Adam was between spirit and body, the moment when the covenant was taken from me."[28]

Even if Muhammad came from a pure lineage, tension between his genealogical excellence and the jahiliyya of his historical setting persists in the question of his parents' fates. As the biographical tradition reports that Muhammad's father died before his birth, and Muhammad's mother died when he was a small child, neither of his parents could have witnessed his prophethood. The sources considered here generally favor a position that Muhammad's parents appear to receive the fate of unbelievers, exhibited in two traditions: one in which Muhammad tells a man who had inquired about his own father, "My father and your father are in the fire,"[29] and another in which Muhammad asks that God allow him to pray for his mother's forgiveness, a request that God denies.[30] While Bukhari and Muslim support the view of Muhammad's parents having been condemned to the fire, al-Hakim's supplement to their *Sahih*s vouches for a tradition in which Muhammad, when asked if he saw his parents in the fire, answers that God had promised to fulfill his requests on their behalf.[31]

A late and obscure tradition, appearing beyond the historical range of this study, depicts God granting Muhammad's request for his mother to be resurrected, but just long enough for her to bear witness to his prophethood. "She believed in me," Muhammad recalls, "and then God returned her." In another narration, God grants Muhammad the privilege of intercession for his father, his uncle Abu Talib (who is unambiguously condemned to hellfire in precanonical and canonical proto-Sunni collections),[32] and his milk-brother.[33]

Physiognomy and Logics of the Body

As Patricia Cox observes in her discussion of Greco-Roman biographies of holy men, ancient biographers commonly relied on physiognomy, a discourse of the body that "sought to reveal a man's virtuous or vicious nature by emphasizing certain aspects of the physique and linking these to specific character traits."[34] I would not attempt to forensically trace roots for Muslim physiognomy, but it is worth recognizing that throughout Mediterranean antiquity, writers treated the body and soul (if these were even perceived as truly separated) as signifiers of each other. Expressions of what has been termed a "physiognomic consciousness" appear throughout the literature of the age: it was the water in which ancient intellectuals swam.[35] It appears in the life of Socrates, who defends himself against physiognomic judgment while still upholding the validity of the science: When the physiognomist Zopyrus determines from examining Socrates's eyes that Socrates is consumed with lust, Socrates agrees with Zopyrus's assessment but asserts that with his rational power, he learned to manage his appetite.[36] From the third century BCE, the Mediterranean saw a proliferation of physiognomic literatures that provided detailed instructions for reading signs of the body.[37] Physiognomy also flourished in Mesopotamia, where scholars interpreted bodily features such as skin color and moles for omens of a person's future and professional qualifications (for example, disqualifying diviners with physical abnormalities and inferior lineages).[38]

Jewish literature of the Second Temple period reveals a physiognomic consciousness, exhibited in Philo's presentation of Moses's beautiful body as evidence of his soul's condition,[39] as well as texts from the Qumran community that refer to an enigmatic "Elect of God," theorized to have been Noah, who becomes identifiable at birth via particular hairs and moles on his body.[40] The Hebrew Bible and adjacent literatures offer affirmations of physiognomy as well as resistance to it.[41]

As Callie Callon demonstrates in her work on early Christians, physiognomic consciousness informed a variety of approaches to Jesus's body. Christian writers such as Gregory of Nazianzus and Jerome, faced with the unflattering description of Jesus in Isaiah 53 ("He had no form nor beauty"), sought to mitigate or undo its effects for those readers who could not imagine an ugly god. Others, such as Iranaeus, Clement, Tertullian, and Origen, accepted and utilized an unattractive Jesus in their work. Callon suggests that their advocacy of an "ugly" Jesus relates to theological issues such as proving that Jesus had a body of earthly flesh (rather than a body composed of the same material as angelic bodies) or offering social prescriptions for Christians to avoid vanity.[42]

Sanskrit sources also read character through signs of the body. Demonstrating a "fundamental lexical similarity" between Greek and Sanskrit physiognomic literature, Kenneth Zysk has argued that Hellenic and Indian physiognomies developed in conversation with one another as these sciences flowed between cultures in antiquity.[43] In particular, Zysk identifies a template of bodily signs that were prioritized in Greek and Sanskrit literature: pseudo-Aristotelian clusters of "bodily sources" correspond almost perfectly with Garga's "marks" for their mutual interests in gait and movement, skin complexion, skin texture, hairiness, and overall shape of the body; Garga additionally considers the body's radiant glow and natural fragrance.[44] While observing consistencies and overlaps in ancient physiognomic archives, however, scholars such as Callon offer careful reminders that physiognomy was not a uniformly theorized science with a systematic and consistent method but rather "messy, and often contradictory," both within and beyond the formal physiognomy manuals and even within a single physiognomist's work.[45]

Informed by local as well as "global" flows of physiognomic knowledge, early Muslim intellectuals regarded the body as a text to be read and deciphered. Greek, Persian, and Sanskrit discourses of the body intersected with indigenous traditions of physiognomy such as the pre-Islamic Arab practice of *qiyafa*, the science of determining paternity by assessment of a child's appearance. In a widely disseminated tradition, A'isha recalls that the controversy over Zayd's paternity of Usama was settled by the verdict of a *qa'if*, an expert in local physiognomic sciences, who identifies their relationship by looking at their feet.[46] The broader Arabic term for physiognomic knowledge, *firasa*, can also signify intuitive judgment and appears in one of the canonical Six Books with an ambiguous statement from the Prophet: "Beware of the believer's firasa, for he sees with the light of God."

According to the narrating Companion, Abu Sa'id al-Khudri, Muhammad then recited the Qur'an's promise, "In that are signs for those who can look closely" (15:75).[47]

Amid these circulating sciences, Muslim traditionists disseminated accounts of Muhammad's physical appearance that seemed to prioritize details popular in physiognomic sciences. Descriptions of Muhammad's moderate bodily proportions, hair texture, body hair, and skin color (in particular, variants describing his skin as white mixed with red)[48] overlap considerably with Polemon's description of "the man who loves knowledge" in his *Physiognomy*, disseminated in Arabic via the 'Abbasid translation movement (Polemon himself was hailed as *Sahib al-Firasa*, "Master of Physiognomy").[49] Hellenic physiognomists idealized a body of perfect proportion and balance as free from the negative personality traits related to various bodily excesses.[50] Polemon's description of the man who loves knowledge includes notes on his complexion (white mixed with red), hair texture (wavy hair inclining to ruddiness, lank hair neither overly curly nor projecting), and body (evenly proportioned, with heavy surfaces, neither too much body hair nor too little).[51] In another section from his *Physiognomy*, Polemon describes the "pure Greek" as having medium stature, standing neither too tall nor too short, with his complexion a mixture of white and red, and hair having some curliness and some waviness.[52] As this chapter demonstrates, reports attributed to various Companions echo Polemon in privileging moderation as a virtue of the prophetic body.

As a mode of learning internal personality traits through external bodily ones, physiognomy was practiced by such foundational Muslim figures as al-Shafi'i, who harshly judged the character of people with thick lips, long noses, fair and ruddy complexions, bulging foreheads, blue eyes, and various physical defects or disabilities (*naqis al-khalq*), identifying them as devils.[53] These scholarly giants became objects of physiognomic judgments in their own right, as in hagiographic reports of Malik ibn Anas as "one of the most handsome people in his face and the sweetest of them in eye, the purest of them in whiteness and the most perfect of them in height and the most excellent in body."[54] Ibn al-Jawzi's medieval biography of Ibn Hanbal includes testimonies to Ibn Hanbal's handsome face, dark complexion, and tall or medium height.[55]

The Qur'an, while repeatedly describing disbelief and hypocrisy as diseases of the heart (2:10, 5:52, 8:49, 9:125, 22:53, 24:50, 33:12, 33:32, 33:60, 47:20, 47:29) and in one verse describing faces on the Day of Judgment as either white or black in accordance with their spiritual conditions (3:106), does not disclose a clear theory of physiognomy. Nor does the Qur'an express concern with interpreting the details of Muhammad's body. When the Qur'an makes arguments for its own status as a divine revelation sent to a genuine prophet, it does not use Muhammad's physical appearance as evidence.

While depicting Muhammad's prenatal presence in his parents' bodies as light, early sira/maghazi literature also remains largely unconcerned with details of Muhammad's appearance. The sources offer their most overt example of Muhammad's body proving his station in their reports of the Seal of Prophethood, which appears as a mark on Muhammad's back. While the Seal will be discussed in a later chapter as an example of the prophetic body undergoing modification, its status varies between sources, and the sira/maghazi literature seems to prefer presentations of the Seal as a birthmark, an organic part of Muhammad's body. The Seal reads as a physiognomic secret of the prophetic body, a signifier noted in Jewish or Christian omen literature that will reveal Muhammad's status to those who already know to look for it.[56] The Seal becomes a sign to be deciphered.

Physiognomic interests find expression in Muhammad's heavenly ascension, as hierarchical relations seemingly become mapped onto the details of bodies. Among the reports of Muhammad's ascension found in Ibn Ishaq's *Sira*, Muhammad describes the bodies of Moses and Jesus with attention to their height, skin color, and hair texture: Moses was a "ruddy faced man, tall, thinly fleshed, curly haired with a hooked nose as though he were of the Shanu'a"; Jesus was a "reddish man of medium height with lank hair with many freckles on his face as though he had just come from a bath. One would suppose that his head was dripping with water, though there was no water in it."[57] Muhammad further compares Jesus's bodily details to the appearance of 'Urwa ibn Mas'ud al-Thaqafi. Muhammad also reports seeing Abraham but gives no information concerning Abraham's physical appearance, explaining only that he had never seen a man more like himself. In this narration, bodies serve a polemical point: with the apparent implication that if Moses, Jesus, and Muhammad appear as stand-ins for their respective communities, Muhammad's body proves his superior correspondence to Abraham's religion.[58] While claiming this embodied resonance between Muhammad and Abraham, the *Sira* never describes either man in detail. In his notes, however, Ibn Hisham supplements the ascension narrative with a detailed description of Muhammad's appearance from 'Ali through his grandson Ibrahim.[59]

Turning to Muhammad's physical description requires a critical pause on the point of his skin color. While some traditions describe Muhammad's complexion as white, this whiteness should not be read in correspondence with modern racial categories. In classical Arabic vocabularies of skin color, "white" (*abyad*) signifies a shade of brown lighter than *asmar*. A pale complexion would have been termed "red" (*ahmar* or *hamra*, as seen in Humayra—"little red one"—the Prophet's pet name for A'isha).[60] In terms of skin color, "red" is just as likely as "white" to be treated as the opposite of "black," as in traditions in which the Prophet implies the full range of humanity by referring to "the Blacks and the Reds."[61]

Muhammad's skin color and other physiognomic details appear from the earliest formations of the hadith corpus. Malik's *Muwatta* operates almost entirely as a collection of legal and ritual precedents, displaying virtually no investment in special qualities of Muhammad's body; but in his chapter, "The Attributes of the Prophet," Malik provides Anas's short description of Muhammad's physical appearance. Anas states that Muhammad was neither too tall nor too short, neither exceedingly white (*al-abyad al-amhaq*) nor very dark (*al-adam*); his hair was neither curly nor lank; God commissioned his prophethood at the age of forty; he spent a decade in Mecca, followed by a decade in Medina; God caused him to die at the age of sixty; and there were fewer than twenty white hairs on his head or in his beard.[62] Variations in which Anas, 'Ali, Abu Hurayra, or other Companions survey Muhammad's observable bodily traits appear throughout the hadith corpus.[63] Some versions conclude with a recollection, "The likes of him had not been seen before or since,"[64] or the more personal reflection "*I* have not seen his likeness since."[65]

Ibn Abi Shayba's *Kitab al-Fada'il* in his *Musannaf* begins with traditions on varied excellences of Muhammad, including his corporeal features. A narration attributed to 'Ali and reported by his grandson Ibrahim mentions Muhammad's moderation in height and hair color, the roundness of his face, and his skin color (white mixed with red), deep-black eyes, long eyelashes, body hair, and stride, as well as the Seal of Prophethood between his shoulders. In the same section, another transmission from 'Ali provides a compatible account; both 'Ali narrations share the concluding note of having never seen Muhammad's likeness before or since.[66] In a *Tabaqat* report with transmission via Kufan pro-'Alid narrators, Ali's son (and the Prophet's grandson) Hasan recalls having asked his uncle Hind ibn Abi Hala al-Tamimi to recall Muhammad's physical attributes. Hind discusses details such as the size of Muhammad's forehead, the broadness of his chest, his balanced proportions, and his complexion's resemblance to silver or the moon.[67]

In the *Kitab al-Jami'* of 'Abd al-Razzaq's *Musannaf*, attributed to his teacher

Ma'mar, the "Attributes of the Prophet" subsection consists of two reports, both of which discuss visually observable details of the prophetic body. The first narrates that when asked about the attributes of Muhammad, Abu Hurayra answered by referring to Muhammad's height, the broadness of his shoulders, his black hair, long eyelashes, and fully fleshed feet, and added that when Muhammad removed his cloak from his shoulders, he appeared to have been cast in silver, concluding that Muhammad's likeness had not been seen before or since.[68] In the second report, 'Abd al-Razzaq narrates that Ma'mar narrated from al-Zuhri that Muhammad was "white in color" (*abyad al-lawn*), adding, "Ma'mar said: 'I heard another than al-Zuhri saying, 'He was brown [*asmar*].''"[69] In other remarks on Muhammad's complexion, Hasan ibn 'Ali describes Muhammad as "radiant" or "illuminating" white (*abyad azhar*),[70] Ibn 'Abbas terms Muhammad's skin as "brown to white" (*asmar ila al-bayad*),[71] and Abu Hurayra remembers Muhammad simply as the "best of humanity in color."[72] A'isha does not emerge in these sources as a prominent reporter of her husband's appearance but in an obscure narration recites her father's praise of Muhammad as a white man, a supporter of widows and orphans, who brings the rain by virtue of his face.[73]

Comparing accounts of Muhammad's body attributed to various Companions, I find some patterns. Narrations attributed to 'Ali tend to describe Muhammad's complexion as a mixture of white and red; narrations attributed to Anas describe Muhammad's skin tone as brown (*asmar*) or a medium complexion between excessively white (*al-abyad al-amhaq*) and dark (*al-adam*).[74] Echoing the association of Muhammad with light, both 'Ali and Anas recollect Muhammad's complexion as glowing or luminous in color (*azhar al-lawn*); an 'Ali narration in Ibn Hanbal's *Musnad* describes Muhammad as "white of extreme illumination" (*abyad shadid al-wadah*).[75] Anas and other Basran reporters further celebrate Muhammad's body with details such as the extreme softness of his hand and the sweetness of his bodily fragrance, superior respectively to silk and musk.[76] Motifs such as Muhammad's radiant and/or medium complexion, medium stature, medium hair texture, and unique stride (walking as if descending from a height) appear broadly throughout narrations attributed to multiple Companions.[77]

Multiple hadiths present Muhammad's body as fulfilling expectations of a future prophet foretold in Jewish and Christian texts. A narration transmitted by descendants of 'Ali depicts an encounter between 'Ali and "a scholar from the scholars of the Jews" in which observable facts of

Muhammad's body compel recognition of his prophethood. In this report, the Jewish scholar listens as ʿAli gives a sermon in Yemen. While examining a book in his hands, the Jewish scholar asks ʿAli to describe Abu-l-Qasim ("Father of Qasim," Muhammad's *kunya* or familial honorific). ʿAli gives a familiar account of Muhammad's height, hair, head, skin color, shoulders, hands and feet, body hair, eyelashes, eyebrows, and stride, concluding that he had never witnessed Muhammad's likeness before or since. The scholar asks for more information, but ʿAli insists that he has reported what he remembers. The scholar then adds details on Muhammad's eyes, beard, mouth, and ears, and describes the particular way that Muhammad turned to face toward or away from something, which the scholar recalls having read in "the scriptures of my ancestors." He then recites details of Muhammad's biography, all of which are familiar to ʿAli. Resonances between the scholar's own archive and ʿAli's eyewitness report of Muhammad prompt the scholar to accept Muhammad's mission as genuine.[78] Muhammad's body, measured against Jewish prophecies of a future body, confirms Muhammad's supersession over Jewish tradition.

The Seal between Muhammad's shoulders becomes increasingly significant as the corpus expands. The Qur'an refers to Muhammad as the "Seal of Prophets" (33:40), though this appears to signify a particular status rather than a feature of his body. Biographical representations of Muhammad, while preserving the Seal of Prophets as a distinct title for him, also describe a material *khatam al-nubuwwa* or "Seal of Prophethood" locatable on his flesh. This Seal marks Muhammad's body with a sign for those who can understand it intertextually through their prior knowledge. In the account of Muhammad's flight to Medina in Wahb's *Maghazi*, the sight of the Seal sparks a conversion experience for Muhammad's hired trail guide. Upon observing this corporeal sign when Muhammad's cloak falls from his shoulder, the learned ʿAbd Allah ibn Urayqat ("a man who was passionate about reading books") immediately recognizes the mark on Muhammad's body. He kisses Muhammad (possibly on the Seal itself, as the Arabic does not allow for distinction between "him" and "it") and bears witness to the oneness of God.[79] The account does not clarify whether the Seal constitutes an organic part *of* Muhammad's body, as in a cyst or mole, or something that happened *to* his body, like the literal stamping of a seal. Nonetheless, the Seal operates as a center of gravity on Muhammad's body, an attractor to which people are drawn and through which they come to perceive Muhammad as extraordinary.

Ibn Ishaq's *Sira* treats the Seal as an apparently organic birthmark by which witnesses (particularly those with access to sacred literatures) can recognize Muhammad's status both before and after the start of his mission. In Muhammad's youth, the Christian monk Bahira recognizes him as a future prophet in part through witnessing the Seal. Observing a number of signs in Muhammad, Bahira looks at Muhammad's back and finds the Seal as it had been described in his books; Ibn Hisham's notes compare the Seal's appearance to the mark left by a cupping-glass.[80] The *Sira* also refers to the Seal in the conversion narrative of Salman al-Farisi. Under the tutelage of a pious and learned man, Salman learns of a future prophet in Arabia who would be identifiable by the Seal of Prophethood between his shoulders. When Salman later meets Muhammad, he turns to look at Muhammad's back; Muhammad realizes what Salman desires and removes his cloak. Salman recognizes the Seal and weepingly kisses Muhammad, bearing witness to the prophetic body as the site at which he encountered the fulfillment of divine promise.[81]

Hadith collections expand upon references to the Seal of Prophethood as a natural bodily omen through which a trained eye can recognize Muhammad's status. Companions testifying to their own experiences of having seen or touched the Seal treat it as a natural part of Muhammad's body, describing the Seal as a mass of hair or accumulation of warts, and comparing its appearance to a bird's egg or camel dung. The Seal remains linked to Jewish or Christian knowledge, as in the above tradition of Salman learning from a monk to identify the coming prophet by his bodily signs.[82] A report attributed to A'isha in the *Tabaqat*, thematically echoing 'Ali's exchange with the Jewish scholar in Yemen, presents the Seal's appearance as a fulfillment of prophecy. This isolated account is particularly rare for presenting a possible reference to the Seal with attribution to A'isha (though she does not call it the Seal). A'isha narrates that on the night of Muhammad's birth, a Meccan Jew asked the Quraysh if any of them had given birth to a boy with a blackish-yellow mole between his shoulders, covered in thick hair; the awaited Arab prophet had just been born, the Jew explained, and his name would be Ahmad. When brought to newborn Muhammad, the Jew witnessed the baby's mole and fainted as he recognized that the Arab prophet had come.[83]

The *Tabaqat*, which devotes a subsection to reports of the Seal, includes four narrations in which a Companion perceives the Seal as requiring medical treatment, thus pathologizing the prophetic body. All four narrations convey the experience of a physician who visits Muhammad and are related by the Companion Abu Rimtha. In three of the narrations, Abu Rimtha himself is the physician; of these, two mention that he is accompanied by his son. The fourth account presents Abu Rimtha himself as the son, accompanying his physician father. In each of these four reports, the physician, upon observing the Seal, offers to treat it; in two of these, he diagnoses the Seal as a cyst. One report portrays Abu Rimtha as stating that he could treat it medically and that God would then "cure" his prophet. In another, Abu Rimtha's son trembles in fear or awe upon seeing Muhammad, which is immediately followed by Abu Rimtha suggesting that Muhammad allow him to treat the Seal. In each of the reports, Muhammad declines the offer, answering variously that the Seal's only physician is he who created it, that it will be treated by he who placed it, or more explicitly that it has no physician except God.[84]

A tradition in the *Musnad* depicts a man from the Banu ʿAmir asking Muhammad, "Show me the Seal that is between your shoulders, for I am the best healer of people." Muhammad responds simply by asking the man if he wants to see a sign (*ayat*), to which the man answers yes. Muhammad then shows bushels of dates becoming animated by his verbal command, after which the man announces to his people that he had never seen a more magical man than on that day.[85] In this depiction of a doctor's meeting with the Prophet, Muhammad's body becomes a site to which access is denied in favor of an alternative demonstration of his prophetic status.

After Muhammad's death, details of his body confirm his visits to later Muslims in dreams. Basran traditionist Yazid al-Farisi recalls that he mentioned his dream of Muhammad to the Prophet's cousin Ibn ʿAbbas, who asks him to describe the man he had seen. When Yazid describes the dream visitor's medium size, medium complexion (brown inclining to white), smile, eyes, beautiful face, and the thickness of his beard, Ibn ʿAbbas affirms that Yazid had indeed received a visit from the Prophet.[86] This exchange between the traditionist and the Companion affirms and authorizes both men: Yazid al-Farisi, who had not seen Muhammad in person, proves that he had been privileged by a genuine encounter with Muhammad in his dream; Ibn ʿAbbas, confirming the truth of Yazid's dream for him, maintains his own privilege as an eyewitness of the late Prophet's body.

Ibn Sa'd organizes many of the above traditions within his *Tabaqat*'s chapter on attributes of Muhammad's *khalq*, his nature. The range of meanings drawn from the *kh-l-q* root, immediately signifying the act of creation, includes signifiers for both innate disposition and physical form. Discussions of Muhammad's khalq in early hadith sources engage both possibilities, discussing Muhammad's character as well as his physical body. In Ibn

Sa'd's section on Muhammad's khalq, the narrations conceptualize khalq as referring chiefly to physical appearance. It is here that Ibn Sa'd presents ʿAli, Anas, and others providing "sketch-artist" accounts of Muhammad's body.

While these eyewitness accounts enforce relations of power by definition, four reports from the section explicitly present the reciting of Muhammad's bodily details as evidence that can enhance or diminish one's authority. Like Ibn Abi Shayba's section on Muhammad in his fada'il chapter, Ibn Sa'd's narrations on Muhammad's khalq include the account of Ibn ʿAbbas confirming the truth of Yazid al-Farisi's dream, with an added statement from Ibn ʿAbbas that because the Devil cannot impersonate Muhammad's form, anyone who sees Muhammad in a dream has truly seen him.[87] Also in this section, Abu Tufayl boldly presents himself as the last living person to have seen Muhammad. When asked for Muhammad's description, Abu Tufayl confirms his position as the final eyewitness custodian of Muhammad's legacy by recalling Muhammad's complexion, handsomeness, and medium height.[88] In a report attributed to Ibn ʿAbbas, I again encounter Muhammad giving accounts of Jesus (curly hair, red complexion, broad chest) and Moses (lank hair, dark brown skin, sturdy body) in comparison to Abraham, whom Muhammad describes only with a simple instruction: "Look at your companion," that is, Muhammad himself. Muhammad identifies himself as the closest to Abraham and also a golden mean between the oppositional skin colors and hair textures that set Jesus and Moses apart from one another.[89]

Even in narrations that do not name their stakes so clearly, accounts of direct encounters with Muhammad's body can exert claims for truth-making power. To recall having touched and smelled Muhammad, particularly in Anas's context of Basra (in which hadith transmitters, perhaps including the allegedly centenarian Anas, often exaggerated their ages to forge greater connections to the past and thus acquire greater prestige for their narrations[90]), bolsters Anas's position as a legitimate eyewitness to the Prophet. The prestige and baraka of contact with this extraordinary body extends through Anas to his students, as illustrated in Thabit kissing Anas's hands and eyes, exclaiming that these hands and eyes had touched and seen the Prophet.[91]

Investments in Muhammad's appearance provoke diverse consequences for competing partisan networks. While a handful of Companions offer accounts of Muhammad's physical description, Muhammad's patrilineal cousin ʿAli and Companions with favorable relationships to ʿAli's household appear with particular prominence. In Ibn Sa'd's khalq section, several chains of transmission from 'Ali travel through his biological descendants (who are descended not only from Muhammad's patrilineal cousin but also Muhammad himself through Fatima), and his son Hasan also appears as the original source for narrations. Other narrators in Ibn Sa'd's khalq section include pro-'Alid Companions such as 'Ali's cousin Ibn 'Abbas, Jabir ibn Samura, Jabir ibn 'Abd Allah, Abu Tufayl, and Bara' ibn al-'Azib. If reporting the excellences of Muhammad's body privileges 'Ali, his family, and supporters, 'Ali's prime antagonist in the Battle of the Camel becomes notable for her lack of a similar "sketch-artist" account of Muhammad's bodily details. A'isha only appears with two reports in the khalq section: one in which she describes Muhammad's manner of turning, another in which she describes his standing and sitting in prayer.[92] While these reports do not exactly offer a *dis*embodied representation of Muhammad—A'isha still speaks with/to an interest in her husband's body—she breaks from the ways 'Ali, Anas, and others map a prophetic corporeagraphy.

While some narrations incorporate both physical attributes and moral character into their discussions of the prophetic khalq, even presenting the former as proof of the latter, A'isha's narrations emphasize Muhammad's khalq as his personality. Though a minor presence in Ibn Sa'd's section on the prophetic khalq, A'isha becomes extraordinarily prolific in Ibn Sa'd's collected narrations on Muhammad's akhlaq, his character and ethics.[93] In Ibn Sa'd's akhlaq section, A'isha provides more than a third of the reports, dominating over familiar narrators such as Anas and Ibn 'Abbas and describing matters such as Muhammad's abstinence from spousal violence.[94] The section opens with four accounts of A'isha's famous declaration that Muhammad's khalq was the Qur'an itself. Three of the accounts describe an exchange in which a man asks A'isha to inform him of Muhammad's khalq, to which she answers simply that Muhammad's khalq was the Qur'an (sometimes with snark, asking, "Don't you read the Qur'an?"). Qatada supplements A'isha's statement in this account with his note, "And the Qur'an came with the best akhlaq of humanity."[95] The fourth account does not mention A'isha by name but presents the statement as reflecting the position of Muhammad's wives.[96] These narrations of the prophetic khalq are followed in the chapter by Anas's statement that Muhammad was "the best of humanity in manners [*khuluqan*]."[97]

Knowledge of Muhammad's khalq features in a tradition in which A'isha demonstrates her superior authority over other Companions. When Sa'd ibn Hisham asks Ibn 'Abbas about Muhammad's performance of *witr* prayer, Ibn ʿAbbas replies that he can either answer Saʾd himself, "or I can point you to the one with the most knowledge of all the people of Earth concerning the witr of the Messenger of God." "Who is that?" asks Saʾd. Ibn ʿAbbas answers, "Aʾisha. Go to her and ask her on that. Then return and relate to me what she has told you." Saʾd asks Aʾisha about Muhammad's khalq, night prayer, and witr, after which he goes back to Ibn ʿAbbas and tells him what Aʾisha had said, prompting Ibn ʿAbbas's wistful reply, "If only I could go to her and receive her speech verbally."[98] Beyond its claim on Muhammad, the report can make a compelling argument about authority in the postprophetic era for its depiction of Ibn ʿAbbas, who led a wing of his cousin ʿAli's army against Aʾisha's forces in the Battle of the Camel, deferring to Aʾisha's knowledge as superior to his own. The narration orders a value hierarchy among Companions—one that even reverses the hierarchy found elsewhere, as in Maʾmar's declaration that he would not favor Aʾisha over Ibn ʿAbbas on the controversy over Muhammad seeing God.[99]

In his commentary on the Qurʾan, ʿAbd al-Razzaq cites Aʾisha's naming the Qurʾan as Muhammad's khalq for his note on 68:4.[100] At first reading, Aʾisha's statement simply affirms that her late husband's moral character corresponded to the essence of the divine revelation with which he had been entrusted. As Geissinger's work on Aʾisha's Qurʾanic exegesis has shown, this reflects the broader tafsir tradition's reading of her statement.[101] When reexamined in conversation with the detailed celebrations of her husband's body found elsewhere, Aʾisha reads as shutting down the interest in her husband's embodied khalq, denying a request for physiognomic data and deflecting its political consequences. When Saʾd ibn Hisham, born too late to have seen Muhammad with his own eyes, asks Aʾisha to describe her husband's khalq, does he seek prophetic ethics or a vision of the prophetic body? Does Aʾisha articulate Muhammad's khalq in a different way than Saʾd might have heard from ʿAli's cousin and ally Ibn ʿAbbas, who shares in Muhammad's genealogy as a paternal grandson of ʿAbd al-Muttalib and appears in the sources as a prominent reporter of Muhammad's exceptional bodily signs? Aʾisha does not absolutely deprive the body of its truth-making significance, but her narrations point to the presence of variegated logics of corporeality among the Companions and their transmission networks.

As the literary corpus grows, Aʾisha's personal corpus of narrations expands and enables new possibilities for an "Aʾisha position" on Muhammad's body. For example, Abu Nuʿaym's *Dalaʾil al-Nubuwwa* presents Aʾisha giving a checklist-styled account of her husband, a doubly rare narration for the way that she describes his body with transcendental superlatives that one would expect from Anas or Ibn ʿAbbas: the sweat on Muhammad's face resembled pearls, Muhammad smelled better than strong perfume, he had the most handsome face of all humanity, and he was the most illuminating in color.[102] The report also comes with a notable transmission history that includes Kufan traditionist Muhammad ibn Fudayl (d. 195), who was highly regarded in Sunni hadith scholarship while also linked to Shiʾism.[103]

Seeing Muhammad

Muhammad became knowable as the Prophet in part for his knowable body: the lineage of bodies from which it emerged and the details of his body as indicators of his internal condition. This observably exceptional body also impacted bodies with which it became linked through ocular witness. As a diachronic reading of the sources exposes an intensifying investment in Muhammad's body over time, the traditions exhibit growing confidence in the idea that a person's destiny could be altered by his or her eyes having seen that body. Muhammad's body not only comes from a privileged class of ancestors but also creates a privileged class of inheritors, those who have been transformed by their intercorporeal connections with him.

This chapter first considered Muhammad as a body that came from bodies, examining the construction of his lineage as well as the possibility of his prenatal existence among his ancestors. If early hadith transmitters, living in a world in which facts of the body were regarded as signs of personality and character, believed that Muhammad was blessed with the best physical form, they also emphasized purity and privilege among the bodies from which he came. Muhammad's genealogy, connecting him to past prophets and protecting him from stains of his jahiliyya context, becomes evidence that effectively demonstrates his prophetic station. Meanwhile, Muhammad's genealogical privilege in turn authorizes communities with connections to his divinely favored family tree, such as the ʿAbbasid caliphate and proto-Shiʾi networks. Examining the chains of transmission for reports of Muhammad's genealogical privilege, I often find transmitters with direct stakes in that lineage, thereby privileging their own genealogies through connections to him. Next, this chapter asked how the product of such a pure lineage might manifest as a body that proves Muhammad's status to its eyewitnesses. Examining reports of Muhammad's physical appearance, I argue that there is no singular context for seeing his body. Rather, the sources reveal multiple competing contexts—geographic, sectarian, caliphal, gendered, and so on—in which imaginaries of the prophetic body as an ideal type differ between transmitter networks. Narratives of Muhammad's physical appearance developed amid physiognomic archives that flowed between cultures in late antiquity. Reported facts of Muhammad's body echo priorities found in Greek and Sanskrit literatures for what reporters considered notable about him.

Varied systems for revealing souls through bodies encountered varied local contexts and transmission networks, informing the visions of Muhammad's body attributed to specific Companions. Constructing an idea of Muhammad's physical appearance from only Anas's reports, for example, would paint a different picture than the narrations attributed to ʿAli. Relying on narrations from Aʾisha's transmission network would mean losing reports of Muhammad's skin color, hair texture, height, gait, and body hair that come from other Companions. The transmissions attributed to Aʾisha do contain outliers: Aʾisha and Ibn Masʾud alike report that Muhammad prayed, "O God, you made my form [*khalqi*] beautiful, so make my character [*khuluqi*] beautiful."[104] Nonetheless, Aʾisha—whose own authority comes in part from the privileged intimacy between her husband and herself, as well as the special friendship between her husband and her father—does not display the same interest as Anas or other Companions in cataloguing names of Muhammad's ancestors or offering accounts of his physical appearance. The variegated Companion networks that took pains to describe features of Muhammad's body did so with their own priorities in terms of the body parts and qualities worth knowing, assumptions about what constituted an ideal body, and values inscribed upon the body for the ways that contact changed their own status.

At first glance, the exceptional nature of Muhammad's body most obviously supports ʿAlid discourses that would authorize ʿAli and his descendants, who share Muhammad's patrilineal genealogy as the best family tree from the best clan from the best tribe from the best son of Ishmael, best son of Abraham. Likewise, the ʿAbbasid caliphate, named for Muhammad's patrilineal uncle ʿAbbas, benefits from this genetic authorization. Without erasing or rejecting Muhammad's biological advantage, however, the proto-Sunni hadith corpus expands the powers of Muhammad's body in ways that decenter familial ties. As the hadith sources imagine Muhammad's body transforming bodies that interact with it, the literary corpus makes the Sunni category of "Companions" possible as an authorizing discourse that can absorb and counter ʿAlid claims of genealogical privilege. Among the Six Books, Tirmidhi's collection includes a report in which Muhammad announces, "The fire will not touch a Muslim who saw me, or saw one who saw me."[105] The hadith is notable for its contribution to a Sunni reading of history, in which the generation of Muslims who personally witnessed Muhammad became a privileged class of authorized—and *authorizing*—bodies themselves, capable of transmitting their authority through intercorporeality with the next generation. The eyes that saw Muhammad have been changed by this contact and can in turn change the future, as Companion bodies make Follower bodies. The tradition develops in later sources to produce a third privileged class—the "Followers of the Followers"—thereby constructing a model of the three-generation Salaf as collectively authorized by their intercorporeal networks. Eyewitness accounts of Muhammad's physical appearance not only establish his embodied perfection and thereby prove his status as a prophet but also affirm the eyewitnesses. When Anas describes the softness of Muhammad's hand, he presents himself as someone who has touched it; when his students transmit this narration, they in turn claim an advantage for themselves. As the Followers of the Followers teach pioneering hadith scholars, the imaginary of Muhammad's body as a material conduit for broadcasting baraka gives critical support to the embodied networks that would make the hadith corpus possible. The hadith corpus becomes a web of baraka circulation through face-to-face intercorporealities.

Just as multiple physiognomic logics circulated throughout the diverse milieus that produced the hadith corpus, competing theories of vision also offered varied implications for what it meant to see Muhammad. Depending on how one conceptualized vision, to see Muhammad's body was something like touching it via invisible rays (in an extramission model) or having the prophetic body imprinted on one's own consciousness (in an intromission model). Vision was a kind of physical contact with the object; at the very least, an ocular encounter would have meant that the witness's "vision spirit" and witnessed object were both in contact with the same mediating air.[106] Despite the explicit denials of contagion that appear in hadith sources (with some narrations in the sources offering a less clear verdict than others), Arabic medical texts from the period do recognize contagion and even present a possibility of diseases spreading through the visual observation of infected bodies.[107] If the mediating air between an observer's gaze and the observed object can be corrupted, can it also be blessed? Does the theological anxiety surrounding contagion as a secondary cause impact the movement of baraka between bodies?

Hadith sources, while broadly expressing an "official" theological resistance to belief in contagion, also conceptualize baraka as a materially accessible resource, potentially a communicable flow between eyes and skin. The thousands of traditionists who participated in the making of the corpus, after all, did not represent a united ideological movement or share a singular vision of how energies and forces could circulate in the world. Masters of transmitter evaluation (*'ilm al-rijal*, "science of men") branded participants in these transmission networks as heretics for their sectarian affiliations and stances on doctrinal points such as God's absolute predeterminism, but they did not necessarily throw out the narrations of the "heretics."[108] Even though master critics increasingly disqualify and marginalize sectarian minorities from their networks, this attempt at ideological purity only comes long after multiplicity has already become embedded in the traditions (starting with the fragmented and factionalized Companions themselves).[109] After the Sahih/Sunan movement of the "Six Books" compilers, the myth of purity again disintegrates as scholars produce massive collections that further expand and destabilize the textual corpus. The following chapters will continue to emphasize the surprising heterogeneity that remains largely invisible in the hadith materials, obscured beneath the appearance of a monolithic "Hadith Folk" project.

CHAPTER TWO

Muhammad's Heart

The Modified Body

Muhammad was born from a pure, ontologically privileged, and prophetic line of ancestors and appeared in the world with a body that matched his station. Even with the best body made from the best ingredients, however, Muhammad still appears in numerous traditions to have required some modification at the hands of supernatural agents. His knowledge, wisdom, and faith develop not merely through tutelage under angelic teachers or reception of divinely authored discourse but also through work performed on his organs. These upgrades qualify Muhammad for his prophetic vocation, provide observable evidence of his prophethood, and enhance Muhammad's function as a mediator between human bodies of this world and supernatural bodies of the unseen.

The question "What can a prophetic body do?" calls for examination not only of Muhammad's capacity to form connections with other bodies and change their conditions but also of his body's openness to interventions from other bodies. Through acts of physical modification, Muhammad's body becomes a node of intensified connection between his Companions and the unseen forces that act upon it. The extended intercorporeal network includes humans and nonhumans, including angelic and possibly divine bodies, as well as potentially demonic bodies.

In multiple reports from the *Musnad*, Muhammad explains that every human being has been given a companion (*qarin*), with variants stating either that each human has both a jinn qarin and an angel qarin or that each human has a qarin strictly from among the devils. When Muhammad's interlocutors inquire as to whether this also pertains to him, Muhammad answers that he has a qarin of his own but that God has caused it to surrender; Muhammad's qarin thus commands him only toward good or truth.[1]

While Muhammad remains vulnerable to the effects from his qarin, the qarin and its effects in turn remain subject to God's interventions, making the prophetic body a site at which numerous forces act upon each other.

These traditions present Muhammad as undergoing modifications to become the prophetic body. However, even the modified prophetic body's access to the divine and angelic remains vulnerable to the effects of other humans. Companion bodies impact Muhammad's access to the unseen, as seen in a tradition in which Muhammad complains that the Companions' poor hygiene causes delays in revelation. When an interlocutor notes that Gabriel has "slowed down" on Muhammad, the Prophet answers, "And why would he not slow down on me when you around me do not clean your teeth and you do not cut your fingernails, and you do not cut your moustaches, and you do not clean your finger joints?"[2] The narration, traced to Ibn ʿAbbas and found in the *Musnad*, presents connections between angelic, prophetic human, and nonprophetic human bodies as enabled or disabled by conditions of the bodies themselves. Though angels personally modify and upgrade Muhammad's body, the dirt of Companion bodies can apparently render the prophetic body unacceptable, even abject in relation to angels. As members of the Muhammadi assemblage, Companions join angels and the divine as forces acting upon Muhammad's body, changing its powers. The significance of Companion corporeality in these traditions calls attention to the instability of Muhammad's body, the limits and possibilities of which remain linked to the powers of other bodies.

Nonhuman bodies can also redirect angels away from the Prophet. A number of canonical traditions depict canine bodies as natural angel repellants, as angels will not enter a house in which there is a dog; in an account that provides context, Gabriel skips a scheduled visit with Muhammad and blames his absence on the presence of a puppy in Muhammad's house.[3]

Such traditions construct an unstable idea of the prophetic body, conveying numerous logics of corporeality both in terms of what exactly makes Muhammad's body special and the precise limits of that body in terms of its interaction with the unseen. This chapter gives focused attention to three incidents from Muhammad's life in which his body becomes the object of a supernatural enhancement: the opening of his chest, in which angels appearing as men (or birds) apprehended him, made an incision in his torso, and purified his insides; the Seal of Prophethood, the visibly observable mark on his body that confirms his genuine status, particularly for readers of Jewish and Christian scriptures; and the controversial tradition of Muhammad seeing God and possibly even feeling the touch of God's hand. These three traditions overlap significantly: while reports often depict the Seal as an organic birthmark rather than a supernatural modification, for example, some present it as the literal *sealing* of Muhammad's surgical incision. Most pointedly, the traditions share an emphasis on the space between Muhammad's shoulders—that is, the location of his heart—as the point on his body where the modifying and perfecting of his mental condition must occur.

The Opening of Muhammad's Chest

The first verse of the ninety-fourth sura asks Muhammad, "Did we not open your chest for you?" but leaves the precise nature of this opening unsaid. The rest of the short sura adds that God had relieved Muhammad of his burden and raised his status, reminding him that relief comes after hardship (94:1–8). The sura neither explicitly enables nor denies a reading of the event as literally corporeal. Early Qur'an commentator Muqatil b. Sulayman (d. 767) interprets the verse as stating that God expanded Muhammad's chest when it had been restricted, and that faith could not enter it/him until God guided him.[4] While Muqatil does not demand a reading of Muhammad's opened chest as a reference to a physical event, later sources do present Muhammad's chest as subject to a literal cutting of his skin that allows for his supernatural surgeons to implant faith—apparently as a material substance—into his opened torso. Moreover, traditions depict Muhammad's chest-opening to also involve the removal of an undesirable portion from inside his body, specifically his heart.

Ibn Ishaq's *Sira* describes an incident in which Muhammad's body is subjected to surgical intervention and seemingly modified to purify him or prepare his body for prophethood. The account of Muhammad's bodily opening appears among a number of signs from his early life that evidenced his future significance, such as astrological readings, miracles of abundant milk (in Muhammad's own wet-nurse as well as in animals that he shepherded), the fact of his having taken part in the prophetic vocation of shepherding flocks, and the light shining from his mother during her pregnancy with him.[5] It is reported here that during Muhammad's childhood, two men dressed in white seized him, held him down, opened his stomach, and began "stirring it up"; Muhammad later narrates that the men were searching inside him, but for what he did not know. The *Sira* provides another account in which Muhammad narrates that two men in white approached him with a gold basin containing snow, seized him, opened his body, took out his heart, and split it. They then removed a black spot from his heart, threw it away, and washed his heart and stomach with the snow. They weighed Muhammad against ten of his people, finding that he outweighed them; he was then weighed against a hundred of his people, then a thousand, with the same result, causing one of the men to remark that Muhammad would outweigh all of his people. When Muhammad's wet-nurse reports the incident to his mother and confesses her fear that Muhammad had been possessed by demons, his mother confidently states that he will be fine, revealing the secret of his miraculous light that had shone from her body during pregnancy.[6]

What was the "black spot" that required removal from the child's heart? Moving from Ibn Ishaq to the early hadith masters, I encounter more traditions in which Muhammad's body appears to contain an abject or even demonic portion that must be removed. Ibn Hanbal's *Musnad* includes reports in which Gabriel comes to young Muhammad and cuts open Muhammad's torso, removing his heart and extracting a clot (*'alaqa*), then washing the heart with Zamzam water before restoring it to Muhammad's body. Gabriel explains to Muhammad regarding the clot, "This is Satan's share of you."[7] Other reports from Ibn Hanbal, however, do not explicitly link Satan to the removed portion.[8] In their treatments of Muhammad's angelic surgery, early hadith masters express tensions in regard to Satan's "share" of the prophetic body. While the reports maintain that Muhammad's body requires some act of internal purification, these sources display less confidence in asserting that within Muhammad's body existed an element of evil or demonic association, hence the nondescription of the extracted flesh in Tayalisi's *Musnad* as simply "what God willed."[9]

Depictions of the chest-opening also locate the event at different points in Muhammad's life. Hadith sources contain reports that repeat the sira/maghazi literature's placement of the event in Muhammad's childhood but also include narrations that locate the chest-opening after the start of Muhammad's prophethood, as preparation for his heavenly ascension.[10] Anas reports the childhood version, though Anas himself was born years after the event would have taken place. Anas recovers his narrative authority with reference to observable physical evidence: "I used to see the trace of stitching in his chest."[11] The scar on Muhammad's outer surface bears testimony to events under his skin, the angelic operation on his heart.

The Six Books and contemporary collections from the Sahih/Sunan era preserve representations of Muhammad's body as subject to modification by angelic or divine forces. The significant shrinking of the corpus that occurs between Ibn Hanbal's massive *Musnad* and the less inclusive texts of the Sahih/Sunan movement constrains some of the variation within these traditions. In *Eye of the Beholder*, Rubin examines this constriction of the corpus with attention to the story of Muhammad's angelic surgery, arguing that changes in the tradition demonstrate a rigid and systematic editorial project among the hadith scholars and sira authors.[12] Rubin argues that a definitive change in the imaginary of Muhammad's body establishes itself at a clear moment in the development of the corpus. As Brooke Olson Vuckovic points out in her critique of Rubin's thesis, however, Rubin overestimates the coherence of this trend within the sira and hadith literatures.[13] While sources do appear to move away from a childhood chest-opening in favor of narrations that relocate the angelic surgery prior to Muhammad's ascension, Muslim's *Sahih* retains a report, attributed to Anas, in which Gabriel cuts open and cleanses Muhammad's body during Muhammad's childhood. The narration includes Anas's statement that he observed the marks of the stitching on Muhammad's chest and also describes Gabriel's removal of a clot from Muhammad's chest, explaining that the clot represents Satan's share in him.[14] While the reports included in these sources certainly marginalize the possibility of a *hazz al-Shaytan* or "black spot" and additionally favor the surgery taking place later in Muhammad's life, reading the chest-opening tradition for a Deleuzian question of "What can a body do?"—examining Muhammad's body as the sum of its powers and limits in relation to forming interconnections with other bodies—the sources continue to present a degree of instability.

Between variant possibilities for the chest-opening found in these sources, the narrations present different consequences for Muhammad's body. The depiction of Muhammad's surgery as taking place prior to his ascension presents bodily modification as a prerequisite for Muhammad's physical entry into another realm and interaction with a host of extrahuman forces. These narrations do not refer to an undesirable or abjected portion of Muhammad's body that must be removed, but they nonetheless establish that his body requires purification and the corporeal implantation of enhanced wisdom and belief. These interventions properly modify Muhammad's body to enable its entry into a domain beyond the world of typical human bodies. Muslim's outlier hadith, meanwhile, does not clearly specify the function of the surgery beyond removal of a demonic portion from within Muhammad's body. Even without Rubin's assertion of a mass expunging and the sweeping rigid ideological cohesion that his thesis demands, it remains noteworthy that the tradition of preascension surgery becomes privileged within the sources over variants placing the surgery in Muhammad's preprophetic childhood.

Beyond Muslim's outlier and the collections that would later attain canonical prestige as the Six Books, reports on the chest-opening further destabilize the coherence of the prophetic body for their representation of the forces acting upon that body. The collections of Ibn Abi ʿAsim and al-Darimi both preserve the narration, seen in earlier sources, in which two white birds perform the surgery on young Muhammad's chest.[15] Later sources, such as al-Hakim's *Al-Mustadrak* and Bayhaqi's *Dala'il*, also include the tradition of ornithomorphic angels removing two "black clots" from Muhammad's heart, preserving the potential to imagine prophetic bodies as containing abjected portions that require surgical intervention.[16] Perhaps even more remarkable, the Anas tradition of Muhammad's body containing a specifically named "share of Satan," after experiencing significant (but not absolute) marginalization in the Six Books, flourishes in later centuries, included by Ibn Hibban, al-Hakim, Abu Ya'la, Abu Nu'aym, and Bayhaqi in their collections.[17] Another tradition reports that when Gabriel purified (*tahhara*) Muhammad's heart, he also performed Muhammad's circumcision.[18] The reports that associate Muhammad's heart cleansing with the removal of his foreskin do not mention the extraction of a demonic portion from inside Muhammad's body, nor do they assign special significance to the abjected fragment removed from Muhammad's exterior.

The Seal

The precise nature of the Seal varies from one report to the next, and the Seal's relationship—if any—to the opening of Muhammad's chest is not settled. Reports tend to discuss *either* the Seal *or* the opening of Muhammad's chest without mentioning the other. I could not find narrations in which both the Seal and the chest-opening (or the traces of Muhammad's stitches) appear in the same narrative unit but are otherwise treated as unrelated; the sources do not provide reports that refer to Muhammad's stitches while also describing the Seal as an organic growth on his body.

Two outliers combine the opening of Muhammad's chest and the placement of the Seal into a single event, transpiring not in Muhammad's childhood but at the start of his prophetic mission. In Tayalisi's *Musnad*, the opening of Muhammad's body occurs immediately prior to the first revelation (the report is also unique in that it places Khadija in the cave with Muhammad). Gabriel descends to perform the surgery alone, though the report notes that the angel Michael remained at a midpoint between heaven and Earth; Gabriel removes "what God willed" from Muhammad's belly, then seals Muhammad's back until Muhammad feels the placement of the Seal; it appears that Gabriel had cut into Muhammad's body through his back, rather than his front, and that the Seal of Prophethood closed the wound. Gabriel then commands Muhammad to recite the ninety-sixth sura, as in popular accounts of the first revelation. The report is an outlier both in its details—the association of the cutting with the first revelation, the presence of Khadija and Michael, and the cutting into Muhammad's back—and its chain of transmission, traced to A'isha rather than Anas.[19] If I were seeking to date the narration, Motzki's isnad-cum-matn method of forensic hadith analysis would find the report, isolated from more prominent versions both in attribution and content, to be a marginal departure from the more widely transmitted—and presumably original—"mainstream" version of the story. The chain of transmission is Basran and incomplete: Tayalisi reports from Hammad ibn Salama, who reports from Abu ʿImran al-Jawni, who reports from "a man" who had narrated on the authority of A'isha. However, it would also help to remember Shahab Ahmed's reminder that an incomplete isnad could ironically point to an older narration, reflecting an early stage of hadith dissemination before transmission-based methodologies for vetting reports attained their full prestige and complete chains became "the preeminent epistemological device for the establishment of the truth-value of reports."[20]

In a report from Ibn Hanbal's *Musnad*, Muhammad is asked about the "start of your affair" and responds with the story of two "white birds like eagles" descending upon him, cutting open his torso, and extracting his heart. The birds split his heart and removed from it two black clots, then washed his heart with ice and snow. The birds installed *al-sakina*, which can be understood as a pious tranquility and its assorted characteristics, into his chest.[21] After washing Muhammad's heart and restoring it to his body, the birds closed the incision with the Seal of Prophethood.[22] Ibn Hanbal also includes reports in which Muhammad's chest is cut open and purified by Gabriel prior to the heavenly ascension, but these narrations do not connect the Seal to the incision.[23]

The Six Books are more consistent in detaching the chest-opening episode from the presence of the Seal on Muhammad's body. The Seal appears consistently throughout these sources as an organic birthmark, described as a protrusion of flesh or mound of hair, rather than a trace of surgical intervention.[24] Later collections offer representations of the Seal both as an organic birthmark and a literal seal that closed Muhammad's incision from his surgery. Familiar traditions emerge from these sources, such as Salman's recognition of Muhammad by the mark on his back,[25] along with descriptions of the Seal as resembling a bird egg.[26] Such narrations, presented as Companions' recollections of the prophetic body to later generations that could not have known this body firsthand, authorize the Companions for their ocular and tangible experiences of the Seal. In Tabarani's *Mu'jam al-Kabir*, Abu Zayd specifically describes an incident in which Muhammad asks him to approach and touch his back. Abu Zayd reports, "I placed the Seal of Prophethood between my fingers," and is then asked by his interlocutor to explain the appearance of the Seal. He answers, "Hair between his shoulders."[27] Bayhaqi's reproduction of the "two birds" tradition in his *Dala'il* presents the birds sealing Muhammad's body as the conclusion to their surgical intervention.[28] Ibn Hibban's *Sahih* provides an unusual narration, attributed to Ibn 'Umar, in which the meaning of the "seal" (*khatam*) on Muhammad's body appears to be informed by the seal with which he would sign letters: the Seal was on the Prophet's back, "made of flesh, resembling a nut. On it was written, 'Muhammad, Messenger of God.'"[29] In this isolated account, the special bodily mark that evidences Muhammad's prophethood reveals itself as such with a literal inscription of text upon Muhammad's skin.

The *Ru'ya* and Cold Hand

In the opening of his chest, extraction of demonic flesh, and injection of faith and wisdom as material substances, angels operate upon Muhammad's body to enhance it for prophetic function. The hadith corpus also offers traditions in which God himself directly intervenes and modifies the prophetic body, even with what appears to be a body of God's own that Muhammad can see and touch.

Hadiths that depict Muhammad's organs as having privileged access or proximity to God—whether the organ in question is his eye, skin, or heart—confront theological controversies that have shaped Islamic interpretive traditions. Early in Muslim intellectual history, as Josef van Ess writes, the problem of divine anthropomorphism (*tashbih*) became a "vexing issue for Islam as it did for Judaism once both religions started thinking in theological terms."[30] The Qur'an, while asserting God's absolute incomparability and separation from created beings (112:4), also describes God in highly embodied terms: God has hands (3:73, 5:64, 38:75, 48:10), including a right hand (39:67); he also possesses a face (28:88, 55:27), eyes (11:37, 20:39, 52:48, 54:14), and potentially a shin (68:42). While Muslim theologians have debated whether God can be seen by human eyes in this world and/or the next, God at least speaks with a voice that humans can hear, as when he announces himself to Moses (28:30). Over twenty verses describe God as the possessor of a throne;[31] the famous "Throne Verse" also mentions a place for his feet (2:255). God's chair appears to be locatable in place and time, existing above celestial waters before God creates the heavens and Earth; the seven verses that describe God occupying the throne all place God's act of sitting *after* his creation of the universe.[32]

The question of how to understand such verses and their potential implications about God would drive key issues in the development of Qur'an interpretation and Islamic theology. Thinking about God's body grew increasingly unacceptable with the development of Muslim theological camps, "rationalist" and "literalist" alike, that regarded anthropomorphism as a scandalous heresy and devastating charge to wield against one's sectarian rivals. As Livnat Holtzman explains, the designation of "anthropomorphist" (*mushabbih*) developed into a heresiographical category and polemical slur, "always used as a term of opprobrium and never as a title one would willingly assume."[33]

While Muslim theological schools accused each other of anthropomorphism with different ideas about exactly where and how that line was crossed, some Muslims indeed believed that the Qur'an informed them of a divine body. Van Ess looks to the mysterious word *samad*, which appears only once in the Qur'an (112:2) and is typically rendered in modern English translations as "eternal," though van Ess argues that the term meant "massive, compact" to audiences in Islam's second century. He mentions an eighth-century exegete, Dawud al-Jawaribi, who understood the term to signify that God's body lacked a digestive system. In addition to God's body parts mentioned in the Qur'an, al-Jawaribi theorized that God must have a mouth, because he speaks, and a heart, because his wisdom needs a source. Because God does not eat or drink, however, he has no stomach; his torso is solid or compact (i.e., *samad*), as opposed to Adam's "hollow" body.[34] Al-Jawaribi did not perceive his belief in God having flesh and blood to be inconsistent with his belief in God as absolutely incomparable and transcendent above creation, nor did he conflate corporeity with anthropomorphism: for God to be corporeal did not require the divine body to resemble human bodies. God for al-Jawaribi possesses a body, but his body is "unlike other bodies, with flesh unlike other flesh, and blood unlike other blood . . . he does not resemble any creature, nor does any creature resemble him."[35] In his survey of early Muslim anthropomorphists, van Ess additionally mentions Hisham al-Jawaliqi, who believed that God's body was made of light and that a special black light comprised his hair. This divine body possessed organs but no more than what was "functionally necessary," meaning that God had only one eye and one ear.[36] Al-Jawaliqi's rival Hisham ibn al-Hakam was also a theological corporealist but not an anthropomorphist: God's body bore no resemblance to human bodies. The divine body in his theology was a "mass of light without any limbs" that obtained knowledge of the world through tentacle-like rays of light and was more analogous to geometric shapes than human forms.[37]

While Qur'an exegetes deployed various strategies for shutting down the implications of divine corporeality in particular verses, hadith traditions could exacerbate the controversy. While the Qur'an makes vague reference to a shin that will be revealed on the Day of Resurrection, for example, a tradition in Bukhari's *Sahih* confirms that it is God's shin. When people on the Day are asked to name the sign by which they would know God, they will answer, "the shin," to which God will respond by exposing his own shin, causing all of the believers to prostrate.[38] While the Qur'an states that God has a right hand (39:67), a canonical tradition clarifies that God does not have a left hand, as "both of his hands are right hands."[39]

The hadith corpus also tells us that God created Adam "in his image" (or "form"), which appears in some versions as a rationale to avoid striking another human in the face. Muslim intellectuals debated the precise meaning of "his image" and whether God or Adam were signified by the possessive pronoun, with some arguing that "his image" meant only "Adam's image." Ibn Hanbal reportedly objected to the "Adam's image" interpretation, asking, "What image had Adam before he created him?" For Ibn Hanbal, this mention of "his image" must refer to God creating Adam in *God's* own image. Examining prophetic traditions that prohibit striking a human's face, with some versions including the explanation that God created Adam in his image and others omitting that detail, Melchert suggests that transmitters edited the tradition due to anxieties over its anthropomorphic implications.[40]

The notorious "Hadith of the Goats," found in three of the Six Books (Abu Dawud, Tirmidhi, and Ibn Maja), explicitly locates God in measurable physical space. Muhammad explains to a group (including his uncle 'Abbas, to whom the report is attributed) that each of the seven heavens are separated by a distance that would take seventy-one, seventy-two, or seventy-three years to cross; the seventh heaven exists under an ocean, with the distance from this ocean's depths to its surface being the same distance as that between two heavens. Above the celestial sea, eight mountain goats—the distance between their hooves and knees equal to the space between two heavens—support God's throne, its height also equal to the distance between two heavens, on their backs; finally, "God is above that."[41] The Hadith of the Goats was famously weaponized against Ibn Taymiyya, who found his acceptance of the hadith cited in court as evidence of his alleged heretical anthropomorphism.[42] Elsewhere in the hadith corpus, the angels who support the throne are portrayed in more anthropomorphic than zoomorphic terms, with the distance between each angel's earlobe and shoulder amounting to a journey of 700 years.[43]

The hadith corpus presents God's body and his throne as though they take up space. When God sits upon the throne, it groans under his size and weight.[44] Imagining the divine body in spatial terms, with other bodies apparently in measurable distance from it, traditions serve to authorize Muhammad's body for his physical proximity to the divine. In al-Darimi's version of the "groaning throne" tradition, Muhammad conceptualizes God as an apparent body with tremendous (but still theoretically measurable) mass that grants Muhammad spatial prestige: "The day God descends upon his throne, it will groan like a new saddle from its tightening with him, and its range is like that between the heavens and the earth.... I will be stationed, standing on the right side of God, envied by the ancients and others."[45]

The possibilities for Muhammad's interaction with God during his earthly life remain ambiguous within the text of the Qur'an, as a sequence of verses possibly refers to God having *descended* and become visible to Muhammad on two occasions, one of which including a proximity between the two that could be measured in physical space—that is, "two bow-lengths or nearer" (53:1–18). Interpretive tradition has come to privilege a reading of 53:5's "one fierce in power" (*shadid al-quwwa*) as referring to Gabriel rather than God, a position most prominently associated with A'isha. Van Ess likens this approach to a tendency in Jewish interpretive traditions, in which theologians navigated around difficult descriptions of God by rereading them as references to angels.[46] The sira/maghazi literatures examined here do not depict Muhammad witnessing God with his eyes, or having an encounter with God that would potentially locate God in physical space and time. In hadith sources, however, the possibility of Muhammad's directly encountering God becomes reopened.

Multiple traditions in the hadith corpus engage the question, reportedly disputed even among the Companions themselves, of Muhammad's capacity for witnessing God. Ibn ʿAbbas appears prominently among those reporting that Muhammad did see God, while A'isha gives the most vehement denials of Muhammad seeing God, insisting that Muhammad only saw Gabriel and that anyone who claims otherwise has lied.[47] Some accounts give only a bare affirmation that Muhammad had in fact seen his lord, but they provide no further details of exactly what Muhammad saw (or, if he saw God, *how* he saw him). Others give qualifiers that Muhammad had seen with his heart, not his eyes, or experienced his vision in the theologically safe context of a dream.[48] An Abu Dharr tradition that appears in a number of variants, some more theologically provocative or conservative than others for their potential consequences, depicts Muhammad answering the question of whether he saw his lord by stating that he saw "light." The ambiguity concerning this unidentified light allows for multiple readings. It can shut down corporeal anthropomorphism by denying the vision of a divine body, but, as discussed above, it can also speak to early Muslims who conceptualized God as having a body made of light, with or without also having the shape of a human body.[49] In different versions of Abu Dharr's narration, it seems to be implied either that Muhammad saw God *as* light or that a blinding light makes the vision of God impossible; in one variant, Abu Dharr clarifies that Muhammad saw God with his heart but not his eyes.[50]

Another tradition, likewise appearing with variation across the transmitter networks, narrates an encounter in which God appears to Muhammad, asks questions that Muhammad cannot answer, and then places his hand between Muhammad's shoulders. In the moment that Muhammad feels the coolness of God's palm between his nipples, he obtains knowledge and can answer God's queries. Through his power of ostensibly physical touch, God changes Muhammad. A version from Ibn Hanbal's *Musnad* describes the touch as revealing to Muhammad everything between the heavens and Earth.[51] Ibn Abi Shayba's *Musannaf* includes an account in which Muhammad asks God to teach him; God then places his hand between Muhammad's shoulders. Muhammad recalls that after the touch, "He did not ask me anything except that I knew it."[52] Muhammad's mention of the physical sensation, emphasizing the tangibility of his contact with God, affirms the encounter as an event in space and time, one body modifying another through direct contact: God penetrates the body of Muhammad and implants knowledge into it.

As demonstrated elsewhere in these materials, contact with Muhammad's body or its by-products can communicate baraka from within his body to others. Reports of the divine "cold hand" insert God's body directly in the matrix of relations through which baraka flows between bodies: to touch or be touched by Muhammad places a Companion within just one degree of separation from physical contact with God.

A tradition in the *Tabaqat*, attributed to Anas, describes the placement of an extrahuman hand between Muhammad's shoulders in connection to his receiving knowledge; in this account, the touch comes not from God but rather Gabriel and is not a cold palm but a punch. After Gabriel punches Muhammad between the shoulders, Muhammad walks to a tree in which he finds things resembling birds' nests. Muhammad sits in one "nest," Gabriel sits in another, and the two then ascend until reaching the junction of east and west at such a height that Muhammad can touch the heavens. He then turns on his side and faces Gabriel, who is described as resembling a saddle blanket. At this point in the narrative, Muhammad recalls, "I recognized the excellence of his knowledge of God." The gates of the heavens are opened for Muhammad and he sees a veil (*hijab*) adorned with precious stones; at this point, "God revealed to me what he willed to reveal."[53] The narration depicts Gabriel punching Muhammad between the shoulders to provoke an ascension in which Muhammad transcends the limits of this world, achieves Gabriel's level of knowledge, and then receives access to whatever God chose to reveal to him at or behind the veil. In resonance with reports that depict Muhammad in embodied interactions with Gabriel (being squeezed by Gabriel, seeing him with his eyes, and traveling with him through the heavens), this narration in particular appears to represent Gabriel's punch as a catalyst for Muhammad's transformation. The angelic fist sparks a sequence of events that leads to Muhammad attaining and then perhaps transcending angelic degrees of knowledge and access to God.

The capacity for Muhammad's body to link with a divine body, either through the divine body's direct modification upon Muhammad through tangible encounter or through Muhammad witnessing the divine body with his physical eyes, undergoes some regulation in the sources. Of the Six Books, only Tirmidhi's collection preserves the intimately corporeal encounter between Muhammad and God, in which God appears in the "best form" (*ahsan sura*) and transmits knowledge into Muhammad's body by placing his cold hand between Muhammad's shoulders. This account, attributed to Ibn 'Abbas through a chain of transmitters that includes 'Abd al-Razzaq reporting from Ma'mar, specifies that God came to Muhammad at night and includes the narrator's note, "I think he said, 'in a dream,'" serving to safeguard the narration against a fully corporeal anthropomorphism.[54] Tirmidhi also provides a version of A'isha's emphatic rejection of Muhammad seeing God,[55] as well as Abu Dharr's ambiguous compromise, in which Muhammad is portrayed as stating only that he "saw light."[56] Finally, Tirmidhi offers a narration in which 'Ikrima recalls his argument with Ibn 'Abbas over the issue, presenting Ibn 'Abbas's engagement of both A'isha's Qur'an-based objection to the vision and Abu Dharr's report of light: "He said, 'Muhammad saw his lord.' I said, 'Did God not say, "No vision captures him, but he captures all vision?"' [6:103]. He said, 'Woe to you, that is when he manifests his light. Muhammad saw his lord two times.'"[57]

Muslim's collection includes Abu Dharr's report of Muhammad seeing an undefined light,[58] along with an Ibn 'Abbas report that Muhammad "saw with his heart,"[59] as well as A'isha's rejection.[60] Bukhari's *Sahih* stands resolutely against the vision, excluding Ibn 'Abbas's affirmation of the vision and giving preference to A'isha's denial.[61] Nonetheless, an account from Anas in Bukhari's *Sahih* mentions God's descent to Muhammad until the distance between them was no more than two bow-lengths, recalling the ambiguous verse in the Qur'an (53:9) that Anas clarifies with precise mention of "his lord."[62] Melchert attributes Bukhari's resistance to the divine vision to his "general wariness of anthropomorphism," noting Bukhari's approach to traditions in which God is said to have created Adam in God's own image.[63]

Beyond the Six Books canon, Abd Allah ibn Ahmad ibn Hanbal's *Kitab as-Sunna* includes Muhammad's narration that God came to him in "the best form," asked him questions, and transmitted knowledge to him of all things in the heavens and Earth by placing his hand between Muhammad's shoulders, causing Muhammad to feel the coolness of the divine hand between his nipples. Muhammad reports that God visited him at night, allowing the implication of a dream.[64] Al-Darimi and Ibn Abi 'Asim also preserve versions of this tradition without disclaimers that the encounter took place in Muhammad's sleep.[65]

Ibn Abi 'Asim's *Kitab as-Sunna* presents numerous reports of Muhammad's theophanic vision in separate chapters distinguishing reports of Muhammad's vision with his eye from accounts of the vision taking place in a dream (with affirmations that prophets' dreams are no less real than wakeful reality).[66] In his chapter, "What Has Been Mentioned of the

Prophet's Vision of His Lord," Ibn Abi ʿAsim includes a report of Muhammad's statement, "I saw my lord" without further clarification, while also providing the tradition that God had favored Abraham, Moses, and Muhammad respectively with intimate friendship, speech, and vision, as well as the compromise tradition of Muhammad seeing an unnamed light.[67] Ibn Abi ʿAsim specifically provides versions of the "best form" tradition in a separate chapter (also including the touch of the divine hand), further isolating an account in which the vision of God's best form takes place during a dream in its own chapter.[68] These chapters on Muhammad's witness of God appear in a cluster of chapters concerning God's accessibility to believers, including the sight of God (and specifically God's face) in the afterlife[69] and God's communication to believers in dreams,[70] as well as polemically loaded traditions prominent in debates over corporeal anthropomorphism and the location of God in a measurable spatial relation to this world. Such traditions include God's creation of Adam in "his own image,"[71] God's descent into the lower heaven for greater proximity to the believers,[72] descriptions of God's throne,[73] and the Hadith of the Goats.[74] In Ibn Abi ʿAsim's collection, accounts of God as visible and tangible serve to simultaneously privilege Muhammad's unique position and more broadly establish the possibility of human access to God.

Like God, Muhammad's hand is reported as cool by those who felt it on their chests. In al-Waqidi's *Maghazi*, Muhammad examines the ailing Saʾd's condition by touching his chest, which the Companion remembers for its coolness.[75] The tradition also appears in Abu Dawud's *Sunan*: Muhammad places his hand between Saʾd's nipples, and the coolness of Muhammad's hand penetrates his body, sensible to Saʾd at his own heart. The report does not present the touch of Muhammad's cold hand as transmitting knowledge into the Companion's body but rather as a diagnostic method by which Muhammad can identify the illness and prescribe a remedy (in this case, seven ʿAjwa dates).[76]

After being relatively marginalized in the Six Books, the tradition of Muhammad directly encountering God via sight and possibly touch resurfaces and proliferates in later sources. The tradition appears in collections such as Tabarani's *Muʾjam al-Kabir* and Daraqutni's *Kitab al-Ruʾya*, disseminated in numerous variants and not always with cautionary disclaimers that the event took place in a dream.[77] As the corpus develops, narrations of God touching Muhammad with a tangible hand also appear in connection with detailed accounts of the divine body. As I will discuss in chapter 4, which gives attention to the gendering of God's body in these traditions, reports of the divine body become increasingly vivid, specifying that God appeared to Muhammad in the form of a young man and providing details of God's hair, clothing, jewelry, and furniture.

The intensifying corporeality of God and his visual or tangible exposure to Muhammad do not simply overtake the corpus to replace one construction of divine-prophetic encounter with another. While some narrations intensify the embodied divine anthropomorphism in treatments of God's interaction with Muhammad, the tradition of A'isha vehemently denying the possibility of theophanic vision does not disappear but continues to find inclusion in later collections.[78] The divine body, like the prophetic body and the possibility and limits of interactions between the two, remains significantly unpredictable across these collected reports, even within an individual scholar's archive.

"The Eye Sleeps but the Heart Is Awake"

What can a prophetic heart do? It can change other bodies, and be changed by them. Operation on a preprophetic child's heart by angelic surgeons can excise the abject or demonic from his flesh, enhance his body with material quantities of faith, knowledge, and wisdom, and prepare his body to receive the revelation of the Qur'an. Before his ascension, this work on his heart can enable him to enter realms otherwise inaccessible to human bodies. When God penetrates Muhammad's heart with his cold hand, Muhammad's knowledge can become divinely supplemented to the point that he can answer any question. It is with this upgraded heart that Muhammad fulfills his vocation as prophet in the world.

In his discussion of Muhammad's encounter with God, Melchert offers a reminder that in antiquity, prominent theories of cognition identified the heart, rather than the brain, as the organ that hosts the mind.[79] The Qur'an speaks to this perception in its frequent treatment of knowledge, ignorance, faith, and disbelief as conditions of the heart. For one example, 22:46 describes humans as having "hearts with which they reason." Elsewhere, God claims knowledge of what is in chests (3:119, 3:154, 5:7 for just a few examples) and describes ignorance or unbelief as the "sealing" of hearts (2:7, 6:46, 42:24, 45:23). In 6:125, the Qur'an speaks of God expanding one's chest for surrender (or Islam) and contrasts this to God leading others astray or constraining their chests. Modern readers might understand these references to the heart as a popular metaphor, but in Mediterranean antiquity, it was medical science. Hadith sources also express a view of the heart as seat of the mind. According to a tradition found in

Bukhari's *Al-Adab al-Mufrad*, 'Ali explicitly asserted, "The intellect is in the heart, mercy is in the liver, compassion is in the spleen, and the self/soul [*nafs*] is in the lungs."[80] A rare variant of the "cold hand" tradition names not the heart but the liver, which was also regarded in Greek medicine as home to a portion of the soul and linked to dreams and divination, as the place where Muhammad felt the coolness of God's touch.[81]

Muhammad's heart increases his capacity to enter into relations with other bodies, in part for the ways his heart can enhance or compensate for the limits of his eyes. As a qualifier that negotiates between oppositional claims concerning Muhammad's vision of God, the more careful versions of Ibn 'Abbas's affirmation specify that Muhammad saw God with his heart; an even more overt disclaimer attributed to Abu Dharr, found in Nasa'i's *Sunan*, makes clear that Muhammad saw with his heart and *not* his eyes.[82] The tradition of Muhammad's vision occurring with his heart appears in sources such as Tirmidhi's *kitab al-tafsir* chapter with connection to the Qur'an's statement, "The heart did not lie in what it saw" (53:11).[83]

Narrations that contextualize Muhammad's vision of God within a dream, while negotiating with theological anxieties over the possibility of seeing God with one's eyes, do not surrender the vision's truth-making gravity: even in a dream, the vision of God was still genuine because while Muhammad's eyes sleep, his heart remains awake and perceptive. In a canonical tradition, Abu Salama asks A'isha about her husband's practice during Ramadan, to which A'isha responds with an anecdote of Muhammad sleeping—which would typically break one's ritual purity—and then praying without first performing ablution. When A'isha asks Muhammad about his prayer, he explains to her that while his eyes sleep, his heart does not.[84] Marion Katz has observed a tension provoked by this tradition in early formulations of Islamic purity law, as jurists such as al-Shafi'i argued for *wudu'* from sleep as proved by Muhammad's own precedent while "available reports about the behavior of the Prophet seemed to document the opposite."[85] For those who asserted that sleep broke wudu', Muhammad's privileged exemption stemmed from the privilege of his heart: because he remained conscious and aware of his body while asleep, his body was not vulnerable to the unaware farts or accidental touches that threatened typical sleeping bodies.[86]

While the A'isha tradition reveals the condition of Muhammad's heart in a discussion of his embodied practice, a less-circulated but still canonically archived Anas tradition depicts the prophetic heart's wakefulness as a subject of conversation between angels. The tradition, which appears in the section of Bukhari's *kitab al-manaqib* devoted to Muhammad's wakeful heart (with a longer version in Bukhari's *kitab al-tawhid*), presents Muhammad narrating the night of his ascension. Muhammad reports that while asleep at the Ka'ba, he was visited by three figures (apparently angels); one asked, "Which is he?" to which another answered, "The best of them." Muhammad narrates that even though he was asleep, his heart saw these visitors, explaining that while his eyes sleep, his heart does not. The tradition adds that this wakeful heart is the condition of all prophets. The longer of the reports provides a complete ascension narrative and establishes that Gabriel performed his surgery on Muhammad's heart after Muhammad's heart observed the three angelic visitors, meaning that Muhammad's heart already reflected his prophetic station prior to Gabriel's modification.[87] A tradition from Jabir ibn 'Abd Allah recalls the three visitors and explicitly identifies them as angels but does not connect their visit to the ascension. Jabir also provides an exchange in which the angels disagree as to the state of Muhammad's consciousness: "Some of them said, 'He is sleeping.' And some of them said, 'The eye sleeps but the heart is awake.'"[88] While Muhammad's heart places him in the category of prophets, this quality is also found with the antichrist figure al-Dajjal, whom David J. Halperin terms "a satanic parody of the true prophet" for the way his heart's condition imitates the hearts of the prophets.[89] Tirmidhi provides a tradition with a chain of Basran transmitters in which Muhammad describes the future al-Dajjal as a boy born to parents who had gone thirty years without having a child. Though the boy's eyes sleep (one of the eyes will be defective, itself a sign in physiognomic literature of malice or iniquity),[90] his heart does not. When Abu Bakr and Zubayr learn of a boy born to Jewish parents in Medina, they decide to investigate. Meeting the boy's parents, Abu Bakr and Zubayr see that they are just as the Prophet had described (the father being fat with a nose like a beak, the mother with long hands). The parents explain that they had waited thirty years for a child, also noting that his eye is defective and that while his eyes sleep, his heart does not. The child himself then appears, uncovers his head and asks, "What were you saying?" Abu Bakr and Zubayr ask the boy, "Did you hear what we were saying?" to which he answers, "Yes. My eyes sleep but my heart does not sleep."[91]

Reports of Muhammad encountering God do not necessarily locate the event at a specific stage in Muhammad's prophetic career (some later sources, discussed in future chapters, situate the touch within narratives of Muhammad's ascension, as with the chest-opening); nor do they clearly link the touch to the chest-opening or the Seal. With traditions of the chest-opening and the Seal, however, the "cold hand" tradition shares an investment in Muhammad's chest as the site at which Muhammad's prophetic station requires modification of his body. With or without reference to a corrupt or corruptible part of Muhammad's body that required surgical extraction, the opening of Muhammad's chest specifically overlaps with the Seal and "cold hand" traditions in its focus on the heart. The Seal is typically located on Muhammad's back, between his shoulders; God places his palm on Muhammad's back, between his shoulders, causing him to sense the hand's coolness between his nipples; both traditions place divine activity and its material trace in the neighborhood of Muhammad's heart. The "cold hand" tradition departs from the chest-opening tradition in that while the two share a theme of extrahuman forces acting upon Muhammad's torso to alter his condition, the "cold hand" narrations treat Muhammad's body as one that requires modification without that body necessarily containing a "black spot" or "share of Satan." With or without an abject portion to be removed, the angelic injection of faith and wisdom into Muhammad's surgical cavity and God's penetrative transmission of knowledge via his cool palm both locate the heart as the object of modification.

While the idea of Muhammad's heart being afflicted with a demonic black portion may come and go between collections, sources preserve a logic of the heart as corporeally blackened by evil. A well-circulated and canonically esteemed tradition materializes sin as a black spot on the heart that grows with each transgression and diminishes with acts of repentance. The tradition relates this black spot to the Qur'an's mention of what has overtaken or covered the unbelievers' hearts (83:14).[92] Another version, found in Malik's *Muwatta* and presented as a saying of Ibn Mas'ud rather than the Prophet, specifically refers to the sin of lying, which causes the black spot to grow until the heart becomes completely black; the sinner then becomes counted among the liars in God's sight.[93] A tradition in Muslim's *Sahih* draws a contrast between hearts colored either black or white as markers of their responses to temptation.[94] Given the physiognomic connections drawn between the heart, face, and condition of the soul, Christian Lange has suggested a connection between these reports and the Qur'an's account of faces that would become blackened on the Day of Judgment (3:106, 39:60), which interpreters such as Fakhr al-Din al-Razi (d. 1209) and al-Ghazali (d. 1111) read as a literal blackening of the face.[95]

Beyond their overlaps and continuities, the sources exhibit an entanglement of intersecting values and anxieties concerning a number of bodies—not only prophetic but also angelic, divine, and even demonic. Certainly, the notion that God can be seen by human eyes or lay a tangible hand upon a human body can have extraordinary and potentially devastating theological consequences. On this point, A'isha appears in the sources to accuse other Companions of lying about Muhammad. The suggestion that Muhammad's body could contain an undesirable element that conceivably subjected his body to claims by demonic forces can also have troubling implications. Narrations in which extrahuman agents modify Muhammad's body, particularly reports in which these forces subject Muhammad to invasive surgery and extract an undesirable "black spot" or "share of Satan," produce a tension between Muhammad's body and ideas of the abject. The extraction of this impurity from Muhammad and subsequent washing of his insides, presented in sira/maghazi literature as an incident prior to his prophetic career, ostensibly transforms his body into an exceptional one that can mediate between metaphysical and physical worlds. Simultaneously, however, the location of "Satan's share" within Muhammad's chest presents his body as one that is naturally impure and imperfect prior to angelic intervention. The sira/maghazi literature presents a prophetic corporeality threatened by elements internal to itself. The presence of demonic material within Muhammad's body, specifically in or near his heart, demonstrates—as Grosz writes of the abject—"the impossibility of clear-cut borders, lines of demarcation, divisions between the clean and unclean, the proper and the improper, order and disorder."[96]

"Abjection," in Grosz's articulation, "involves the paradoxically necessary but impossible desire to transcend corporeality. It is a refusal of the defiling, impure, uncontrollable materiality of the subject's embodied existence."[97] As seen in the preceding discussion of bodily waste, abjection concerns anxieties surrounding substances produced within and ejected from the body, which retain ambiguous relationships to that body. Abjection enforces the image of a coherent and united body through disgust and discomfort at the substances and processes that undermine that image: Kristeva writes that these phenomena signify what one must "thrust aside in order to live."[98] What does it mean if a piece of Muhammad must be thrust aside in order for him to be fully "Muhammad?" If one were to encounter the piece that was thrust aside, should it be defined by its origins within the prophetic body or the fact that Muhammad's special destiny required its separation from him? Is the rejected portion most meaningfully connected to its owner (Satan) or its host body (Muhammad)? These questions of the prophetic body's capacity for abjection will receive further attention in the following chapter's discussions of Muhammad's bodily substances, including his blood and digestive waste.

CHAPTER THREE

Bottling Muhammad

Corporeal Traces

Muhammad's body, while exceptional, maintained and regulated itself via typical human processes. These processes operated at his body's liminal zones, openings in the border between Muhammad's insides and the outside world. At these liminal zones, substances could cross the threshold from one side to the other. Remnants of the food and drink Muhammad consumed would leave his body as waste. Glands in his mouth produced saliva to help his digestion. The pores of his skin released sweat, apparently in profuse amounts when he received divine revelation. His blood could spill out of him when he was wounded in battle or treated with cupping. His acts of personal maintenance also severed materials from his body, such as fingernails and hair. By-products of Muhammad's body were not exactly his body itself, though they came from or through his body, and some perhaps had been parts of his body at one time. Muhammad's disjecta provoke the question of where his body begins and ends, and how these artifacts can extend his body's limits and the reach of its baraka.

Concerning Muhammad's corporeal by-products, the Qur'an remains silent. It does not give us any information about Muhammad's bodily fluids or hair and fingernail clippings, let alone a systematic theory of their relationship to baraka. The Qur'an neither responds to nor prescribes Companions' investment in substances related to his body. If the Qur'an's only acknowledgment of Muhammad's bodily by-products appears in prescriptions regarding ritual purity, the text leaves his body unexceptional; what matters is not Muhammad's body itself but the precedents set by Muhammad's bodily practices, since his processes and products result in the same pollutions as those of his Companions. The bodies of Muhammad and his wives, therefore, enter the text's imagination only for instructional purposes.

Within sira/maghazi sources, products emerging from Muhammad's body hold an ambiguous status, neither fully part of Muhammad nor absolutely differentiated from him. They sometimes appear to be capable of transporting baraka from within Muhammad's body to other bodies, yet they apparently remain bound to a hierarchy that would construct some substances as more desirable resources than others. In comparison, hadith collections provide an abundance of traditions concerning Muhammad's bodily traces. Substances such as Muhammad's digestive waste, while ignored in sira/maghazi works, receive attention in multiple hadith sources as possible evidence of Muhammad's station and even as a source of baraka. However, the values of Muhammad's bodily by-products do not shift unilaterally. Reading the sources for their multiplicities and changes over time, I find some substances prioritized over others as conductors of baraka. For example, Muhammad's saliva and sweat appear early and persist throughout the corpus as valuable. In contrast, Muhammad's blood receives brief consideration in sira/maghazi literature as a conduit for baraka, largely disappears from the developing hadith corpus, and then resurfaces in later sources. While early materials do offer reports that link Muhammad's acts of excretion with marvelous phenomena, such as trees moving to shield his modesty or the earth concealing his waste from the view of others, Muhammad's digestive waste is generally excluded from imagination as potentially a baraka-transmitting substance, but in the collections of later masters, such as Tabarani, these same materials receive increasing attention as powerful traces of the prophetic body. While reading for change, asking these sources questions of Muhammad's material traces also showcases the heterogeneity of ways that Companions and their transmitter networks conceptualize his body.

Baraka Water

Beyond the expected leakages and disjecta that emerge from typical human bodies, Muhammad's body also exhibits a marvelous flow that I have termed "baraka water." Similar to miracles in which Muhammad's spit or skin contact causes a dry well or empty vessel to overflow,[1] Muhammad's production of baraka water supports his communities with miraculous intervention in times of need. Unlike blood, digestive waster, and other bodily products that come into being through normal human processes, baraka water does not come from a conventional "border zone" opening where Muhammad's interior meets the outside world (such as his mouth or a wound), but rather comes from his hands. In al-Waqidi's *Maghazi*, Muhammad puts his fingers into an empty pot, at which point water gushes from between his fingers. This flow provides ample water for not only 30,000 people but also for their 10,000 horses and 12,000 or 15,000 camels.[2] As in the sira/maghazi works, numerous early hadith sources—the *Musnad* collections of Ibn Hanbal and Tayalisi, Ibn Abi Shayba's *Musannaf*, and Ibn Sa'd's *Tabaqat*—present Muhammad as ejecting baraka water from his hands, providing water to large numbers of his Companions, whether for drinking or for ritual ablution.[3] Prominent narrators of these incidents include Anas, Jabir, and Ibn Mas'ud, who quotes Muhammad as calling people to blessed purification and/or baraka from God, and also narrates that he filled his stomach with what had flowed from Muhammad's hands.[4] While the water comes from inside Muhammad's body, it is not stated to be *of* his body, a product of a system internal to him; the baraka water is not bodily waste or otherwise necessarily made *by* his body. While Muhammad's precise relationship to the water that flows from his hands remains unarticulated, these reports affirm his body as a site of divine activity and locus of baraka for those who encounter its emissions. Baraka water continues to appear in later sources. Traditions of Muhammad producing water for drinking and/or ablution from his body, attributed to Companions such as Anas, Jabir ibn 'Abd Allah, and Ibn Mas'ud, appear in four of the Six Books, including both of the *Sahihayn*.[5] A report from Bukhari's *Sahih*, traced to Jabir ibn 'Abd Allah, locates the flows of baraka in these flows. Jabir narrates that Muhammad's hands provided water to enable ablutions for nearly 1,500 worshipers, and that Muhammad told them, "Hurry, people of wudu'. The baraka is from God." Jabir adds that the people not only performed ablution but also drank the water, and that Jabir also "eagerly tried to put what I could in my stomach, as I knew that it was baraka."[6] This flow is not typical water, nor does its origin within Muhammad's body serve only as an intellectual proof of his prophethood: Jabir does not simply observe the incident to confirm that Muhammad is a prophet but also ingests the water to bring its baraka into his body. The water facilitates Muhammad's ejection of baraka from his own body into Jabir's stomach, producing a new Companion body infused with material linkage to the Prophet. Jabir's narration authorizes not only Muhammad's body but also his own as one transformed by their exchange.

Saliva

From the earliest materials through the development of the corpus, Muhammad's saliva appears as a powerful conduit through which baraka flows from Muhammad into the world. In Ma'mar's *Maghazi*, 'Urwa ibn

Mas'ud al-Thaqafi conveys his shock at the intensity of the Muslims' love for Muhammad by describing their treatment of his oral expectorations. "When the Messenger of God hawks up his phlegm," ʿUrwa exclaims, "one of these men catches it in his hand and smears it on his face and skin . . . and when he performs his ablutions, they nearly kill themselves over the ablution water."[7] While the Companions are represented as desiring enhanced closeness to Muhammad through his bodily ejections, whether the Companions value these substances specifically for their potency as baraka transmitters remains unclear in ʿUrwa's remark. Otherwise, reports of Companions expressing desire for contact with products from Muhammad's body remain absent from the text. Nor does Ma'mar's *Maghazi* report Muhammad's saliva or other bodily products being employed in the performance of miracles.

Ma'mar's treatment of Fatima's wedding to ʿAli, however, does depict Muhammad using his saliva in the ceremony. In Ma'mar's first account of the wedding, Muhammad uses water but not saliva: he recites words over a vessel of water, then uses the water to anoint ʿAli's chest and face, and sprinkles some on Fatima. In Ma'mar's second account, Muhammad spits into the vessel and uses the mixture of water and saliva to wash his own face and feet. He then pours it onto Fatima, accompanying the act with a prayer for God to purify Fatima as he had been purified, as "she is from me, and I am from her." Muhammad requests a second basin of water and performs the same action for ʿAli, which he supplements with another prayer. This account also portrays Muhammad applying his saliva to the celebratory dinner, reporting that he spat on it and blessed it (or "did baraka" to it).[8] Muhammad achieves something by transferring his saliva to water and food, and through these substances, to the people who consume them. However, the precise mode by which these transfers benefit their recipients goes unsaid. It is not clear whether Muhammad simply adheres to a particular ritual script that happens to involve saliva, or whether his saliva itself contains baraka that can spread like a beneficient contagion to other bodies.

Al-Waqidi portrays Muhammad making similar use of his saliva, giving water in which he had washed his hands and mouth to the bereaved mother and sister of Haritha ibn Suraqa, who drank the water and splashed it on their chests. Muhammad's saliva appears to act as a psychotropic medication: the report adds that after this incident, they became the most content and joyful women in Medina.[9] Muhammad also applies his saliva to the dead: he commands that Ibn Ubayy's corpse be removed from the grave, after which Muhammad sprays his saliva over the body, then dresses the body in his own shirt (which, the text notes, was one of two shirts that Muhammad was wearing, and the one that had been in closer contact with his skin).[10] In contrast to the relative conservatism regarding Muhammad's body in Ma'mar's *Maghazi*, al-Waqidi presents Muhammad's saliva as endowed with exceptional powers, providing several incidents in which Muhammad uses his saliva to cure the injured and sick, either by spitting directly onto their wounds or into a handful of soil, with instructions for the sick person to heat the soil with water and consume it.[11] Al-Waqidi portrays Muhammad spitting his ablution water into a fatigued camel's mouth and pouring the rest over its body, which empowers the camel to run. After the camel completes its journey, the owner's brother sacrifices it and distributes the meat as charity.[12] The episode represents baraka as a flow that moves both through substances and intentions. Water from Muhammad's ritual washing, charged by contact with Muhammad's skin and also mixed with his saliva, becomes a conductor of forces and energies between Muhammad (who himself operates as a conductor and mediator between extrahuman powers and the world) and an animal, charging the camel's muscles with baraka. The camel in turn becomes a vehicle through which baraka flows to others: its owner's brother, who slaughters the camel and then shares its meat with the community, and then the recipients of this charity, who are eating meat that was apparently transformed by its absorption of prophetic saliva. Baraka moves between human and animal bodies in this report both through a chain of substances (the ablution water, Muhammad's skin, his saliva, and potentially their energies in the camel's meat when it is consumed) and actions performed with devotional intention (the ritual script of ablution, the giving of blessed meat in charity). The narration's detail of the camel's slaughter suggests that even if the owner's brother does not necessarily ingest baraka through the meat itself, he recognizes a special property to the meat and is rewarded by distributing it piously. It becomes apparent that Muhammad's bodily fluid transfers a special property to the camel; through his spit and used water, Muhammad extends his corporeality into a nonhuman animal which then carries a trace of Muhammad and his effects across a long journey to be accessed by others.

Elsewhere, contact with Muhammad's saliva engages a power that can both destroy obstacles and provide material abundance. In Ibn Ishaq's *Sira*, Muhammad spits into water and then pours the water over a large rock that trench diggers had not been able to break or move; the mixture of water with prophetic saliva crushes the rock into powder.[13] Another report presents Muhammad's mouth (and thus likely saliva) as a source for contacting baraka, as Muhammad splits a morsel of meat with his teeth before throwing it back into a communal dish; through this intervention, a quantity of food small enough to have been consumed by a single person feeds the entire group to satisfaction.[14]

The powers of Muhammad's saliva, the most prolific of his baraka-transmitting bodily substances in the sira/maghazi sources, receive further attention in early hadith collections. In addition to the ability of Muhammad's saliva to heal injuries and produce water miracles, hadith sources from early masters such Ibn Hanbal also report his saliva transmitting baraka to newborn boys. Several narrations represent Muhammad using dates as vehicles to transfer his saliva to male infants. The reports associate (but do not exactly conflate) this act with his practice of *tahnik*, the rubbing of a baby boy's palate with a date by his father.[15] Though Muhammad was "not the father of any of your men," as the Qur'an reports,[16] he performed the patriarchal act of tahnik and saliva transferal for male infants in his community. These practices do not appear in the sira/maghazi works but can be found in hadith collections. Ibn Hanbal's *Musnad*, Ibn Sa'd's *Tabaqat* and Ibn Abi Shayba's *Musannaf* include accounts, attributed to Anas, of Anas's mother Umm Sulaym or stepfather 'Abd Allah ibn Abi Talha bringing their newborn son to Muhammad; longer versions of this narration depict Umm Sulaym losing a baby, then becoming pregnant again after Muhammad prays for God to send baraka to her and her husband. When she gives birth, Muhammad performs tahnik for the boy and names him 'Abd Allah.[17]

Ibn Hanbal's *Musnad* and Ibn Abi Shayba's *Musannaf* also provide traditions in which Asma' bint Abi Bakr's infant son and "the first born in Islam," 'Abd Allah ibn al-Zubayr, is brought to Muhammad, who then asks for a date, chews it, and spits it into the baby's mouth. Asma' thus narrates, "The first thing that entered his stomach [or mouth, depending on the version] was the saliva of the Messenger of God." Muhammad then performs tahnik with the date, prays for the baby, and "does baraka on him" (*baraka 'alayhi*).[18] Ibn Abi Shayba's version includes Muhammad naming the baby 'Abd Allah.[19] The narration appears in numerous variants and achieves high canonical privilege in the collections of Bukhari and Muslim.[20]

These two traditions of Muhammad performing tahnik and naming baby boys 'Abd Allah, depicting a pair of thematically overlapping but apparently distinct events, do not necessarily oppose each other with competing truth claims. Ibn Abi Shayba also reports Muhammad naming Abu Musa's boy Ibrahim and giving him tahnik, and presents A'isha describing tahnik for boys as a regular prophetic practice.[21] Bayhaqi's *Dala'il* also provides an account of 'Amir ibn Kariz bringing his son 'Abd Allah, at the time only five or six years old, to the Prophet, who spits into the child's mouth. The saliva of the Prophet causes the boy to swallow and lick his lips. The report concludes with a note on the prophetic saliva's effects: "They used to say, 'If 'Abd Allah struck a stone in front of him, water would come from the stone due to his baraka."[22] While the existence of separate stories depicting "'Abd Allah babies" Ibn Abi Talha and Ibn al-Zubayr does not overtly threaten the continuity of a shared narrative universe, these narratives privilege different geographic and familial networks. In each tradition, the respective 'Abd Allah's brother becomes our crucial source for learning of this infant's special connection to the Prophet. The tradition in which Muhammad gives tahnik and the name 'Abd Allah to the son of Abu Talha and Umm Sulaym enters the corpus through Basra-based chains of reporters from Umm Sulaym's son Anas. The tradition that presents baby 'Abd Allah as Ibn al-Zubayr appears with Kufan chains that lead back to Hisham ibn 'Urwa from his father 'Urwa ibn al-Zubayr, who in turn narrates his brother's saliva exchange with the Prophet and names his source as either their mother Asma' or aunt A'isha.

In the case of 'Abd Allah ibn al-Zubayr, Muhammad offering his saliva as a baby's first food constructs an intercorporeal linkage between the prophetic body and a figure who would later become controversial amid the factional conflicts that followed Muhammad's death. Ibn al-Zubayr appeared repeatedly as a rebel against the reigning caliphate—first siding with his aunt A'isha and father Zubayr against his father's cousin 'Ali, then with 'Ali's son Husayn against Yazid, and after Husayn's death launching his own caliphate.[23] The revolution was ultimately crushed but informed apocalyptic expectations, as hadith traditions circulated in which the Prophet gives an outline of the Mahdi's career—going from Medina to Mecca after a caliph's death, fighting Syrians and the Kalb, and persisting for nine years until his death—based on the events of Ibn al-Zubayr's life.[24]

Discussing tahnik and saliva transferal, Mohammad Ali Amir-Moezzi notes the ideological stakes in narrations of who does or does not receive prophetic saliva, observing the curious absence of 'Ali and his sons in these narrations from Sunni sources. For Muhammad to have favored Companions in this patriarchal ritual while neglecting males of his own family, Amir-Moezzi argues, suggests that such narrations express an anti-'Alid project to authorize men outside the prophetic household.[25] Amir-Moezzi rightfully points to the power of tahnik and saliva-transferal narratives to construct authorizing relations to the prophetic body. However, the exclusion of ʿAli and his sons from prophetic saliva transmission is not as absolute as Amir-Moezzi suggests, as Ibn Hanbal's *Musnad* reports Muhammad protecting ʿAli's son Hasan, the second Shi'i Imam, from afterlife punishments through mouth-to-mouth contact. Noteworthy for its potential political consequences, the witness who reports Hasan's prophetic favor is none other than ʿAli's opponent, the caliph Mu'awiya, who narrates that he saw Muhammad sucking Hasan's tongue (or lips), "as whoever had his tongue or his lips sucked by the Messenger of God would not have torment."[26]

ʿAli also receives prophetic saliva, as Ibn Hanbal's *Musnad* and both *Musannaf* collections report Muhammad spitting into his infected eye. The *Musannaf* narrations connect the incident with Muhammad handing his flag to ʿAli on the day of the battle at Khaybar, and Muhammad naming ʿAli as one who is loved by, and loves, God and Muhammad. In Ibn Abi Shayba's chapter on the excellences (*fada'il*) of ʿAli, ʿAli rejects the duties of flagbearer on the grounds that he cannot see anything; Muhammad then spits into ʿAli's eyes and prays for ʿAli to be protected from heat and cold. ʿAli later narrates that he was not affected by heat or cold after that day.[27] In the *Musnad*, ʿAli states that he never experienced eye infection after Muhammad spit into his eye.[28]

Beyond the capacity of prophetic saliva to transmit baraka through direct contact, as in Muhammad spitting into mouths or eyes, Muhammad's saliva also enables an extended prophetic corporeality through its potential to permanently alter the condition of water sources with which it makes contact. In the *Tabaqat*, Ibn Sa'd devotes an entire section to listing wells from which Muhammad drank. All seventeen reports in this section were transmitted to Ibn Sa'd by his teacher, al-Waqidi.[29] Adding to the significance of Muhammad having drunk *from* the wells are details of his adding material *to* them, namely water that had been in contact with his body or produced within it, which seems to alter the well forever. Some reports in this section add details of Muhammad praising a particular well's water for its sweetness, performing ablutions with its water, or pouring his used ablution water and/or saliva into a bucket and lowering the bucket into the well. One narration, attributed to Anas, presents Muhammad's saliva as causing Bir Ghars, which had previously dried up, to overflow with water.[30] Another report, attributed to Sahl ibn Sa'd, narrates that Muhammad blessed Bir Buda'a with his ablution water and saliva, and then prescribed the well's water as medicine for the sick; the report notes its success for treating patients.[31] The commingling of Muhammad's materiality with well water transforms the well into a point of convergence between Muhammad's body and the bodies not only of his Companions who drink from it but also those of future generations. For Anas to assert that Muhammad "drank from this well of ours,"[32] given the contagious energies and forces that flow from Muhammad's body, presents Anas's well (and those drinking from it, including of course Anas himself) as a linkage to Muhammad that can outlast the life of the prophetic body.

Umm Sulaym and her son Anas, prominent reporters of Muhammad's saliva as a mode of contacting his baraka, appear at the center of another tradition that locates baraka in contact with Muhammad's lips. The tradition, appearing in the *Tabaqat*'s entry on Umm Sulaym via two reports that share in their transmission from Anas to his grandson al-Bara', presents Muhammad drinking from a waterskin that he found hanging in Umm Sulaym's house. Umm Sulaym then cuts out the waterskin's mouth and keeps it.[33] Like Anas's well from which Muhammad drank, the waterskin mouth in Umm Sulaym's house offers a trace of the prophetic mouth and access to the baraka that passed through it.

In representations of the end of Muhammad's life, Companions' encounters with prophetic saliva during his final illness produce his body as a map on which ideological struggles are inscribed. While Ma'mar and al-Waqidi do not cover the death of Muhammad, and Ibn Ishaq's *Sira* depicts Muhammad dying in A'isha's arms, Ibn Sa'd gives coverage to opposing accounts that alternately position A'isha or 'Ali as the one holding Muhammad for his final breath. In one of the pro-'Ali narrations, 'Ali states that Muhammad reclined on his chest and did not stop talking until his saliva fell onto 'Ali. At that moment Muhammad expired and his body became heavy in 'Ali's lap. Muhammad's saliva appears at the moment of his death to perform a final act of baraka transferal.[34] One pro-A'isha narration asserts that as she held him, cold water poured from his mouth onto her collarbone, causing her to shiver.[35] Another pro-A'isha account establishes their intercorporeal connection in a dramatically alterior fashion, since A'isha does not receive Muhammad's saliva but the opposite: he receives hers. A'isha narrates that Muhammad desired a *miswak* to clean his teeth but that she softened the miswak for him by chewing it herself. Muhammad then used the miswak to clean his teeth until the moment of death, at which it fell from his hand. She thus narrates, "God mixed my saliva with his in the last hour of his worldly life and the first day of the hereafter."[36] A'isha privileges her link to Muhammad through the mingling of their fluids as he transitioned out of this world, though she reverses the direction in which these connections typically occur. The narration favors A'isha through her intimacy with Muhammad during his last breath, rather than a transmission of baraka directly from his body to hers.

The hadith collections of masters from the later ninth century CE preserve this imaginary of Muhammad's saliva as ritually efficacious and a transmitter of the beneficent energies that flow through his body. Traditions such as Jabir's narration of Muhammad covering the body of 'Abd Allah ibn Ubayy with his shirt and saliva, Yazid ibn Abi Ubayd's report of Muhammad healing Salama's leg by spitting into his wound, and Muhammad healing 'Ali's eyes by spitting into them, appear in the Six Books.[37] Moreover, later collections such as Tabarani's *Mu'jam al-Kabir*, Bayhaqi's *Sunan al-Kubra*, and Khatib's *Tarikh* include a tradition that presents Muhammad seemingly performing a kind of *metzitzah*—the rabbinical practice of sucking blood from a circumcision wound—on his grandson Husayn, parting his legs and kissing his penis.[38] The precise significance of Muhammad's act (that is, the question of whether he performs a ritual, medical, or baraka-transmitting function upon Husayn, though these need not be mutually exclusive) remains unsaid. In the longest variant of the tradition, Muhammad additionally tells his grandson, "God curse your killer."[39]

As the literary corpus constricts and expands with Bukhari's generation and postcanonical sources, saliva remains distinguished among Muhammad's bodily products as the mode of mediation and corporeal linkage to be privileged by A'isha. Her narrations of Muhammad performing tahnik and saliva transferal to infants (specifically 'Abd Allah Ibn al-Zubayr) and incorporating his saliva into rituals of healing, as well as her assertion that saliva had poured from Muhammad's mouth onto her during his final illness, appear throughout the sources.[40] In addition, A'isha also reports that she had softened Muhammad's miswak with her own mouth, causing her saliva to mix with his at the time of his death.[41] In reports that appear with minor variations in four of the Six Books, A'isha narrates to 'Amra bint 'Abd al-Rahman that Muhammad used his saliva in healing practices and explained that "the dust of our land with the saliva of some of us" could cure the sick.[42] With her assertion that the Prophet said "some of us," A'isha's claim for saliva's ritual efficacy democratizes its power beyond her husband: rather than boast of her husband's bodily marvels, she reports his practice as a part of his *sunna* that could theoretically be imitated by anyone. Additionally, narrations from other Companions attest to members of the original Muslim community using their own saliva for healing.[43]

Of Muhammad's bodily products, his saliva appears early in the sources as an extension of prophetic corporeality, a resource through which Muhammad can energize fatigued camels, crush boulders into dust, or bestow his daughter's wedding with baraka. Saliva appears with this power in early sira/maghazi literature to the virtual exclusion of other bodily products, and maintains its privilege over other substances and fluids in later sources, provoking the question of a hierarchy among Muhammad's fluids and excreta. While the sira hadith corpus does contain reports that treat substances such as blood and urine as conduits of baraka, these fluids enjoy nothing remotely comparable to the literature's consistent and prolific treatment of prophetic saliva—a substance that Muhammad could produce from his body instantly, at seemingly any time without harm to himself, and one that could be accessed by Muhammad's Companions in less invasive or intimate fashion than other products of the body.

Sweat

While saliva dominates the corpus as the primary material trace of Muhammad's body that can transmit his baraka into other bodies, the sources also give considerable priority to his sweat, an even more "public" and easily accessible fluid than his saliva. The meanings and values of Muhammad's sweat observably change with the development of the corpus. In early sira/maghazi texts, the Companions report their sensory experiences of Muhammad's sweat in ocular terms, as a readable symptom through which they can recognize events taking place inside Muhammad's body. Perspiration appears as a side effect of revelation; in their recollections of Muhammad's sweat, the Companions report a symptom that reveals the flows of transcendent forces through his body. These traditions authorize not only Muhammad as the locus of divine activity but also the Companions themselves as witnesses to the event of the Qur'an and privileged accessors to Muhammad's corporeal baraka.

In sira and maghazi texts of the early third/ninth century, Companions recall Muhammad sweating during revelations, even in cold weather. Both Ibn Ishaq's *Sira* and al-Waqidi's *Maghazi* include A'isha's narration that after Muhammad received the revelation that confirmed her innocence, she observed the sweat falling from him as he sat up. In Ibn Ishaq's version, A'isha compares his sweat to "drops of water on a winter day."[44] Al-Waqidi's version depicts A'isha as likening the sweat drops to pearls, a comparison that will persist in the literature.[45] Al-Waqidi additionally includes an episode in which a convulsion that overtakes Muhammad causes observers to suspect that he is receiving revelations, and the resultant drops of sweat from his brow are compared to pearls.[46]

In comparison to the sira/maghazi literatures, in which Muhammad's excessive perspiration serves primarily to signal the event of divine revelation, hadith sources present his sweat as a baraka-fused material that merits collection and preservation. Whereas the sira/maghazi works emphasize the ocular encounter with Muhammad's sweat as a sign of the Qur'an's descent, reports of olfactory encounters in the hadith collections affirm Muhammad's body as a site of divine intervention while also privileging themselves as the generation that could directly access his body. Ibn Hanbal and Ibn Sa'd include a tradition in which 'Ali ibn Abu Talib is asked by unnamed interlocutors to describe Muhammad; among details such as Muhammad's height, stride, and color, and the statement that he had never seen Muhammad's likeness before or since, 'Ali recalls that the drops of perspiration on Muhammad's face resembled pearls.[47] The *Tabaqat* also provides Anas's recollection of various details of Muhammad's body, including Anas's statement that he had never smelled musk more pleasing than Muhammad's sweat or personal scent.[48]

Umm Sulaym appears at the center of a tradition that portrays Muhammad's sweat as a coveted substance. In this tradition, Muhammad falls asleep, with some narrations specifying that he does so on a leather mat. During Muhammad's nap, he sweats. Upon awakening, Muhammad discovers that Umm Sulaym is collecting or has collected his perspiration. Muhammad then asks what Umm Sulaym is doing. In reports from Ibn Hanbal's *Musnad* and the *Tabaqat*, Umm Sulaym answers that she wants Muhammad's sweat for her perfume, in some variants adding that his sweat is superior to any other perfume.[49] Umm Sulaym also shares some of her prophetic-sweat-infused perfume with Ibn Sirin, whose father had been a slave of Anas.[50] Ibn Sirin arranges to have the perfume used in his own embalming; the source for this information in the *Tabaqat*, Ayyub ibn Kaysan, adds that he still possesses a portion of what Umm Sulaym had given to Ibn Sirin.[51]

Umm Sulaym's rationalizations for collecting the prophetic sweat are not limited to its pleasing smell. In another report from the *Tabaqat*, Umm Sulaym tells Muhammad, "I take this for the baraka that exudes from you."[52] Umm Sulaym locates baraka as a property that can exit Muhammad's body through the waste that streams from his pores. Like the body of the camel that had ingested Muhammad's saliva, the collection of Muhammad's sweat in a bottle can preserve his baraka and transport it to others when Muhammad is absent or even deceased.

While examining the Companions' representations of Muhammad's sweat as emitting a pleasurable fragrance, proving his prophetic station, and transmitting baraka, there remains the question of whether Muhammad experienced his own sweat in this manner, as well as the ways Companions may depart from one another in their treatments of the sweat. In tension with these traditions of Companions finding pleasure in the smell of Muhammad's sweat, Ibn Hanbal's *Musnad* and Ibn Sa'd's *Tabaqat* also contain a tradition, attributed to A'isha, in which Muhammad appears to be displeased with his own smell. In this tradition, a sheet is made for Muhammad of black wool. In some versions, A'isha draws attention to the stark contrast between the blackness of the wool and the whiteness of Muhammad's skin. Muhammad wears the sheet but is then displeased by the smell of the wool after he sweats. He throws it away, with A'isha explaining, "He liked good smell." At no point in the narration does A'isha or another Companion express interest in the sweat-soaked wool as a conduit of baraka.[53] Placing this tradition in conversation with reports of Companions fondly remembering Muhammad's odor and using his sweat for perfume, I find a potential departure between Muhammad's experience of his own body and his body as experienced by his Companions, in addition to diversity in the Companions' perspectives. Though a handful of reports present the possibility that Muhammad was displeased by the smell of his sweat, the Companions do not treat his bodily scent as anything less than sublime. Whether or not Muhammad could find his own sweat to have an offensive odor, the Companions appear to experience his sweat only as a sensory delight or as a sign of divine activity upon his person.

Nonetheless, Muhammad's unfavorable perception of his own scent also enters the sources through the mediation of a Companion, namely A'isha. These reports depict A'isha explaining matter-of-factly that Muhammad did not like the smell of his sweat in the black wool garment, and that he threw the garment away because he preferred good smells. Narrations in which A'isha describes her husband's sweat as a visual signifier of revelation do not offer recollections of its scent. In her narrations of the black wool garment, A'isha does not confirm or deny that the smell that upset Muhammad would have also been unpleasant to others, let alone that she had smelled the sweaty garment herself and found it offensive. A'isha refrains from offering her personal opinion of the smell but does not appear threatened or surprised by the possibility of her husband smelling bad.

As in the treatment of Muhammad's saliva, the Six Books and their contemporary hadith collections do not meaningfully depart from earlier hadith collections in their representations of Muhammad's sweat. Prophetic perspiration continues to signify a special relationship to divine forces when seen or smelled by Companions. Bukhari includes a narration from Anas in which Anas recalls that he has never smelled perfume sweeter than Muhammad's sweat; in the narration, Anas also mentions that he had never touched silk softer than the palm of Muhammad's hand.[54] In a report of the Umm Sulaym perfume tradition, Bukhari adds that as Anas's death approached (roughly eighty years after the death of Muhammad), Anas still possessed the perfume made from Muhammad's sweat, and that Anas requested that the perfume be mixed with the *hanut* that would be used in his funeral preparations.[55] Following the works of the previous generation, these reports of transcendent qualities in Muhammad's sweat are countered by A'isha's narration of the black wool cloak that Muhammad throws away, which she attributes to his not liking its smell after he sweats in it. The tradition appears in Nasa'i's *Kubra* collection and Abu Dawud's *Sunan*.[56] Also consistent with earlier sources, A'isha appears as a source for the representation of Muhammad's sweat as a symptom of divine activity upon his body, namely the descent of the Qur'an. In reports included by Bukhari, Nasa'i, and Tirmidhi, A'isha quotes Muhammad's explanation of the various forms in which revelation came to him, adding her own remark that she had witnessed profuse perspiration from his forehead even on an intensely cold day.[57] Another set of reports from A'isha directly relate Muhammad's excessive sweat during his reception of revelation with her exoneration from rumors of adultery, as A'isha observes Muhammad sweating profusely prior to his announcing that God had confirmed her innocence.[58] Though A'isha's narrations do not treat the sweat itself as endowed with special qualities, the change in Muhammad's bodily condition establishes his body as the site of mediation between God and the community. The appearance of profuse sweat, establishing that Muhammad's judgment is not his own, becomes evidence in his wife's favor.

Hair and Fingernails

While Ma'mar makes no reference to the collection of Muhammad's hair or nails, al-Waqidi includes a report of Khalid ibn Walid coveting Muhammad's hair, placing it on his mouth and eyes and carrying it in his cap,[59] as well as Suhayl placing Muhammad's hair on his eyes.[60] Al-Waqidi additionally provides a narration from A'isha in which she is questioned by her father regarding hairs in her possession. She explains that Muhammad had distributed the hairs from his head-shaving at hajj, and that she was among the recipients: "We took what the people took."[61] The narration does not name a specific benefit related to the hair, nor does A'isha articulate a personal interest in possessing her husband's posthajj trimmings. These narrations are accompanied by a report in which Muhammad is said to have ordered the burial of his hair and nails.[62]

Thematically faithful to their representations in the sira/maghazi literatures, early hadith collections present Muhammad's hair and fingernails as efficacious extensions of prophetic corporeality. These items bestow Muhammad's bodily baraka upon their possessors, and also intensify their possessors' power as links between Muhammad and later generations who could not have witnessed him in person. In the *Tabaqat* and Ibn Hanbal's *Musnad*, Anas narrates that as Muhammad got his hair cut, the Companions would gather around him, with every hair falling into someone's hands.[63] Though Muhammad's hair and nail clippings do not appear as the focus of miracle accounts from his lifetime, they were reportedly preserved by the community after his death and prized as traces of his bodily baraka. Anas tells us that as a barber cut Muhammad's hair and men caught the clippings as they fell, his stepfather, Abu Talha, took one of the hairs to Anas's mother, Umm Sulaym, who mixed it in her perfume.[64] Abu Talha appears in multiple canonical narrations as a Companion particularly interested in obtaining clippings from Muhammad's haircuts.[65] Anas even tells us that while most people received one or two strands of hair from the Prophet's postpilgrimage shaving of his head, Anas's stepfather received an enormous share: all of the clippings from the left side of Muhammad's head.[66] In one version, Anas adds that Abu Talha was appointed distributor of prophetic hairs to members of the community.[67] Ibn Hanbal and Ibn Sa'd provide accounts of Umm Sulaym keeping a hair of Muhammad and showing it to visitors.[68] Ibn Sa'd shares two accounts in his *Tabaqat* of Mu'awiya, the first Umayyad caliph, giving instructions for Muhammad's hair and fingernails to be used in his own burial. In one report, Mu'awiya asks to be clothed in Muhammad's shirt and buried with Muhammad's fingernail parings that he had stored in a bottle; in the second report, he requests that both the hairs and fingernails he had collected from Muhammad be placed in his mouth and nose.[69]

One tradition involving Muhammad's hair reveals that his bodily products, while potentially operating as pathways for baraka to travel between his body and those of his Companions, can also facilitate undesired connections and expose him to malevolent forces. A number of accounts portray Jewish sorcerer Labid ibn ʿAsim acquiring hairs from Muhammad, which renders Muhammad vulnerable to Labid's technologies of harm. Using Muhammad's hairs, the sorcerer manages to temporarily impair Muhammad's sexual performance before angelic intervention restores him. The tradition of Labid's attack is mentioned only briefly in the *Sira* (reporting the sorcery against Muhammad's sexuality but not the use of his hairs) but appears with greater detail and some variation in Ibn Hanbal's *Musnad*, the *Tabaqat*, and both *Musannaf* collections.[70] In order for his assault on Muhammad to work, Labid needs material from Muhammad's body. Labid's use of Muhammad's hair as a weapon operates on a perceived relationship between the body and its by-products (or even inorganic artifacts marked by intimate interactions with the body, such as the teeth of Muhammad's comb). Muhammad's hair remains sufficiently bound to him, even after a barber has severed its connection to his body, to empower sorcery against him. While Labid can temporarily bring harm to Muhammad by manipulation of his hairs, however, there is no indication that Labid derived further personal benefit from possessing them, as though the baraka in the hairs might have been indiscriminately contagious.

While I could not find reports of people directly ingesting hairs from Muhammad, reports do present prophetic hairs as potent transmitters of baraka, particularly to liquids in which they have been placed. In Bukhari's report of Umm Sulaym making perfume from Muhammad's sweat, the mixture also includes prophetic hairs.[71] Bukhari's *Sahih* additionally preserves reports in which Umm Salama shows men hairs of Muhammad that she keeps in a container; in one narration, ʿUthman ibn ʿAbd Allah recalls his people sending him to Umm Salama with a bowl of water, explaining that anyone suffering from the evil eye or other ailments would send water to Umm Salama. He also mentions the small container in which she kept hairs of Muhammad, adding that he had looked into the container and seen the red hairs for himself.[72] By dipping the hairs into the bowl, Umm Salama transmits Muhammad's healing baraka into someone who drinks the water. Umm Salama thereby extends the reach of Muhammad's body across space and time, healing those who are both geographically distant (as ʿUthman narrates, "My people sent me") and temporally removed, living in the generations after Muhammad's death. Possession of the prophetic hairs also empowers Umm Salama as a controller of access to prophetic baraka in a postprophetic time. For Bukhari, the report becomes valuable primarily as an eyewitness account of Muhammad's personal practice, since it confirms that the Prophet dyed his hair. Bukhari's organization of his *Sahih* does not present these reports with an expressed interest in theorizing about the corporeal transmission of baraka but rather places them in his section, "What Is Said about Gray Hair" to establish a prophetic norm.[73] In this case, Muhammad's preserved hair becomes meaningful as evidence of correct praxis rather than as a transmitter of beneficent energies.

Blood

Did baraka literally flow through Muhammad's veins? If so, what would happen if a wound on the prophetic body, opening a new zone of movement between inside and outside, directed that flow from his insides into the world—or into other bodies? The question of whether Muhammad's blood could transmit baraka provokes a possible tension with dietary prescriptions and issues of ritual purity. The Qur'an expressly forbids the consumption of animal blood (5:3), and early Muslim jurists debated whether human blood was substantively pure or polluting.[74] While blood cannot become legally permissible food, and the leakage of blood from one's own body possibly invalidates prayer (depending on the kind of blood and the specific legal school), a handful of traditions depict Companions consuming Muhammad's blood. In these traditions, Muhammad's blood becomes defined by its origins within his ontologically privileged body, rather than by blood's broader legal status in discussions of diet regulation or ritual purity.

In early sira/maghazi literature's economy of fluids dominated by the relatively benign saliva and sweat, a rare account of prophetic blood consumption appears in an account that at the battle of Uhud, two helmet rings were removed from Muhammad's cheeks, causing blood to flow "as though from a water bag." Witnessing the Prophet's injury, Malik ibn Sinan decided to suck blood from the wound and swallow it. In response, Muhammad declared, "Whoever desires to see one who mixes his blood with mine, let him look at Malik ibn Sinan." Muhammad is also quoted in the report as stating, "Whoever touches his blood and my blood, the fire of hell will not wound him." When asked if he drank the blood, Malik would answer, "Yes, I drank the blood of the Messenger of God." The narration goes on to describe Malik's son, prolific hadith narrator Abu Sa'id al-

Khudri, kissing Muhammad's knees, and Muhammad exclaiming to him, "May God reward you in your father."[75] In Ibn Ishaq's version, Muhammad remarks that the person whose blood mixed with his own would not be touched by hellfire.[76] The tradition is reported through Abu Sa'id to his grandson, Rubayh ibn 'Abd ar-Rahman ibn Abu Sa'id. Like the incident of Muhammad spitting into a Companion's wound, the violent opening of his own flesh creates a new threshold between inside and outside at which bodies can connect. When Malik places his mouth on the Prophet's wound, a flow from Muhammad's insides crosses the threshold out of his body to mix with Malik's insides.

Another Companion who encounters prophetic blood in Ibn Ishaq's material, Muhammad's daughter Fatima, wipes the blood from Muhammad's face and treats the wound but does not display a personal interest in contact with his blood as a means of connection.[77] While it might seem intuitive that Muhammad's biological daughter does not need to consume his blood to achieve the intercorporeality with him that other Companions desire, her lack of interest in the blood remains notable, as these sources do not present Fatima as having necessarily inherited her father's relationship to baraka.

The representation of drinking Muhammad's blood as metaphysically transformative does not appear in Ma'mar's *Maghazi* or otherwise flourish across the sources. While the tradition of Malik ibn Sinan's blood consumption appears in Ibn Sa'd's *Tabaqat*, prophetic blood remains virtually invisible in early hadith sources as a baraka transmitter.[78] Ibn Sa'd also devotes a section of reports to Muhammad's participation in cupping, providing reports that cover topics such as cupping's efficacy for treating various ailments, payment of the cupper's wages, the points on Muhammad's body at which he would get cupped, the days of the week and month on which to get cupped, and Muhammad's cupping while in the mosque, the state of ihram, or fasting. One hadith narrates that a Companion who was unfamiliar with cupping expressed shock that Muhammad paid a man who ripped his skin, until Muhammad explained the practice. Multiple reports authorize cupping as an order that Muhammad had received from Gabriel and other angels. In regard to the substance of Muhammad's blood, the section only narrates that Muhammad ordered for his blood to be buried so that no dog might search for it, and that he advised this method of disposal as a general practice for others. Muhammad states that whoever "sprinkles this blood" will not be harmed, but the section's reports read as a prophetic prescription for cupping rather than a claim specifically regarding his own blood's special qualities.[79]

Ibn Abi ʿAsim provides an outlier among ninth-century hadith masters in his report of an encounter between ʿAbd Allah ibn al-Zubayr and Muhammad's blood. As discussed earlier, Ibn al-Zubayr had received Muhammad's saliva directly into his mouth as an infant. Distinguished in traditions by his ingestion of Muhammad's saliva or blood, Ibn al-Zubayr's interior nature and future significance become marked (or produced) in part through these acts of consumption. When he encountered Muhammad's blood, Ibn al-Zubayr—born roughly two years after Muhammad's migration to Medina—would not have been more than eight years old. The account appears as Ibn al-Zubayr's recollection of the event a generation later to his own son, ʿAmir ibn ʿAbd Allah ibn al-Zubayr. ʿAmir reports that his father came to the Prophet when he was getting cupped. Muhammad gave the blood to young Ibn al-Zubayr with the instructions "Go with this blood and pour it out so that no one will see it." Ibn al-Zubayr left the Prophet and drank the blood. When Muhammad later asked, "O ʿAbd Allah, what did you do with the blood?" Ibn al-Zubayr answered, "I put it in a hiding place where I thought that it would be hidden from the people." Muhammad replied, "Perhaps you drank it," prompting the child to confess. "O ʿAbd Allah," Muhammad said to him. "Why did you drink the blood? Woe to you from the people, and woe to the people from you."[80]

While prophetic blood reemerges with this tradition as a thinkable resource for baraka, Muhammad's response to Ibn al-Zubayr reflects ways different products and portions of Muhammad's body, when detached from his body, acquire different meanings and values. In depictions of Ibn al-Zubayr as the newborn baby who receives prophetic expectoration as his first food, the consumption of Muhammad's saliva offers an unambiguous privilege.[81] In contrast to the Kufa-based saliva tradition in which Ibn al-Zubayr receives prophetic saliva, this Basra-based tradition presents Ibn al-Zubayr's drinking blood as a perverted attempt at intercorporeality that Muhammad seems to reject (or at least read as an ominous indicator of Ibn al-Zubayr's destiny as defeated rebel and slain "anti-Caliph").[82] In the hands of different narrators who describe Ibn al-Zubayr's consumption of prophetic saliva or blood, his mouth becomes a machine that succeeds or fails at linking to the prophetic body.

Canonical collections erase the tradition of prophetic blood consumption. As the hadith corpus continues to expand after the Sahih/Sunan era, however, possibilities reopen for prophetic blood as a carrier of contagious baraka. Al-Hakim's *Al-Mustadrak* includes the tradition of Ibn al-Zubayr ingesting Muhammad's blood, reported by ʿAbd Allah's son ʿAmir, with a slight variation: Muhammad asks Ibn al-Zubayr, "Was it your decision to drink the blood?"[83] An alternate version reported by Abu Nu'aym in his *Hilya*, attributed to Ibn al-Zubayr's client (*mawla*) Kaysan, presents Salman al-Farisi as revealing Ibn al-Zubayr's actions to Muhammad. Kaysan's account maintains Muhammad's ominous if vague forecasting of Ibn al-Zubayr's destiny but expands the episode to provide both Ibn al-Zubayr's clear expression of a desire for Muhammad's blood and Muhammad's assurance that the future countercaliph will be (mostly) immune to otherworldly punishment:

> Salman entered upon the Messenger of God . . . as ʿAbd Allah ibn al-Zubayr had a basin and was drinking its contents. ʿAbd Allah entered upon the Messenger of God . . . [Muhammad] said to him, "You emptied it?" [Ibn al-Zubayr] said, "Yes." Salman asked, "What is that, Messenger of God?" [Muhammad] said, "I gave him the leftovers from my cupping for him to spill." Salman said, "He actually drank what you had dispatched him with." [Muhammad] said, "You drank it?" [Ibn al-Zubayr] said, "Yes." He asked, "Why?" [Ibn al-Zubayr] said, "I loved that the blood of the Messenger of God, God bless him and give him peace, was in my stomach." [Muhammad] said with his hand on Ibn al-Zubayr's head, "Woe to you from humanity, and woe to humanity from you. The fire will not touch you except for the oath."[84]

Tabarani's *Mu'jam al-Kabir* restores the early sira/maghazi tradition in which Malik ibn Sinan drinks Muhammad's blood directly from his wound and Muhammad declares salvation for Malik due to his having mixed their blood together. The incident appears in the *Mu'jam* with a full isnad that starts with Malik's son, Companion and prolific hadith reporter Abu Sa'id al-Khudri, and extends through three subsequent generations of Malik's descendents.[85] In addition to the resurfacing of the Malik ibn Sinan tradition, later sources include other narrations of Companions ingesting Muhammad's blood. Bayhaqi's *Sunan al-Kubra* includes the tradition of Muhammad's blood consumed by his mawla Safina, which significantly mirrors the Ibn al-Zubayr tradition. In both, Muhammad gives the Companion his blood after cupping with instructions for its disposal. In the Safina tradition, Muhammad tells Safina to bury the blood in order to hide it from animals and birds (or humans and animals, as one transmitter suggests). Safina recalls, "I vanished with it and drank it. Then he asked me, and I reported to him, 'I drank it.' Then he laughed."[86] Unlike the Malik ibn Sinan tradition and other narrations of Companions consuming Muhammad's bodily substances, but, in resonance with versions of the Ibn al-Zubayr blood-drinking tradition, Muhammad does not name a medical or soteriological benefit of Safina's act of consumption. However, Safina's narration adheres to the formula for other traditions in that the report minimizes Muhammad's agency in the matter, limiting his role to that of surprised witness and respondent. Muhammad gives no indication that Safina should consume his blood; Safina in fact disobeys Muhammad's instructions to pour out the blood and only drinks it after leaving Muhammad's sight. Muhammad's concern to hide his blood from people could express an awareness of others' interest in the substance, whether to consume for baraka as Safina does or for malicious sorcery, as Labid intends with prophetic hairs. The narrative gives Muhammad a chance to assure Safina (and, by extension, the readers of this narrative) that he found no offense. Upon discovering Safina's action, Muhammad laughs but does not further comment: the significance of this corporeal border crossing remains unsaid. At the very least, Muhammad's laughter seems to reflect a lesser gravity than his ominous remarks to Ibn al-Zubayr. Finally, it should be noted that like the other blood-drinking traditions, the Safina tradition reaches us through Safina's family tree: Safina narrates the event to his grandson, Ibrahim ibn ʿAmr ibn Safina.[87] While the effects and meanings of drinking Muhammad's blood remain unstable among these traditions, all three traditions of Companions drinking Muhammad's blood enter the corpus through reporters who are direct descendants of the drinkers. Their own bodies conceivably become linked to the Prophet by their ancestors' consumption of his fluids—even if, as in the case of Malik ibn Sinan, his reporting son was already born when he ate prophetic blood.

Digestive Waste

Muhammad's acts of making waste, unexamined in the Qur'an and earliest sira/maghazi works, appear in early hadith collections not as moments at which baraka becomes more materially accessible to his Companions but rather as prescriptive precedents and occasionally as stories of marvels related to his prophetic station. In the *Tabaqat*, reports associated with Muhammad's defecation and urination call attention to his control over forces of nature and the divine protection of his modesty, rather than the substances themselves. Ibn Sa'd's section regarding signs of prophethood that followed the start of Qur'anic revelation includes two reports in which Muhammad feels the need to relieve himself but has no shelter from the eyes of his Companions. He instructs a Companion to inform two trees that he had ordered them to come closer together for him. The Companion relates Muhammad's command to the trees, causing one to move closer to the other to veil Muhammad from view. After Muhammad has finished, the tree moves back to its original place.[88] In another hadith from this section, A'isha asks Muhammad why she cannot detect any traces of his waste. Muhammad explains that the earth swallows what prophets excrete so that none of it can be seen.[89] These traditions present the forces of nature as compelled to protect Muhammad's dignity, shielding not only Muhammad's nakedness and vulnerability in making waste but also the material waste as an artifact that can cause him embarrassment.

Left ambiguous in these reports is the nature of the waste itself. There is no portrayal in the *Tabaqat* of Muhammad's urine or feces holding special properties. In contrast to narrations concerning Muhammad's sweat, in which the sensory experience of the waste brings pleasure to his Companions, the earth's concealment of his excreta could suggest that Muhammad's waste was typical in its capacity to be offensive or embarrassing. As with Muhammad's sweat, A'isha constricts the possibilities for Muhammad's excreta, suggesting that there is nothing particularly noteworthy about substances from her husband's body. Nor do reports in the *Tabaqat* depict Muhammad's Companions more broadly as interested in his digestive excreta as a source of baraka. Similarly, though Muhammad experienced the same violations of ritual purity as his Companions and gave prescriptive instructions for dealing with these bodily processes, I found no narrations that reported specific incidents of prophetic gas or Companions' olfactory witness of Muhammad breaking wind.

As in earlier sources, the Six Books and most sources from the period considered do not generally treat prophetic urine as remarkable. In relation to the transmission of baraka through substances produced by Muhammad, his urine seems to remain unthinkable as a resource. The silence of the sources is observable in A'isha's account of Muhammad on his deathbed from Tirmidhi's *Shama'il*, in which A'isha reports that before expiring, Muhammad requested a container in which he could urinate; consistent with A'isha's broader corpus of reports concerning Muhammad's body, the narration does not present Muhammad's final urination as materially special. No one is portrayed as desiring contact with the urine or hoping to bottle it, as Umm Sulaym had done with his sweat.[90] This tradition can be found in sources such as the *Tabaqat* and Nasa'i's *Sunan* works, though in most reports it is unclear whether Muhammad receives the container and manages to urinate before passing away.[91] Tirmidhi's version mentions that prior to the moment of his expiration, Muhammad did urinate, but it does not say what the Companions did with the urine after Muhammad's death. These reports do not present the Companions as imagining that Muhammad's urine could provide the same beneficent energies as his sweat, saliva, blood, hair, or fingernails. Though Muhammad's deathbed saliva specifically appears in traditions of his final illness as a mode of meaningful connection to other Companions ('Ali or A'isha), reports neglect his deathbed urine.

Muhammad's excretory system receives attention in the canon for the salience of his personal habits to questions of correct practice and ritual purity, not the substance of his waste itself. The collections offer reports on questions of whether Muhammad stood or squatted to urinate,[92] the direction he faced,[93] and the way he cleaned himself.[94] A minor tradition, found in the collections of Nasa'i and Abu Dawud, represents Muhammad as keeping a vessel under his bed for urinating at night.[95] Again, these reports serve purely legal considerations, answering the question of whether keeping a vessel for such purposes (and therefore having urine in the house, which some reporters would condemn as a repellant to angels)[96] is permitted. Information on Muhammad's acts of making waste present these events as establishing precedents rather than narrations of proximity between the Companions and baraka-laden materials. Companions who assisted Muhammad by carrying water or providing him with stones might become privileged by their degree of intimacy with Muhammad, but these collections do not portray them as caring specifically about the feces or urine that had been produced within the prophetic body.

In a departure from the practice-centered narrations found in these collections, one source from the period does present Muhammad's urine as a conduit of baraka. The tradition of Muhammad's urinating into a jar that he kept under his bed, presented in two of the Six Books as relevant for questions of praxis, appears in Ibn Abi 'Asim's *Al-Ahad wa al-Mathani* as a narrative of encounter between a Companion and Muhammad's bodily baraka. Muhammad "used to have a bowl from date-palm that he urinated into and then put under his bed. Then came a woman—they say that she was Baraka, who came with Umm Habiba from al-Habasha [Ethiopia]—and she drank it, and the Prophet, God bless him and give him peace, looked for it. They say: Baraka drank it and when he asked her, she said, 'I drank it.' He said, 'You have been brought from the fire,' or he said, 'protection' or its meaning."[97]

Salvation from afterlife punishments emerged from Muhammad's body as a literal flow that could be successfully accessed by ingestion. Ibn Abi 'Asim's source for the report of Baraka's drinking, 'Ali ibn Maymun al-'Attar, relates from the same chain of Hajjaj < Ibn Jurayj < Hujayma < Umayma as shorter versions in the collections of Nasa'i and Abu Dawud, which state that Muhammad urinated into a vessel that he kept under the bed but do not mention the urine being consumed. The account of Baraka consuming prophetic urine adheres to the narrative formula found in other accounts of Companions interacting with Muhammad's bodily products. As in the tradition of Umm Sulaym obtaining Muhammad's sweat for her perfume and Malik ibn Sinan consuming Muhammad's blood directly from his open wound, Baraka drinks Muhammad's urine without Muhammad first having a chance to approve or disapprove. Similar to the episode in which Umm Sulaym bottles his sweat, Muhammad asks Baraka for an explanation. As in the case of Malik ibn Sinan and the bloody wound, Muhammad then approves with an announcement of his urine's soteriological benefits for its consumer. Unlike Umm Sulaym, who explains to Muhammad that his sweat makes the greatest perfume (and in one variant, reveals hope that baraka from his sweat will benefit her children), Baraka's interest in Muhammad's urine is not articulated. The report does not address Baraka's perception of the substance, that is, whether or not she recognized it as urine (or specifically as Muhammad's urine) before or during her consumption. Nor is it clear whether she believed that beneficent energies could pass from a prophetic body through his urine and that she could access these energies by drinking it. While the report does not display investment in Baraka's subjectivity, its departure from other versions of the "bowl under the bed" tradition opens a new portal through which Companions can experience the material ejection of baraka from Muhammad's body.

Urine finally receives attention as a prophetic bodily product that could transmit baraka to its consumers in a lone report from Ibn Abi 'Asim's *Al-Ahad wa al-Mathani*. In this report, Muhammad asks Baraka, an Ethiopian servant of Umm Habiba, what had happened to a vessel into which he had urinated, and she confesses to having drunk his urine. Muhammad laughs and declares that by ingesting his waste, she had shielded herself from the fire.[98] In hadith collections following the Bukhari-Muslim era, the field becomes increasingly open for ignored and marginalized substances to resurface or emerge anew as conduits of baraka. Muhammad's urine undergoes a minor proliferation in reports of its powers, represented as miraculous in no less than three variations of the "drinking Ethiopian slave woman" tradition that vary in their claims regarding the consequences of consuming prophetic urine. Additionally, the eleventh century offers a separate tradition in which Muhammad's urination into a well permanently bestows baraka upon its water.

The narration in which Umm Habiba's servant drinks the urine is reported by Bayhaqi, whose *Sunan al-Kubra* includes a section focused on those who drank his urine and blood.[99] Muhammad asks Baraka why the bowl into which he has urinated is empty, and she confesses to having drunk his urine; the report does not provide Muhammad's reaction or judgment. Al-Hakim's *Al-Mustadrak* and Abu Nu'aym's *Dala'il al-Nubuwwa* include a tradition in which a Companion drinks Muhammad's urine, resonant with the narration reported by Ibn Abi ʿAsim and Bayhaqi but also reporting Muhammad's approval and attributing the act to another woman from his household. This version presents the drinker as not Umm Habiba's servant but another Ethiopian servant, also named Baraka though better known by her kunya, Umm Ayman. She had reportedly been a slave of Muhammad's father and was later freed by Muhammad.[100] The narrations appear as Umm Ayman's firsthand account of her encounter with prophetic urine: "I got up in the night and I was thirsty, so I drank what was in the pot and I did not notice." When Muhammad woke up and asked her to pour out the pot's contents, she told him, "I drank what was in it." Umm Ayman reports that Muhammad "laughed until showing his molars, then said, 'There will never be affliction in your belly after this.'"[101]

The narration resonates not only with the other narration of an Ethiopian woman named Baraka, as well as with the broader formula of Companions' consuming or acquiring Muhammad's bodily substances without his prior knowledge or permission, but also with the mixed treatment of Umm Ayman throughout the sources. That Umm Ayman picks up a pot of urine and drinks what she finds inside, apparently consuming *all* of the urine, echoes her depiction in other reports. Asma Sayeed observes that while Umm Ayman emerges from the earliest sira literature as a pious woman, various traditions also portray her as a bumbling, unintelligent, and somewhat comical character, for whom Muhammad holds an undeniable affection despite her flaws. Ibn Sa'd's *Tabaqat* reports that she could not manage to learn the customary greeting of *as-salamu ʿalaykum* ("Peace be upon you"), instead saying *as-salam la ʿalaykum* ("Peace *not* upon you") until Muhammad instructed her to greet others with simply *salam*.[102] Umm Ayman is also depicted as bickering with Muhammad over the size of the camel that should transport her.[103] In her analysis of Umm Ayman's treatment in the hadith corpus, Sayeed observes, "In spite of her proximity to the Prophet, she was clearly not regarded as a good vehicle for conveying his sunna."[104]

Despite her less than glowing representation and role as a comic figure, Umm Ayman also appears as a devoted Companion who supported Muslim soldiers on the battlefield. Ibn Sa'd portrays Umm Ayman as the beneficiary of divine intervention. In her entry in the *Tabaqat*, Ibn Sa'd reports that during the Muslim community's collective migration to Medina, Umm Ayman found herself alone in the desert and without water. Umm Ayman feared that she would soon die of thirst but was saved when a bucket of water descended to her from the heavens. Umm Ayman drank the water and never felt thirst for the rest of her life.[105] As later sources reimagine this bucket of water from heaven as a bucket of urine under the bed, Umm Ayman's miraculous redemption becomes a humorous episode, marked as such by Muhammad's own laughter. Tracking change between the sources demonstrates a profound deabjection of Muhammad's body, in that his urine becomes capable of achieving the same medical transformations within Umm Ayman's body as heavenly water delivered by angels.

A third version of this tradition presents the drinker as Bara, Umm Salama's Ethiopian servant. The drinker in this version benefits not in this world but the next, as Muhammad tells Bara that consuming his urine has shielded her from the fire. The Bara version appears in the *Mu'jam al-Kabir* of Tabarani, which additionally includes both the Baraka and Umm Ayman versions.[106]

Abu Nu'aym's *Dala'il al-Nubuwwa* devotes a subsection to Muhammad's digestive waste with the straightforward title "His Urine or Feces." The section includes the Umm Ayman variant of the "drinking Ethiopian woman" tradition, as well as the tradition of A'isha asking Muhammad why she can observe no traces of his making waste, to which Muhammad answers that the earth consumes what prophets excrete.[107] The "His Urine or Feces" subsection includes a third report, narrated on the authority of Anas, which depicts pleasure and refreshment traceable to an act of prophetic micturition. The Prophet urinated into a well in Anas's house that had been known as "the Coolness" [*al-Burud*] during the jahiliyya period. Anas narrates, "There was no well in Medina sweeter than it . . . when they used to come, I would refresh them with it."[108]

Abu Nu'aym's "cool well" tradition echoes earlier literature. The tradition particularly resonates with the section in Ibn Sa'd's *Tabaqat* devoted to various wells that had received Muhammad's baraka via his contact with their water, including acts of spitting into them.[109] Between the Umm

Ayman, A'isha, and Anas traditions found in Abu Nu'aym's "His Urine or Feces" subsection, the corpus exposes significant incoherence in the prophetic body. The traditions of Umm Ayman and A'isha both provide proofs of prophethood while reflecting a tension in the collective imaginary of Muhammad's bodily processes. In its representation of a woman finding and drinking Muhammad's urine, the Umm Ayman narration establishes Muhammad's prophetic station by demonstrating that waste products flowing from his body, when entering into the bodies of others, can connect their bodies to flows of baraka. In contrast, A'isha's account of her inability to see or smell Muhammad's waste erases his acts of excretion and closes a possible route to his baraka. The contradictory consequences of the A'isha and Anas narrations reflect a broader tension between the archives associated with these two Companions. Between A'isha and Anas, the collective textual imaginary of Muhammad remains fragmented and destabilized, reflecting the multiplicities inherent in the construction of the hadith corpus. For A'isha, her husband's waste remains potentially repulsive in typical human fashion; the miracle is that no one gets to observe its sight or smell. For Anas, prophetic waste is substantively exceptional; Muhammad's waste improves the quality of a well's water, seemingly extending his body's reach not only to his Companions but to generations after his death.

Conflicting imaginaries of Muhammad's digestive waste intersect in an obscure narration reported by al-Khatib al-Baghdadi (cited by al-Suyuti) with a chain of transmission that includes Malik ibn Anas and names its original source as Jabir. In this account, Jabir reports the episode in which Muhammad commands trees to come together to shield him during his defecation, and also presents himself as Muhammad's interlocutor who asks about the missing waste. Both the miracle of the trees and the earth's consumption of prophetic waste echo earlier traditions, of which Jabir himself appears as a narrator. Unique to this narration, however, is Jabir's expressed motive for asking why he cannot find Muhammad's waste: "I pleaded with God that [Muhammad] might show me what he excretes from his stomach, so that I could eat it."[110] For his confession of a desire to eat rather than drink, this narration stands alone as the only example I could find of a Companion seeking to consume Muhammad's solid waste. Jabir's desire goes unfulfilled, since the earth removes prophetic feces from public access. Nor does he make his desire known to Muhammad—he asks God, not the Prophet, for the privilege of eating the Prophet's feces—which would have provided an opportunity for Muhammad to approve or disapprove. Nonetheless, the expressed desire does operate within Jabir's apparent logic of prophetic bodies; this is the same Jabir who drinks the water that gushes forth from between Muhammad's fingers in more canonically approved narrations, later recalling that he sought to fill his stomach with water from Muhammad's body since he "knew that it was baraka." For Jabir, Muhammad's organs and their flows are not hierarchically ordered: the prophetic anus works as effectively as prophetic hands to eject attainable baraka.

Consuming Muhammad

Among variegated logics of bodies that I find in the sira/maghazi literature and hadith corpus, multiple traditions seem to operate on a perception that you are what you eat. Consumption can transform both sides of the transaction: When Hind bint ʿUtba chews the liver of Muhammad's uncle Hamza ibn ʿAbd al-Muttalib on the battlefield of Uhud, she is unable to swallow it, since this would have meant that when Hind receives her due punishment in the afterlife, a portion of Hamza's flesh would go into the fire with her. Muhammad explains, "God did not allow for anything from Hamza to enter the fire."[111] Nadia Maria El Cheikh locates Hind's attempted cannibalism within a broader representation of pre-Islamic irrationality and violence, with special attention to the gendering of this construction: "It is a female who became, ultimately, the principal locus for the cultural monstrosity that defined jahiliyya."[112] Though Hamza's flesh is subjected to mutilation in this world, God protects it from absorption into the matter of an unbeliever's eternally condemned body. Resonant with this logic of the body, the sources provide traditions of Companions whose protection from the fire becomes ensured or signified by their encounters with (or consumption of) Muhammad's bodily traces.

As Muhammad's body is transformed by what goes in, it transforms other bodies with what comes out. As the Qur'an's revelation occurs through transcendent agents' actions upon Muhammad's body, it causes Muhammad to sweat profusely; Muhammad's Companions report this side effect as smelling better than perfume, and women bottle Muhammad's sweat to preserve traces of his baraka for their children. Muhammad's saliva can heal wounds and cause dry wells to overflow. A fatigued camel ingests prophetic saliva and ablution water and can then run at full speed to the next town. Companions drink Muhammad's blood and urine and achieve physical well-being and soteriological security through their consumption. Hairs detached from Muhammad's body, dipped in water, transform the water into medicine. As I will discuss in chapter 4, logics of milk kinship enable Muhammad's semen to transform bodies in exceptional ways: his body's role in the production of his wives' breast milk enables prophetic baraka to travel through the body of Umm Salama into the mouth of famed ascetic Hasan al-Basri, whom she breastfeeds years after Muhammad's death.

Sira/maghazi sources and hadith collections do not offer a singular, systematized view of Muhammad's bodily traces. Reading the sources diachronically reveals an amplification of interest in what products of his body can do. The sources also seem to construct a hierarchy of substances, as not all prophetic bodily products appear to be equally valued as routes through which Muhammad's baraka can flow to others. Some materials (such as Muhammad's saliva and sweat) become privileged even in the earliest literature, while others (such as his urine) appear as baraka conduits only later.

The question of how Muhammad's bodily products can change other bodies receives diverse answers from Companions and their transmission networks. The tangling of these networks into a larger hadith corpus both preserves and obscures the diversity of ways they imagine the prophetic body. Multiple logics of the body coexist alongside each other. Muhammad's capacity for intercorporeal transactions of baraka, while intensifying through the development of the textual corpus, remains unstable even within the bounds of a singular scholar's collection.

A poignant case study for thinking about connections to Muhammad through his bodily products appears in ʿAbd Allah ibn al-Zubayr, the "counter-caliph" who ingests prophetic saliva and blood. Tensions in Ibn al-Zubayr's familial links to the Prophet may provide context, as his genealogy connects him to the prophetic body at multiple points. His father, Zubayr ibn al-ʿAwwam, was not only Muhammad's cousin (the son of Muhammad's aunt Safiyya bint ʿAbd al-Muttalib) but also the son of Khadija's brother. Ibn al-Zubayr's mother, Asma', was the daughter of Abu Bakr and sister of A'isha. With these intersecting relations considered, Ibn al-Zubayr was a first cousin once removed of Muhammad, ʿAli, and Ibn ʿAbbas; a first cousin once removed or second cousin (depending on whether their relation is read from the Khuwaylid or ʿAbd al-Muttalib line) of Fatima; a cousin of Hasan and Husayn; a grand-nephew of Khadija; a nephew of A'isha; and a grandson of Abu Bakr.

Whether fighting for his father Zubayr and aunt A'isha against ʿAli or joining his cousin Husayn against the Umayyads, Ibn al-Zubayr aligns with interests informed by his positions in these crisscrossed familial networks. He also leans on these connections for his own support: during his short-lived caliphate in Mecca, Ibn al-Zubayr demolished and rebuilt the Ka'ba, a controversial project that he apparently defended by claiming that he had heard from his widowed aunt that the Prophet had wanted to do it.[113] But despite his varied connections, Ibn al-Zubayr remains inescapably disadvantaged in comparison to the sons of 'Ali; his father Zubayr was the son of 'Abd al-Muttalib's daughter Safiyya, meaning that Zubayr cannot claim the patrilineal privilege of Muhammad and 'Ali as sons of 'Abd al-Muttalib's sons.

In Sunni archives, Ibn al-Zubayr can draw prestige from his father. While Zubayr's relationship to the Prophet's household is problematized in Shi'i historical memory for his alignment with A'isha in the coalition against 'Ali's caliphate, Zubayr appears in Sunni hadith literature as one of ten Companions who personally received Muhammad's promise of paradise.[114] In narrations attributed to 'Ali and Jabir, Muhammad is said to have declared that every prophet has a disciple, and that his disciple is Zubayr.[115] In one version, 'Ali narrates Muhammad's words as a response to the arrival of Ibn Jurmuz, who had slain Zubayr, and additionally condemns "the killer of Safiyya's son" to hellfire.[116] In another version, Muhammad names his disciple as "Zubayr, son of my aunt," emphasizing their familial bond. This variant appears in Ibn Hanbal's *Musnad* with a chain of transmission between Zubayrid fathers and sons (Hisham ibn 'Urwa ibn al-Zubayr < 'Urwa ibn al-Zubayr < 'Abd Allah ibn al-Zubayr).[117]

Ibn al-Zubayr first enters into intensified relations with Muhammad through the practice of tahnik. A'isha narrates that upon the birth of her nephew, he was brought to Muhammad, who chewed a date and spit it into the baby's mouth. The consumed item of interest is not the chewed date but bodily fluids: "The first thing that entered his stomach," A'isha reports, "was the saliva of the Prophet."[118] Ibn al-Zubayr and Muhammad become even more connected when Muhammad enhances Ibn al-Zubayr's connection to his aunt A'isha. Narrations of Ibn al-Zubayr's nephew Hisham from various Zubayrid transmitters (Hisham's father, 'Urwa ibn al-Zubayr, Hisham's cousin 'Abad ibn Hamza, 'Abad's son Yahya, or an unnamed source, either a "man from the sons of Zubayr" or "mawla of Zubayr") depict A'isha saying to the Prophet, "All of your wives have kunyas except me," which leads Muhammad to name her Umm 'Abd Allah, "Mother of 'Abd Allah."[119] 'Urwa's version explains that his aunt A'isha was called Umm 'Abd Allah until she died, "and she never had children."[120] While Yahya's version of the exchange between Muhammad and A'isha has the Prophet calling Ibn al-Zubayr "the son of your sister," versions attributed to 'Urwa as well as Yahya's father, 'Abad, narrate that Muhammad mentioned Ibn al-Zubayr to A'isha as "your son."[121] Though Muhammad was "not the father of any of your men," as the Qur'an notes, and A'isha did not have children of her own, traditions circulating from the Zubayrid transmission network construct Ibn al-Zubayr as a symbolic son of the Prophet and A'isha.

For the controversies of his political location, Ibn al-Zubayr also makes a troubled attempt at connection to the prophetic body. After young Ibn al-Zubayr sneaks away with Muhammad's blood and drinks it, Muhammad foretells doom for both Ibn al-Zubayr and the community. When read as a pro-'Alid polemic, the tradition presents Ibn al-Zubayr—a second-generation opponent of 'Ali, with a complex relation to 'Ali's son Husayn—attempting to steal what does not rightfully belong to him, namely a privileged blood relation to the Prophet.[122] While some variations of this tradition soften its polemical blow, even allowing that Ibn al-Zubayr achieves a successful transaction through his act of consumption, ambiguities persist concerning the consumption of prophetic blood. Ibn al-Zubayr's body becomes a site of tensions and ambiguities in its own right. Prophetic saliva entering the stomach of baby Ibn al-Zubayr successfully initiates him into the community, even potentially advantaging him as Muhammad's symbolic son; Muhammad's blood in the same stomach provokes a warning of future disaster but might still retain sufficient Muhammad-ness to benefit its consumer.

Material traces of Muhammad's body consistently act as affective forces that enable his body to engage and change a variety of other bodies, whether "bodies" here refers to other living things (humans, animals, and plants), inanimate objects (such as a rock destroyed by his saliva), or a body of water that flows in abundance and becomes sweeter due to his saliva or urine. However, the precise terms by which his body can extend its powers change from one reporter to the next. The case of Ibn al-Zubayr's body demonstrates the difficulties in reducing these varied imaginaries of the prophetic body to a singular binary opposition, such as one that would contrast proto-Sunni representations to proto-Shi'i claims for the body. Such a clear division would be tempting, given A'isha's treatments of Muhammad's body when compared to pro-'Alid narrators. For traditions that either authorize or condemn Ibn al-Zubayr, the truth becomes marked in his body's capacity for linkage to the body of the Prophet.

CHAPTER FOUR

The Sex of Revelation

Prophethood and Gendered Bodies

In her discussion of the crisis in Islamic legal tradition posed by intersex bodies, Paula Sanders observes that medieval Muslim jurists understood the world "as a place with only two sexes, male and female. . . . In this world where everyone had to be gendered, a person without gender could not be socialized."[1] Prayers, pilgrimage, marriage, slavery, funerals, inheritance, clothing, legal testimony, and essentially every aspect of living as an adult in human society were defined and regulated by gender. The Prophet's capacity for achieving linkages with other bodies would also navigate gendered opportunities and limitations that defined Islamic jurisprudence, upholding what Sanders calls "the gendered integrity of their world as a whole."[2]

According to the late tradition referenced by Bashir in *Sufi Bodies*, some bodies can access prophetic baraka through the shaking of hands, whether by directly shaking Muhammad's hand, a hand that shook his hand, or the hands that shook *those* hands, and so on up to seven degrees of separation.[3] By definition, the shaking of hands requires touching between bodies, which means that access to this exponentially expanding web of baraka transmissions becomes open and closed by gender. Muhammad shook the hands of men who pledged their allegiance to him, but canonical hadiths assert that women declared their pledges with strictly verbal oaths. While Muhammad promises paradise to an extended network of men who have connected with each other (and him) through handshakes, A'isha narrates, "By God, the hand of the Messenger of God, God bless him and give him peace, never touched the hand of a woman."[4] When men such as Anas compare Muhammad's skin to silk, they report a knowledge that would have been theoretically public for all men in Muhammad's community to directly access but available only to a select category of women. Not every node in the network of Muhammad's extended corporeality can easily connect with every other node. If baraka becomes accessible through varying types of interaction with Muhammad's body, and Muhammad interacts differently with women and men, then the gendering of Muhammad's body directly impacts his capacity for circulating baraka among the bodies in his community.

Sanders's insight that in the gendered organization of Muslim societies, "Human beings had to be either male or female" holds consequences for nonhuman agents that are described in anthropomorphic terms or appear with anthropomorphic form. When Gabriel appears with embodiment to enter human social worlds and walk and speak with humans, he does so in adherence to a blueprint that requires such embodiment to be unambiguously gendered—and also one that orders a social hierarchy in which male dominates female. Whether or not Gabriel is "really" masculine, he performs as such. As discussed in this chapter, master scholars (men) such as Bukhari regarded Gabriel's interactions with women as a template for how *they* could interact with women, perceiving Gabriel's gendered position as analogous to their own. Similarly, God's engagement of humans, whether through his self-descriptions in the Qur'an or depictions of his encounter with the Prophet—in which God appears with a visible and even touchable body—becomes a performance of gender. When God and Gabriel appear with bodies, their bodies are exclusively presented as masculine. In turn, their interactions with humans operate in line with their genders, as when Muhammad promises that God will someday engage 'Umar in the homosocial interaction of a handshake, or when Gabriel is repeatedly mistaken for a man from Muhammad's community. Wherever there is anthropomorphism, there is gender. Moreover, as I will discuss in this chapter, the question of gender does not disappear if we erase divine and angelic bodies to imagine God and the angels only as ethereal transcendent intellects.

Prophethood's nature as an embodied experience, a phenomenon that occurs in, to, through, and between bodies, means that Muhammad's status as a prophet might relate to the gendered codings of his body. At the risk of using presentist language, classical physiognomists were certainly sexist: their science privileged masculine bodies. In reports of Muhammad's appearance, gender becomes the unarticulated but necessary detail of his physiognomy. As much as his medium height, medium complexion, distinct gait, and the material omen between his shoulders, Muhammad's body fulfills an expectation of prophetic physiognomy for the marking of his body as masculine.

As much as any other force, categories of gender regulate the encounters between human, angelic, and possibly divine bodies. To ask how Muhammad's body encounters the unseen remains a gendered question. This chapter explores the significance of Muhammad's gendered body, starting first with ways the transcendent agents that act upon his body are themselves, with or without bodies, consistently gendered masculine.

Allah versus al-Lat: Gendering Light

In her work on literary traditions of Muslim philosophical ethics (*akhlaq*), Zahra Ayubi makes a cautious but compelling observation: "To be clear, God in Muslim thought is not male, at least not consciously."[5] But despite God's presumed genderlessness, Ayubi explains, Muslim intellectuals (men) virtually deified masculinity. As these men "conceived of the entire cosmos as belonging to men," they freely imagined themselves as "miniatures of the Ultimate (patriarchal) ruler of the universe" and thus "projected male attributes onto God."[6] Ayubi's analysis preserves the revelation's innocence from becoming implicated in the gendering of God, but I argue that the Qur'an and hadith sources *do* consciously gender God as—if not exactly "male"—a masculine agent, both with and without the appearance of a gendered *body*. These sources even define monotheism itself as masculine against a feminine polytheism.

Modern Muslim discourses often dismiss God's masculine pronoun as a mere accident of Arabic grammar, which lacks a gender-neutral pronoun and thereby requires the inscription of "he" or "she" on every noun. By this argument, the gendered pronoun conveys no more meaning as a description of God than it would for any inanimate object or abstract concept, since all of these things technically have "gender" in Arabic. A developing tradition of gender-progressive Muslim theology treats God's transcendence of gender as a prerequisite for true Islamic monotheism, on the grounds that assigning human gender constructions to God would amount to crude anthropomorphism. This theological intervention, Aysha Hidayatullah explains, aims for a social consequence, as "debunking masculinized understandings of God becomes a tool in fighting Qur'anic interpretations that tout male supremacy and seek to legitimate a hierarchy of male authority over women."[7] On another reading, which interrogates God's gendering in the Qur'an and hadith corpus beyond the question of pronouns, the sources can be seen advocating for a masculine god. Even if Arabic possessed a gender-neutral pronoun with which the sources could refer to God, God would still appear in the sources on one side of a gender binary as explicitly *not* feminine.

The Qur'an states that God created all things in gendered pairs (36:36, 43:12, 51:49, 53:45) but does not self-evidently present God as transcending that binary. Countering the Christian claim that God had fathered a son, the Qur'an argues that this is impossible because God has not taken a wife (6:101), more precisely a female companion (*sahibat*). Asserting that God remains exalted above the possibility of having partners, the Qur'an states that God has no female companion or son (72:3). In the monotheism constructed here, God stands alone as a solitary masculine figure without a feminine counterpart; there is only one god because God does not *take* a wife who can mother children for him. Whether God would *be* a wife or mother does not appear as a thinkable possibility for the Qur'an or the monotheists against which it argues.

The Qur'an further masculinizes God in its gendered polemic against polytheism with the charge, "Besides him, they invoke but females; they call upon a rebellious Satan" (*Inni ya'una min dunihi ila innathan wa inna yad'una ila shaytanan maridan*), drawing a line between masculinist monotheism and goddess-centered polytheism (4:117). To worship the God of Abraham is to serve a singular *he*, in contrast to the religion of jahiliyya, characterized here by the worship of feminine entities. The Qur'an's antipolytheism polemic gives focused attention to the triad of al-Lat (whose name is literally the feminine equivalent of Allah and thus translatable as "Goddess"), al-ʿUzza (feminine of the divine name al-ʿAziz), and Manat, whom the Meccans apparently conceptualized as angels and/or God's daughters. Early Qur'an exegetes, operating with what Ayesha S. Chaudhry calls a "patriarchal idealized cosmology" that took masculinity's ontological supremacy for a natural given,[8] read the Qur'an's antigoddess polemic in gendered terms. God's ontological masculinity would have been unquestioned "common sense" in the patriarchal cosmological orientations of the sacred sources and their historical milieus. In his tafsir work, al-Tabari cites commentary on 4:117 from Hasan al-Basri that interpreted "females" as a reference to inanimate matter with no spirit, like dry wood or dry stone. Al-Tabari also acknowledges an alternative vocalization of 4:117 that mitigates its gendered consequences, noting that A'isha and Ibn ʿAbbas recited not *innathan* ("females") but *wuthunan* ("idols").[9]

Controversies regarding the sources' potential for divine anthropomorphism sometimes approached ideas of God's *corporeal* masculinity, potentially inscribing gender codes onto divine body parts not referenced in the sources. Sunni theologian Ash'ari apparently accused an eighth-century sectarian mystic, Mughira ibn Sa'id, of teaching followers that God had human body parts that corresponded to Arabic letters and that Mughira himself had seen God's genitalia.[10] Al-Jawaribi, the eighth-century anthropomorphist who believed that God's body lacked a digestive system, reportedly said, "Do not ask me about the genitals or the beard, but you can ask me about anything else."[11]

With questions of God's genitalia and beard left unasked, do God's actions with his other body parts—as in Muhammad's canonical statement that ʿUmar will be the first man in paradise with whom God (al-Haqq) shares in the homosocial connection of a handshake[12]—locate God within social expectations for how a gender-specific body should behave? Accounts of God placing his hand between Muhammad's shoulders describe God's visible and tangible embodiment as the "best form" (*ahsan sura*).[13] When hadiths that refer to the "best form" appear in canonical collections, its precise nature generally goes unarticulated. However, Bukhari's contemporary and fellow hadith partisan Ibn Qutayba (828–89) mentions an account that describes God's best form in details that many would find surprising. Discussing the "cold hand" tradition in his *Ta'wil Mukhtalif al-Hadith*, Ibn Qutayba refers to an Umm Tufayl narration that Muhammad "saw his lord in sleep in the form of a young man with abundant hair [*surati shabban murfirin*] in green, reclining on his bed of gold, wearing sandals of gold."[14]

With variations in God's clothing, jewelry, veil, furniture, variations of this explicitly corporeal tradition proliferate in later sources. Khatib presents Muhammad telling Anas, "The night of my ascension into the heavens, I saw my lord, powerful and sublime. Between him and I was a blazing veil. Then I saw everything until I saw a crown made from pearls."[15] Another narration from Khatib, attributed to Ibn ʿAbbas, quotes Muhammad recalling, "I saw my lord in the form of a beardless young man wearing a red cloak."[16] In Khatib's *Tarikh* and Tabarani's *Mu'jam al-Kabir*, Muhammad tells Umm Tufayl, "I saw my lord in the form of a long-haired youth dressed in green, wearing sandals of gold and a gold veil on his face."[17] Daraqutni also includes variations of the Umm Tufayl tradition.[18] Among versions of the encounter in Bayhaqi's *Al-Asma' wa-l-Sifat*, one narration describes God as beardless and curly-haired, wearing a veil of pearls.[19] Van Ess notes that in descriptions of God as beardless, the precise word used, *amrad*, signifies a boy whose moustache is "beginning to show."[20] Beyond the scope of the literature examined here, Hellmut Ritter finds sixteenth-century scholar Jalal ad-Din Suyuti (d. 1505) attributing a version of this tradition (with God a young man on a throne, his feet in "greenery of glittering light") to none other than A'isha, who otherwise appears as the most forceful opponent of the vision.[21]

In his discussion of what he calls the "youthful god" tradition, van Ess writes, "It is remarkable that God was never imagined as a *shaykh*."[22] Representations of God as a young man mirrored popular notions of what constituted an ideal human body. "In the science of physiognomy," Karen Cokayne writes, "the elderly came out badly."[23] Physiognomic prejudice against old age appears even in the previously discussed representations of Muhammad, which mention him living into his sixties but still note his scarcity of gray hairs and call attention to his supreme virility in his later years. Even without a documented chain of "influence" or "borrowing" in the hadith corpus's depiction of God as a beautiful young man, these traditions can be observed echoing imaginaries of divinity that were prominent in Mediterranean antiquity. Van Ess writes that in Persian traditions, Mithra appears as a youth with curls and a crown, and Ahura-Mazda appears in the form of a fifteen-year-old boy.[24] In *Yahweh's Coming of Age*, Jason Bembry examines the Hebrew Bible's depictions of God primarily as a youthful warrior and later pivot in Daniel 7 to depict God as an old man.[25] In contrast to dominant images of Jesus as a bearded man, early Christian art frequently depicts Jesus as a handsome beardless youth. Scholarship has argued that early Christian intellectuals came to prefer imaginaries of Jesus as ugly in order to more clearly demarcate Christianity from the cult of Antinous, another sacrificed man-god who was depicted in monuments and statuary throughout the Roman Empire as a beautiful youth with lush, curly hair and no beard.[26] In short, when the Sunni hadith corpus offers its most detailed articulations of a divine body, it speaks with the popular aesthetic and theological vocabularies of its world. These vocabularies also found different expressions in Muslim traditions. Omid Ghaemmaghami has observed that proto-Sunni hadith networks circulated traditions of a youthful God in roughly the same historical time frame that proto-Shi'i communities constructed their doctrines surrounding the twelfth Imam, who had reportedly disappeared as a small child near the end of the ninth century CE. Muslims who witnessed the twelfth Imam in dreams and visions would often report his appearance in ways that resonated with accounts of Muhammad seeing God.[27]

God appears in reports of Muhammad's theophanic vision as a passive object of the prophetic gaze (narrated with Muhammad's statement

"I saw"). With Muhammad's eyes serving as lenses through which others can visualize God, Muhammad's perception of the divine body provides a portal of mediated access between the metaphysical and physical worlds. In these narrations of divine-prophetic intercorporeality, God appears as a body productive of desire. The reports illustrate investments in erotic bodily foci of youthfulness, abundant or curly hair, and the face as either beardless or shrouded by a veil of gold or pearls, along with the lush accessories of his red or green garments, golden sandals, and the crown of pearls presented as the culmination of Muhammad's account, "I saw everything of him."[28]

The construction of divine masculinity produced within this tradition refers to sexuality at once rendered illicit and affirmed as powerful within the sources. The eroticized imaginaries of handsome young men in poetry contemporary to the sources, as well as the anxieties of jurists and the very hadith traditionists who compiled these collections, has received attention in academic literature.[29] In *Before Homosexuality in the Arab-Islamic World, 1500–1800*, for example, Khaled el-Rouayheb discusses hadith transmitter Sufyan al-Thawri (d. 778) fleeing from an attractive boy in a bath because he believed that seventeen devils accompanied every beardless youth, compared to only one devil for every girl; el-Rouayheb also provides evidence of Ibn Hanbal and Abu Hanifa acknowledging the dangers of attraction to handsome boys.[30] The erotic power of the *hadith al-shabb* is affirmed in the sources via a report from Bayhaqi's *Sunan al-Kubra* in which Muhammad prohibits gazing at the "beardless boy with a beautiful face."[31] For Bayhaqi's *Al-Asma' wa-l-Sifat* to also provide versions of the "youthful god" tradition, as well as a report of the "cold hand" encounter (which he subjects to critical scrutiny through both isnad evaluation and allegorical readings of the divine embodiment),[32] presents God as an object of desires that Bayhaqi constructs elsewhere as illicit. In his appearance as a beautiful young man, God produces the visual fascination and attraction that becomes threatening when directed toward young men in this world, expressing in Bayhaqi's personal corpus a tension between desires that simultaneously provoke anxieties over unlawful sexual acts between men and inform believers' contemplation of the masculine divine.

Descriptions of God's appearance give the suggestion of a sexually specific or gendered divine body: whether or not the beardless young man embodies God's "true form," this was the form in which Muhammad perceived God. But if—as the overwhelming majority of Muslim intellectuals wrestling with theological anthropomorphism have insisted—God does not actually have a body, does this also mean that the sources imagine God to lack (or rather transcend) gender? If Muhammad only saw "light," as in Abu Dharr's narrations, is such a light necessarily beyond gender, or does it perform as masculine or feminine? Given Luce Irigiray's analysis of a male/mind versus female/body binary in Mediterranean antiquity, with the disembodied intellect conceptualized as masculine while women are perceived as more excessively "corporeal" and "biological" than men (a treatment shared by Greek and Islamic philosophical traditions),[33] the presentation of God as light or a mind without a body can ironically enforce divine masculinity. As an example of the incorporeal masculine god, the Qur'an's account of Mary's miraculous pregnancy resists the image of God as a father but nonetheless upholds masculinist imaginaries of reproduction and the soul. Though God remains too transcendent above creation to have a sahibat with whom he can conceive children and therefore cannot be Jesus's father, the notion of a disembodied intellect acting upon passive matter and breathing life/soul into it was not perceived as gender-neutral. As Kueny writes, the Qur'an's portrayal of Jesus's conception echoes "the Aristotelian model of male semen carrying the essential breath of life that activates the inanimate matter in Mary's womb"; God's act was understood by medieval Qur'an exegetes precisely through analogy to a man impregnating a woman.[34] Even while declaring that God has no companion and "begets not, nor is he begotten," the Qur'an genders God's intervention in Mary's reproductive system; father or not, God remains a masculine agent acting upon the feminine. Distancing God from biology and corporeal anthropomorphism, in other words, does not in itself rescue God from undergoing masculinization in the sources.

A masculinist god might appear "universal" and transcendent above gender when he has not been marked with feminine specificities, as in Grosz's observation that "the specificities of the masculine have always been hidden under the generality of the universal, the human."[35] Presented in the sources as blinding light, a formless and disembodied intellect, or with specific embodiment as a beautiful young man—but never with specific embodiment as a woman—God bears the imprint of patriarchal cosmologies that treat the mind as masculine and imagine masculinity as the generic or default setting of human.

Masculine Angels and Feminine Idols

Contrary to suggestions that angels remain ungendered in the Qur'an,[36] the Qur'an's angelology relies on clearly drawn sexual difference to distinguish between genuine angels and false idols: "Those who do not believe in the hereafter name the angels feminine names" (53:27). In the same polemic against polytheists who worship goddesses as angels and/or daughters of God,[37] the Qur'an treats the attribution of daughters to God as a slight against him, since the polytheists only desire sons for themselves: "Is the male for you and for him the female? That is an unfair division" (53:21–22). The Qur'an denounces the idea that God has children, whether sons or daughters; as discussed above, its polemic against Christians rejects the notion of God's fathering a son. Belief in God having daughters, however, is condemned in explicitly gendered terms as a special insult.[38]

When appearing with visible, audible, and tangible human embodiment, angels perform in the world as men. The Qur'an's reference to "Our Spirit" who came to Mary as a "well-proportioned man" (*basharan sawiyyan*) has been historically identified as Gabriel, though this does not appear to have been a self-evident given from the onset of interpretive tradition. In his commentary on the reference in 19:17, Muqatil ibn Sulayman reads the Spirit's appearance as a well-proportioned man to mean a beardless youth with curly hair but does not name him as a specific angel.[39] The identification of the Spirit in 19:17 with Gabriel might not have been the position of A'isha (who has been regarded in Sunni intellectual traditions as a masterful Qur'an exegete),[40] at least not if A'isha's claimed prestige as the only woman to have seen Gabriel applies to all women throughout history.

In sira/maghazi literature, angels appear as men on the battlefield, distinguished by the whiteness of their skin and robes, the varying colors of their turbans, and their wool helmets, to participate as soldiers on behalf of the Prophet.[41] Muhammad's cousin Zubayr ibn 'Awwam, distinguished for wearing a yellow turban in battle, narrates in Ibn Hisham's *Sira* that angels at the battle of Badr shared his preference, wearing yellow.[42] Ibn Hisham's *Sira* presents Gabriel as seen by several Companions riding a white mule with a saddle covered by brocade; these eyewitnesses mistakenly identify Gabriel as a specific man from the community, Dihya al-Kalbi.[43] Al-Waqidi reports that when Mus'ab ibn 'Umayr died carrying the Muslims' flag at Uhud, an angel in Mus'ab's form appeared and picked up the flag in his place. When Muhammad addressed the angel as Mus'ab, the angel replied, "I am not Mus'ab," revealing himself as an angel.[44] The report is followed by an account by Sa'd ibn Abi Waqqas, who narrates that during battle he witnessed "a man, white, with a beautiful face, whom I did not know; later, I thought he must be an angel."[45] Suliman Bashear writes that the name Dihya, "which is non-Arabic, and probably of Latin/late Greek origin," literally means "chief" and adds that Dihya's resemblance to Gabriel can prove useful in tracing "the existence, in the second and third centuries, of conflicting currents concerning anthropomorphism in Islam."[46]

For angels to assume the form of human feminine bodies seems to be more unthinkable than their taking nonhuman animal bodies: while shifting between anthropomorphic and zoomorphic embodiment, as demonstrated in Ibn Hisham's *Sira* when he takes the form of a camel, Gabriel preserves his masculinity.[47] Khadija, who does not see Gabriel, also masculinizes Gabriel in her test to determine whether her husband's extrahuman informant is an angel or demon. After exposing herself and inviting Muhammad to sit in her lap, Khadija asks whether Gabriel is still present; Muhammad answers that Gabriel has left the room. By Gabriel's modest response to exposed feminine bodies, Khadija recognizes him as a genuine angel.[48] Iblis/Satan additionally appears in the form of a man, even impersonating specific individuals.[49]

Sira/maghazi sources engage imaginaries of extrahuman beings marked as feminine in their discussions of pre-Islamic goddesses. Ma'mar reports episodes of both Abu Bakr and ʿUmar insulting polytheists by directing embodied vituperations at their goddesses: Abu Bakr telling ʿUrwa ibn Mas'ud al-Thaqafi, "Suck on al-Lat's clitoris,"[50] and ʿUmar responding to Abu Sufyan's question "What shall I do with al-ʿUzza?" with the answer "Defecate on her."[51] While these embodied expressions of moral disgust do not necessitate that Abu Bakr and ʿUmar literally believe in the goddesses' existence, an altogether different representation can be found in al-Waqidi's *Maghazi*, which depicts an encounter between Khalid ibn Walid and a fully corporeal and apparently *alive* al-ʿUzza. The narration depicts Khalid destroying al-ʿUzza's icon in Nakhla, after which he is confronted by a naked Black woman with wild hair. Khalid kills her with his sword and reports back to Muhammad, who tells him, "That was al-ʿUzza," adding that she despaired of no longer being worshiped.[52] The tradition portrays al-ʿUzza as having an empirically observable existence and physical body, as opposed to merely being a false construct of her worshipers' imagination. While ostensibly an actor in the metaphysical realm from which humans seek baraka, al-ʿUzza exists entirely as an abjected outsider to the divine/angelic system. The narration marks her as such with the body of a wild and unrestrained Black woman, corporealized in gender-coded and color-coded opposition to the angels who appear as white men in clean white robes.[53] Al-ʿUzza appears simultaneously more corporeal and yet less "real" than God, who does not exhibit an observable body, at least not in the same sira/maghazi literature, enacting the binary of male/mind versus female/body as distinct and unequal opposites that Grosz examines in *Volatile Bodies*. Al-ʿUzza's unmanageable corporeality invokes the threatening "metaphorics of uncontrollability" that Grosz observes in imaginaries of menstruation: "the association of femininity with contagion and disorder, the undecidability of the limits of the female body."[54] For her exposed and out-of-control body, al-ʿUzza's mourning over her own demise also resonates with contemporary anxieties regarding women's public funeral lamentations in Kufa.[55] The gendered moral disgust with which the sources judge polytheism becomes intensified with the presence of al-ʿUzza not as an abstract conceptual problem but as a naked and disordered feminine body, a monster out of bounds.

The nexus of women's corporeality and the demonic is further articulated in Ibn Ishaq's account of a temple in Yemen, which emerges in different iterations between the recensions of Ibn Hisham and Ibn Bukayr. Both recensions portray a temple maintained for the worship of a *shaytan* who deceived people with oracles and demanded sacrifices. The Ibn Hisham version narrates that the king gave two rabbis permission to destroy the temple; prior to the temple's destruction, the rabbis commanded a black dog to come out of the temple and then killed it.[56] The Ibn Bukayr version describes a golden temple at which the shaytan was presented with offerings of animal sacrifice performed on a menstruous garment: the animal's throat would be cut on the garment, allowing the garment to absorb its blood, at which point the shaytan would come to receive the doubly blood-soaked garment and provide oracles. In this version, the Jews convinced the king to accept their faith if they could drive out the shaytan. They then recited divine names until the shaytan emerged and then fell into the sea.[57] Menstrual blood figures powerfully in Kristeva's third category of abjection, the markers of sexual difference.[58] In contrast to Malik ibn Sinan's consumption of blood from the masculine prophetic body granting him exemption from hellfire, this narration presents menstrual blood as adding to the horror of shaytan worship. Even as the two recensions of Ibn Ishaq's *Sira* depart from one another in their treatments of this story, they share a compelling overlap. The Ibn Hisham version signifies the shaytan with the presence of a black dog, while the Ibn Bukayr version does not describe the precise form in which the shaytan appears but renders the shaytan an eater of menstrual blood. The signification achieved in one version of the Yemeni temple episode with a demonic black dog is achieved in the other through association with women's corporeal flows.

Gabriel's Body and A'isha's Eyes

Consistent with the gendering of Gabriel in the Qur'an and sira/maghazi sources, Gabriel appears throughout hadith literature with fully corporeal masculinity, as in Muhammad's description of revelation coming to him via the form of a man (*surat al-rajul*) who talks to him.[59] Gabriel appears in multiple traditions as a white-robed, "intensely black-haired" man, and sometimes as a specific man from the community, as Muhammad reports Gabriel's appearance to him in the likeness of Dihya al-Kalbi.[60] Gabriel does not become accessible to earthly bodies only as an "image" or "vision" but is also audible, and even interacts with the world as a body that can touch and be touched. A particularly famous tradition of Gabriel appearing in human form, known popularly as the "Hadith of Gabriel," presents Gabriel engaging Muhammad and a number of the Companions with masculine human embodiment and subjecting Muhammad to a short quiz.[61] In a version from Ibn Abi Shayba's *Musannaf*, Gabriel approaches and sits close to Muhammad until their knees are touching, then places his hands on Muhammad's thighs and asks him, "O Muhammad, When is the time?" to which Muhammad replies, "The asked does not know more than the asker, but from its signs: the slave woman gives birth to her mistress, and you see the barefooted, naked shepherds excelling in buildings."[62] In a version narrated by 'Umar ibn al-Khattab, Gabriel appears again as an unknown man with intensely black hair and white clothing. Though a stranger to the local community, he shows no signs of having traveled. He again sits facing Muhammad, touching knees and placing his hands on Muhammad's thighs, and asks him to explain concepts such as surrender, goodness, charity, and faith, along with information concerning the end of time. After their exchange, Gabriel leaves and Muhammad informs the group, "That was Gabriel. He came to you to teach you your *din*."[63] In Ibn Hanbal's *Musnad*, 'Umar's son also tells us that Gabriel used to come to the Prophet "in the form of Dihya."[64]

The *Musnad* collections of Ibn Hanbal and al-Tayalisi and the *Mustadrak* portray Ibn 'Abbas as seeing Gabriel; Muhammad asks Ibn 'Abbas if he sees him and then clarifies that the man is Gabriel. With a chain of transmission tracing back to Zaynab bint Sulayman, Ibn 'Abbas's great-granddaughter, who in turn narrates from her father Sulayman ibn 'Ali ibn 'Abd Allah ibn 'Abbas, the *Mustadrak* presents an account in which Muhammad additionally explains to his cousin Ibn 'Abbas that with the exception of his uncle (Ibn 'Abbas's father), no one who was not a prophet had ever seen Gabriel.[65]

Ibn Hanbal also includes a narration from the Companion Harith ibn al-Nu'man, who recalls seeing Gabriel and the Prophet together. As he passes them, Harith extends the greeting of "salam" to Gabriel, apparently under the impression that Gabriel is a man. Muhammad later asks Harith, "Did you see who was with me? That was Gabriel. He returns the 'salam' to you."[66] Throughout these narrations, Muhammad expresses surprise that a man saw Gabriel, mirroring what I will discuss in accounts of Gabriel visions among Muhammad's wives.

Throughout these interactions, Muhammad's presence appears to facilitate Companions' access to Gabriel (that is, men tend to see Gabriel when Muhammad is also around), and Muhammad's explanation allows them to understand what they have experienced. Though Muhammad's mediation creates an additional degree of distance, the Companions' witness of Gabriel and exchanges of "salam" with him achieve an intensified access to the realm of the (usually) unseen. The known participants in these accounts—Muhammad, Gabriel, and the Companions narrating the episodes and their own parts in them—are men, or, in Gabriel's case as a supernatural agent, performing human masculinity in a temporary embodiment. As the corpus develops, Gabriel's participation as a mediator between prophetic and divine personalities remains embodied and concretely masculinized. Gabriel appears with a male-sexed body, noted for his handsome face and hair, turban, physical resemblance to a specific man (Dihya al-Kalbi), and the homosocial intimacy of his encounter with Muhammad, when Gabriel faces him and touches their knees together. When Gabriel is seen riding a mule or white horse on his way to Banu Qurayza, Companions mistake him for Dihya.[67] Additionally, a narration from Anas supplements Muhammad's comparison of Gabriel to Dihya with Anas's personal recollection, "And he was a beautiful white man" (*Wa kana rajulan jamilan abyad*).[68]

While the sources abound with accounts of men becoming eyewitnesses to angels who perform in the world with masculine-gendered bodies, women's visual access to these angelic corporealities undergoes further regulation. A'isha's claim to see Gabriel in the *Tabaqat* takes on an added gravity with her assertion of an exclusive privilege: "I saw Gabriel and no other woman saw him except me."[69] Gabriel, therefore, was not one of the unnamed men who seized young Muhammad in his wet-nurse's account from the *Sira*.[70] A figure such as Ibn 'Abbas receives heightened prestige for his perception of Gabriel, but A'isha's gendered exclusivity raises the stakes. A'isha's witness of Gabriel positions her even above Muhammad's first wife, Khadija, who has no knowledge of Gabriel's presence without Muhammad telling her when the angel comes and goes,[71] and even Mary, who only saw an unnamed "spirit"/"messenger" in the Qur'an's account.

Not all hadith transmission networks were willing to accept A'isha as the lone woman to see Gabriel, even if only the singular woman to see him within her own household. A'isha's claim, appearing within a list of her special distinctions, is undermined by her cowife Umm Salama's narrations of encounters with Gabriel, as well as the tradition of Muhammad's angelic chest-opening (presented in some versions as witnessed by his wet-nurse). Like the suggestion that Muhammad saw God with his eyes, the notion of A'isha's eyes seeing Gabriel provokes anxieties and diverse responses. In the most corporeally explicit visions of Gabriel reported by both A'isha and Umm Salama, Gabriel not only occupies a masculine embodiment but specifically resembles Dihya al-Kalbi.[72] Alternate traditions, however, deny that A'isha had ever seen Gabriel. The tradition of Muhammad conveying Gabriel's greeting to A'isha appears in numerous iterations without explicit references to her seeing Gabriel with her own eyes; some even portray A'isha telling Muhammad, "You see what we do not see" or narrating in the past tense, "He used to see what we did not see."[73] Numerous chains present a narration in which Muhammad reveals, "This is Gabriel" and conveys Gabriel's greetings to her, without making it clear whether Muhammad alerted her to an invisible presence or identified a body that she could see. Nonetheless, all accounts of A'isha interacting with Gabriel position her husband as the necessary link between them, reporting greetings from each to the other. This is also the case with narrations of Umm Salama seeing Gabriel; each woman's encounter with the angelic requires mediation from her prophetic husband.[74]

A'isha's accounts of interactions between Muhammad and Gabriel during the battle of Qurayza, including their dialogue and Gabriel's removing dust from his hair and pointing in Qurayza's direction, vary on the question of A'isha's access. While chains from transmitter Ibn Numayr present these accounts without any statement from A'isha that would explicitly portray her as an eyewitness, a version traced to Hammad ibn Salama includes A'isha clearly stating, "I saw him." Positions on A'isha's vision of Gabriel do not appear to be bound within particular geographically defined networks, but the pro-vision Qurayza narrative is traced to the Hisham < 'Urwa < A'isha chain through Basran transmitters, while the more careful versions trace back to Hisham < 'Urwa < A'isha through Kufan chains.[75] Nor does the nature of A'isha's interaction with Gabriel seem to have been necessarily related to the controversy of Muhammad seeing God, at least not in terms of traceable transmission histories. Masruq, a prominent reporter of A'isha's denial that Muhammad had seen God (often appearing as the one who asks her if Muhammad saw his lord), reports that A'isha saw Gabriel. Hammad, who supports Muhammad's vision of God, also reports A'isha's declaration to have seen Gabriel.[76] Ma'mar, who apparently favored Ibn 'Abbas's affirmations of Muhammad's divine vision over A'isha's rejection, reports traditions that deny A'isha's eyewitness of Gabriel.[77]

The Six Books, which favor A'isha's denial that Muhammad had seen God, also favor A'isha's inability to see Gabriel. The Six Books overall present A'isha's interaction with Gabriel either in vague reports that leave the question of vision unresolved or in reports of A'isha denying that she saw Gabriel. In canonically privileged accounts, Muhammad informs A'isha, "This is Gabriel," with her precise degree of access to the angel left unconfirmed, or A'isha clearly tells her husband, "You see what we do not see."[78] Accounts of A'isha telling the Prophet, "I saw him" or claiming an exceptional status as the only woman to have seen Gabriel with her own eyes fail to enter the Six Books. In Bukhari's *Sahih*, this exclusion becomes more overtly gendered; Bukhari clearly locates Gabriel in the social position of men, placing the A'isha-Gabriel exchange of "salam" in his section "Greetings of Peace from Men to Women and from Women to Men."[79] Although not exactly a "man," Gabriel still requires location in the binary gender system with which Islamic jurisprudence orders human society.

The Six Books do not absolutely deny the possibility of women seeing Gabriel, as the reports of Umm Salama's vision achieve inclusion in the canon.[80] While the Sahih/Sunan works marginalize the possibility that A'isha witnessed Gabriel with her own eyes, later sources such as al-Hakim's *Al-Mustadrak* rehabilitate the tradition of A'isha seeing Gabriel. In these reports, Muhammad allows Gabriel into A'isha's chamber, provoking A'isha to ask, "O Messenger of God, who is this?" Muhammad replies by asking, "Who does he look like?" A'isha answers that the man resembles Dihya al-Kalbi, after which Muhammad explains that he is Gabriel. Gabriel and A'isha exchange "salam," with Muhammad conveying the greeting from each to the other.[81] Tabarani's *Mu'jam al-Kabir* devotes an entire section specifically to A'isha's witness of Gabriel, which provides narrations of A'isha seeing Gabriel with her own eyes and misidentifying him as Dihya, as well as her confessed inability to see Gabriel; Tabarani also includes narrations in which Muhammad mediates the greetings of peace between A'isha and Gabriel, leaving her vision of the angel neither clearly affirmed nor denied,[82] and the parallel tradition in which Umm Salama rather than A'isha sees Gabriel and mistakes him for Dihya.[83] Bayhaqi's *Dala'il* reports A'isha observing the embodied Gabriel and Muhammad revealing the angel's identity to her,[84] and also provides chapters devoted to visions of Gabriel and other angels by specific Companions, including figures such as 'Umar, Ibn 'Abbas, and Umm Salama.[85]

Without demanding that the hadith corpus exhibit a singular shared logic regarding women's eyes and their in/ability to witness angels, I ask: When A'isha tells her husband, "You see what we do not see," who is A'isha's "we"? If placed in conversation with other traditions in the corpus, most notably the famous "Hadith of Gabriel," in which multiple Companions (unidentified apart from the narrating witness, 'Umar ibn al-Khattab) observe Gabriel as a man quizzing Muhammad,[86] A'isha's denial of angelic vision becomes gendered. Her restrictions of women's angelophanic experience presumably gender the group of Companions in the Hadith of Gabriel as homosocially male. A'isha's proximity to prophetic experience, while remaining privileged among women for Gabriel's greeting to her, becomes distanced further from the possibilities for male prophets and their male Companions.

Despite A'isha's privileged position among the wives of Muhammad and earthly women at large, her relationship to transcendent angelic forces remains ambiguous: though honored with a greeting from Gabriel, she loses the prestige of angelic vision. Umm Salama's vision complicates the gendering of A'isha's accounts. In this case, A'isha's exclusion from angelic witness stands at an intersection of gendered and sectarian questions, highlighting the significance of relations to Muhammad's body (and relations to angelic bodies through their positionality with Muhammad) for relations of power among his wives and conceivably the Companions at large. A'isha and Umm Salama, after all, were rival cowives and later positioned on opposing sides of the Battle of the Camel, and Umm Salama appears as a source for narrations lauding the virtues of 'Ali, Fatima, and their descendents.[87]

In another tradition from the *Musnad*, Muhammad defends A'isha against the jealousy of her cowives by privileging her with a special proximity to revelation that enforces the gendering of prophethood. When Umm Salama demands equitable treatment, Muhammad tells her not to bother him regarding A'isha, since she was the only woman in whose presence he received revelation (and while sharing a single blanket no less).[88] A'isha's status becomes elevated with the suggestion that women are not only incapable of receiving revelation but generally act as inhibitors of the prophetic faculty in men: unlike other women, A'isha could remain physically present without obstructing her husband's access to the angelic. Whatever the degree to which women can interact with angels, their access to angels consistently remains embedded in a man's sexual access to them; that is, the specific women who can boast either direct or mediated access to angels are wives of Muhammad. In linkages formed between angels and women, a sexual link to the Prophet appears as the crucial force that makes their connections possible.

Gendering Prophethood

While prophetic traditions have counted the total number of prophets at 124,000, our sample is exceedingly small, limited to the roughly two dozen prophets named and discussed in the sources. A survey of these prophets as presented in the Qur'an and sira/maghazi literatures, including Muhammad as well as pre-Islamic prophets both within and beyond biblical rosters, reveals three details so obvious that they might go unnoticed, invisible in plain sight. First, all of the named prophets are humans. Angels deliver divine communications to human prophets, but angels as a species do not themselves require an angelic prophet to teach them. The possibility of jinn prophets, while not explicitly denied in the Qur'an or sira/maghazi literatures, does not appear to have been thinkable.[89] Nor do the sources consider prophets among nonhuman animal species. Second, Muhammad's recollections of his experience and the accounts of his eyewitnesses treat prophethood as a phenomenon of or in prophets' *bodies*. As described vividly in Muhammad's narrations of his first meeting with Gabriel (in which Gabriel nearly crushes him),[90] revelation enters into the prophetic body, inflicts violence and trauma upon it, and produces observable side effects through which the event of divine communication can be recognized by eyewitnesses.[91] It is through the violence performed on Muhammad's body that his reception of revelation becomes demonstrable. Third, this embodied performance constitutes a gendered performance, as the small roster of prophets named in the Qur'an and hadith sources includes only men.

Muhammad's encounters with other human beings in paradise, limited to pre-Islamic prophets, are also entirely homosocial; he does not, for example, interact with Mary or other esteemed women from sacred history. Muhammad does witness women as present in paradise; Ibn Hanbal's *Mus-*

nad provides an Ibn ʿAbbas report that during his visit to paradise, Muhammad smelled the fragrance of Firʿawn's daughter's hairdresser, who was martyred with her children for her monotheism.[92] In Muslim's *Sahih*, the well-known tradition of Muhammad hearing Bilal's footsteps ahead of him in paradise also includes Muhammad narrating that he saw Umm Sulaym there.[93] A variant of this tradition in Bukhari's *Sahih* mentions a palace in paradise reserved for ʿUmar, which includes a woman awaiting him in the courtyard.[94] While reading accounts of Muhammad observing women as present in paradise, I could not find accounts of women in paradise appearing as Muhammad's active interlocutors.

Some representations of women in the sources complicate the significance of gender to this transcendent economy, though these materials can also enforce masculine-exclusive prophethood. Most famously, the Qur'an's depiction of Mary, who receives divine communication and advanced knowledge of future events and whose body becomes a site of miraculous extrahuman modification, seems to challenge the male monopoly on prophethood. While this project's scope does not cover the entirety of Islamic interpretive tradition, it should be noted that feminine prophethood was at least conceivable to one significant figure of the period covered here, Ibn Hazm (994–1064). As Barbara Stowasser has observed, Ibn Hazm recognizes Mary and other women as eligible for prophethood (*nubuwwa*) but still restricts them from messengership (*risalah*). Ibn Hazm's relatively inclusive model of prophethood failed to take hold against arguments that the Qur'an's statement "We sent not before you other than men [*rijalan*] whom we inspired" (12:109 and 16:43) necessarily excluded women, as well as the view that women could not achieve the physical purity of men due to menstruation.[95]

For Mary to ostensibly meet all of the qualifications of prophethood without being counted as a prophet would enforce the male-sexing of prophetic bodies more explicitly than if she had not been mentioned at all. Ambiguities and silences in the Qur'an's discussion of Mary's relation to prophethood could leave her status open to interpretation (as seen with Ibn Hazm and later Ibn ʿArabi),[96] but could also reveal prophethood as a category so entrenched in sexual specificity that a woman's location within it is too radically unthinkable to be considered.

A narration in sira/maghazi works that also simultaneously challenges and affirms the masculine gendering of prophethood appears with ʿAtika bint ʿAbd al-Muttalib, Muhammad's aunt, who dreams that Muhammad's opponent mocks a woman's claim to prophecy. The episode is reported by both al-Waqidi and Ibn Ishaq, with neither providing a complete chain of transmitters: al-Waqidi prefaces the narration simply with "They say," while Ibn Ishaq cites an unnamed "person above suspicion" who transmitted the report to him with an isnad of ʿIkrima < Ibn ʿAbbas and Yazid ibn Ruman < ʿUrwa ibn al-Zubayr.[97] In this tradition, ʿAtika dreams of a rider on a camel shouting warnings and then throwing a rock that shatters into numerous pieces, with every home in Mecca damaged by a fragment. Fearing what the dream might foretell, she seeks out her brother ʿAbbas and confides it to him. ʿAbbas in turn tells his friend Walid ibn ʿUtba, and soon word of the dream begins to spread throughout Mecca. Muhammad's opponent Abu Jahl confronts ʿAbbas with the charge that the descendants of ʿAbd al-Muttalib are not satisfied with only their men prophesying, but now their women prophesy as well.[98] ʿAtika's dream does not itself counter the prevailing gender logic of the sources, as other episodes report of women having similar experiences.[99] Women soothsayers and visionaries seem to have been part of the pre-Islamic landscape; Ibn Bukayr's recension of Ibn Ishaq even reports that prior to Muhammad's prophethood, Khadija used to hire an old woman of Mecca to heal her husband when he suffered from the evil eye.[100] However, mockery of ʿAtika as a supposed prophet sets her outside this mode of knowledge, identified with a biblical roster that appears to have been regarded as entirely comprised of men. Abu Jahl's specific use of the verb *nabaʾa* links ʿAtika's dream to Muhammad's mission with the suggestion that for this woman to claim prophetic activity embarrasses her nephew's claim and exposes a radical arrogance in the Banu Muttalib.[101]

Prophethood undergoes increasing articulation in hadith sources as a masculine office. Numerous traditions suggest ontological inequality between masculine and feminine bodies; examples include Muhammad differentiating between the urine of a baby girl and that of a baby boy, naming the former as the greater impurity,[102] and traditions in which Muhammad describes the bodies of women as interrupters of prayer along with the bodies of donkeys and dogs.[103] More specifically, women's bodies become disqualified from prophetic perfection in the reports of Muhammad naming two gendered deficiencies for which women constitute the majority of people in the hellfire: a deficiency in religious duty (*din*), illustrated in women missing days of the Ramadan fast due to menstruation, and a deficiency in intellect (*ʿaql*), as evidenced by women's testimony equaling half that of men.[104] In her discussion of what she calls "the most notoriously misogynistic hadith in the established corpus," Marion Katz highlights the relationship drawn in this tradition between gender, uncontrolled bodies, and corporeal pollution. In particular, she notes the *ʿa-q-l* root's construction of a link between intellect and restraint, which informed premodern exegesis that linked women's uncontrollable bodies to their deficient mental capacities.[105]

Muhammad's masculinity precedes his materialization as a body. As we saw in chapter 1's discussion of Muhammad's genealogy, Ibn Ishaq's *Sira* presents Muhammad's body as chiefly a product of his forefathers. Many of these forefathers were prophets themselves. The *Sira* constructs the lineage of Muhammad's father ʿAbd Allah through Abraham to Adam on patrilineal terms, naming all of his male ancestors (while also naming the mother of Ishmael's sons as Ra'la bint Mudad ibn ʿAmr al-Jurhumi, who herself is assigned a genealogy of male ancestors).[106] The *Sira* provides a considerably shorter treatment of Muhammad's matrilineal descent, listing his mother Amina, her mother, grandmother, and great-grandmother, and asserts that Muhammad was endowed with superior lineage on both sides.[107] Nonetheless, Muhammad's patrilineal genealogy is prioritized, as shown in the *Sira*'s account of the "blaze" shining between the eyes of Muhammad's father. The *Sira* also reports that according to "popular stories," this light emanated from Amina's body during her pregnancy, allowing her to see castles in Syria. The "other woman" who pursued ʿAbd Allah for his light recalls, "I invited him hoping that that would be in me."[108] In whatever capacity Muhammad's mother contributes to his materialization (that is, whether his conception is imagined within a one-seed or two-seed model), her womb does not actively generate the light that shines from it but rather provides a nesting place for the light from Muhammad's father. Muhammad-as-light shines from within Amina's womb as evidence of an exceptional deposit from outside, a transmission from ʿAbd Allah's body to hers through the vehicle of his seminal fluid.

The capacity for prophethood appears in the Qur'an to be significantly a patrilineal transmission, an inheritance between fathers and sons. Abraham has two prophetic sons and is also the uncle of Lot; Abraham's son Isaac is the father of Jacob and the subsequent line of Israelite prophets, including David, his son Solomon, and his descendent Jesus. In contrast, the only mention of a prophet's daughter appears in the story of Lot, who offers his daughters to men as an alternative to their expressed desire for sex with other men.[109] Lot's daughters are not named or represented as holding any agency of their own; their appearance in the narrative serves only to illumine the characters of the men to whom their bodies have been offered.

Though questions of the precise link in the Qur'an between Muhammad's sonlessness and prophethood's closure in 33:40 ("Muhammad is not the father of any of your men, but he is the Seal of the Prophets") remain contested in academic literature,[110] the hadith corpus constructs prophethood as hereditary in discussions of Muhammad's son Ibrahim, who died in infancy. Ibn Hanbal's *Musnad* and Ibn Sa'd's *Tabaqat* contain Anas's assertion that if there were to be prophets after Muhammad, Ibrahim would have survived, and that Ibrahim would have been a righteous man and prophet (*siddiqan nabiyan*).[111] The treatment of prophethood as a patrilineal inheritance also appears in the Six Books via Bukhari and Ibn Maja, who both include narrations that if there were to have been another prophet after Muhammad, baby Ibrahim would have lived.[112]

The claim that Ibrahim would have become a prophet if he survived to adulthood establishes a possibility for prophets' sons but not their daughters. Fatima reached maturity, outlived Muhammad, and received the designation "master of women" from her father during his final illness,[113] but her position remains subject to a gendered limit. Muhammad authorizes her only above other women (with added qualifiers naming her position as specifically over the women of paradise, and with exceptions such as her mother Khadija and Mary), and assigns her no share of his rank in this world. Hadiths asserting that Muhammad's son would have become a prophet if he reached maturity require that his daughter's maturity and extraordinary metaphysical prestige have no bearing on the issue.

In Sunni hadith canon, this attention to Ibrahim could express a sectarian interest in marginalizing 'Ali and/or the Prophet's grandsons born from 'Ali and Fatima. At any rate, after the death of Muhammad's infant son, his adult daughter's gender handicap seemingly forces the end of prophethood. Throughout the sources, Fatima remains privileged by narrations that she represents a part of Muhammad and that one who angers her also angers him,[114] as well as the traditions of her receiving secret information from Muhammad of his imminent death, becoming the first of his house to join him,[115] and boasting an exceptional rank as master over women.[116] Nonetheless, the fact of Fatima surviving her father is not presented as comparable to the hypothetical survival of his son as having any impact on the continuation of prophethood.

The Prophetic Penis

Beyond Muhammad's light and patrilineal inheritance, the gendering of prophetic bodies becomes more explicitly corporeal in representations of

Muhammad's marked penis as a signifier of his mission. Muhammad's circumcision, while an act of bodily modification and not precisely a "natural" physiognomic marker of his prophethood, becomes compelling evidence for his station early in the literature. Maʿmar's *Maghazi* reports the legend that Roman emperor Heraclius determined through astrological calculations that an anticipated "king of the circumcised" had arrived. Heraclius's courtiers advise him that only Jews practice circumcision, and that he can therefore eliminate the king of the circumcised by simply ordering the execution of all Jews in his cities. After hearing of Muhammad's emergence in Arabia, Heraclius orders his courtiers to find out whether Muhammad had been circumcised. His courtiers report, "They have looked, and he is circumcised," and recognize that Muhammad is indeed the anticipated king.[117] Muhammad's status as circumcised appears to be confirmed by visual inspection—"They looked" (*nazaru*)—rather than by the assertion that Arabs practiced a tradition of circumcision.[118] The *Sira* presents a version of this tradition in which Heraclius receives knowledge of the anticipated king through a dream, rather than through an astrological reading. An Arab man is later brought to Heraclius's court, claiming that a prophet has emerged from among his people. Heraclius orders the man to be stripped naked, revealing the man to be circumcised. Having been shown that the Arabs practice circumcision, Heraclius commands his officials to locate the coming prophet among them.[119]

As in the sira/maghazi literatures, the gendering of Muhammad's body contributes to his prophetic status. In the *Tabaqat*, Muhammad's circumcised status becomes not only a sign of foretold events coming to fruition but also a marvel in its own right, as Ibn Sa'd reports that Muhammad was born already circumcised and with his umbilical cord cut. Upon learning of these signs, Muhammad's grandfather ʿAbd al-Muttalib takes joy in recognizing them as promises of Muhammad's future greatness.[120] The "born circumcised" tradition does not enter into the most canonical sources but resurfaces in the collections of later scholars such as Tabarani, al-Khatib al-Baghdadi, Bayhaqi, and Abu Nu'aym.[121] Several post–Sahih/Sunan collections provide the narration of Anas in which Muhammad states, "Among my marvels [*karamati*] of my lord upon me is that I was born circumcised and no one has seen my private parts [*sawati*]."[122] Reports of Muhammad as born circumcised bring the penis into prophetic physiognomy as a physical symptom of Muhammad's moral condition, but in a betrayal of how physical evidence usually works: this special feature of Muhammad's external form *cannot* be observed. Muhammad renders his penis both as a meaningful sign and a text denied to its readers, meaningful in part for its inaccessibility. The tradition resolves tensions between a necessity for Muhammad to have been circumcised and the idea that no one had seen his genitalia; Muhammad was born without a need for someone to perform the procedure, and he bears witness to this fact himself. In addition to narrations of Muhammad having been born circumcised, Tabarani's *Mu'jam al-Awsat* and Abu Nu'aym's *Dala'il* also provide reports of Gabriel personally circumcising Muhammad (which the narrations combine with Gabriel's washing of Muhammad's heart into a single event), thereby enabling Muhammad to have undergone circumcision while at least protecting him from human eyes.[123]

The unreadability of the prophetic penis becomes a signifier to be read. While not all parts of Muhammad can be seen, the act of witnessing the prophetic body—in whatever ways this is possible—becomes increasingly salient over time as a source of authorizing power. The *Sira* reports an episode from Muhammad's childhood in which, as he carries stones while in a state of exposure, Muhammad is slapped by an "unseen figure" and told to cover himself.[124] Accounts of Muhammad's funeral preparations also reveal concerns over the exposure of his nakedness. One report from the *Sira* portrays 'Ali as performing the ritual washing of Muhammad's body, adding clarification that 'Ali did not remove Muhammad's clothing but instead used it to wash Muhammad's body without direct contact between the body and his own hand.[125] In another narration, A'isha recalls disagreement among the Companions as to whether or not Muhammad's clothing should be removed for his washing. She reports that as they argued, God caused them all to fall into a deep sleep, after which the voice of an unidentified being told them to keep Muhammad fully clothed as they washed his body—which they achieved by rubbing Muhammad's body with his clothing, not their hands.[126] One recension of the *Sira* quotes A'isha as saying, "Had I known at the beginning of my affair what I knew at the end of it, none but his wives would have washed him."[127] This cryptic statement leaves much unsaid regarding the washers' degree of encounter with Muhammad's corpse and what precisely had changed in A'isha's knowledge.

In al-Waqidi's *Maghazi*, Muhammad's modesty remains guarded even against his wives: A'isha states that she had only seen Muhammad naked once, when his garment fell as he rose to meet Zayd, and does not clarify whether she had seen Muhammad from the front or back.[128] As Muhammad's body emerges in these sources' narrations as a heterogeneous assemblage of bits and pieces, parts and by-products, that allow or deny linkages to other bodies, A'isha and 'Ali both stand as gatekeepers between Muhammad's sexed body and communal memory, denying access to his nakedness. The irony of these narrations is that while Muhammad's private parts are shielded from becoming public parts that might be subjected to a collective textual gaze, their denials of access produce his genitals as objects of analysis and proofs of his unique status.

Narrations in ʿAbd al-Razzaq's *Musannaf* and Ibn Hanbal's *Musnad* discuss the episode from Muhammad's preprophetic years in which he and other youths used their clothing to carry stones during the reconstruction of the Ka'ba, and an unidentified voice tells Muhammad to cover himself. One version ends with the reporter's statement, "He was not seen naked after that," suggesting the possibility of a time, perhaps prior to sexual maturity, in which Muhammad's nakedness could have been witnessed by human eyes.[129] In the *Tabaqat*, Ibn ʿAbbas notes, "His private parts [*ʿawra*] were not seen after that day" and identifies the episode as the earliest evidence of Muhammad's special destiny, "the first thing that the Prophet, God bless him and give him peace, saw of prophethood."[130]

Hadith sources preserve A'isha's denials that Muhammad's naked body was witnessed even by his sexual partners. Ibn Hanbal reports A'isha's declaration, "I never looked at the genitalia of the Prophet, God bless him and give him peace, nor did I see the genitalia of the Prophet."[131] Ibn Abi Shayba includes the narration in his chapter on ritual purity, and Ibn Maja includes it in his chapters on ritual purity[132] and marriage,[133] but the narration speaks to more than questions of jurisprudence; Ibn Sa'd places it in his *Tabaqat*'s section on marvelous signs of Muhammad's prophethood that preceded the start of revelation,[134] and Tirmidhi includes it in the *Shama'il*, his collection of reports concerning Muhammad's sublime qualities.[135] In the *Tabaqat*, Ibn Sa'd follows his placement of the Ibn ʿAbbas narration with a report of A'isha's statement, "I never saw that of the Messenger of God."[136] The meaning of A'isha's reference to "that" is not clarified apart from Ibn Sa'd's placement of her report next to Ibn ʿAbbas's narration that Muhammad's private parts had not been seen since his youth.[137]

In another contribution from the *Tabaqat* to this imaginary of prophetic nakedness, the one protecting Muhammad's exposed body from view is not A'isha but ʿAli. The narration relates to the ritual washing of Muhammad's body after his death. ʿAli recalls that Muhammad had said, "No one has seen my private parts except that his eye was obliterated." Al-Fadl and Usama were blindfolded and tasked with giving ʿAli water from behind a curtain.[138] Vision of Muhammad's exposed genitalia as theoretically attainable, but at a cost of devastating injury to the viewer; only ʿAli can perform the funerary washing without becoming permanently disabled. Muhammad's genitalia thus remains a site at which connections between the prophetic body and other bodies are simultaneously forged and denied. 'Ali's insistence on washing the body alone, with an implication that the physical danger of witnessing Muhammad's exposure does not apply to 'Ali's own eyes, turns prophetic nakedness into a mode of achieving or demonstrating privileged relationships. Muhammad's genitalia and 'Ali's eyes form a linkage that is prohibited even to A'isha, who denies her own witness of Muhammad's naked body.

Questions of visual access to Muhammad's naked body persist in hadith collections, via familiar traditions such as the report of Muhammad briefly exposing himself as a child.[139] One canonical account repeats an episode found in al-Waqidi's *Maghazi*, in which Muhammad rushes to see Zayd while in a state of exposure. In this version, A'isha mentions that Muhammad stood naked and embraced Zayd, but adds, "By God, I had not seen him naked before or after."[140] Another narration from the Six Books addresses the issue of washing Muhammad's body after his death, countering earlier narrations that present 'Ali as having special access to a naked prophetic body that would otherwise blind those who witnessed it. Abu Dawud's *Sunan* repeats A'isha's narration from Ibn Ishaq's *Sira* of God's intervention in disputes among the Companions over the exposure of Muhammad's corpse: God causes the Companions to fall asleep, then instructs them to wash the body while keeping it clothed. The Companions wash the body with the shirt that covers it rather than touching the body directly with their hands. The narration also includes A'isha's statement that if she had known then what she knew later, only Muhammad's wives would have washed him. As in the *Sira*, the precise item of knowledge is not articulated.[141] In later sources Muhammad's own penis remains unseen, both in A'isha's denial of having seen her husband naked[142] and the tradition of young Muhammad only briefly exposing himself during the reconstruction of the Ka'ba (with a Bayhaqi report including the coda, "His 'awra was not seen after or before").[143]

Muhammad's penis also demonstrates his exceptionality through its capacity for function. Narrations in Ibn Sa'd's *Tabaqat*, 'Abd al-Razzaq's *Musannaf*, and Ibn Hanbal's *Musnad* depict Muhammad's sexual vigor as superhuman, measured in comparison to the combined power of thirty or forty men;[144] additional reports from 'Abd al-Razzaq measure Muhammad's sex power as that of forty to forty-five men.[145] These narrations are not attributed to Muhammad's wives but rather to male Companions such as Anas. According to a tradition that appears in more than one report in the *Tabaqat*, Muhammad's sex power becomes extraordinary due to further angelic modification of his body. Muhammad explains his vigor as having resulted from Gabriel bringing him a kettle; when Muhammad ate from the kettle, he became endowed with the sexual vigor of forty men.[146] In addition to enhancing Muhammad's sexual power, angelic intervention also defends his sexual performance against enemies' sabotage, as shown in our previous discussion of Labid ibn ʿAsim employing sorcery to prevent Muhammad from having intercourse with his wives.

Reports of Gabriel's interventions in Muhammad's sexuality mark both prophethood and masculinity with a shared act of embodied performance. Ibn Sa'd connects Muhammad's sexual strength of forty men to performative masculinity more broadly, as the section of his *Tabaqat* devoted to Muhammad's sex power also includes the report of Muhammad physically overpowering Rukanah, the great wrestler.[147] The tradition of Muhammad's extraordinary sex power persists throughout the development of the hadith sources. Scholarship has argued that these traditions do not expose Muhammad as having an enhanced libido but emphasize his degree of personal discipline and rational control over the body.[148]

The Six Books canon also preserves a degree of thematic overlap between prophetic sexuality and angelic interventions on the prophetic body, found in reports of angels defending Muhammad's sexual performance from a sorcerer's assault.[149] However, the tradition of Muhammad deriving his privileged sexual vigor from angelically provided supplements, as in the *Tabaqat*'s narration of Gabriel providing Muhammad with a kettle of performance-enhancing food from the heavens, does not find its way into the Six Books. Repeating earlier sources, Muhammad's vigor is compared in these collections to that of multitudes of men, but apart from the angels' defense of Muhammad against Labid, his sexual performance does not appear to have resulted from an angelic modification of his body.[150]

The tradition of Muhammad having intercourse with each of his wives every night, attributed to his having been granted the power of multitudes of men (usually thirty), appears in collections of Bayhaqi,[151] Ibn Hibban,[152] Ibn Khuzayma,[153] Abu Ya'la,[154] and Tabarani, whose variant of this tradition narrates that Muhammad "went around eleven women at one time, and he was given the power of thirty."[155] All of the above reports share an isnad that traces the accounts back not to someone who had experienced prophetic sexuality firsthand, such as A'isha or Umm Salama, but rather Anas. Tabarani's *Mu'jam al-Awsat* additionally provides a narration in which the Companion ʿAbd Allah ibn ʿAmr presents the claim in Muhammad's own words: "I was given the power of forty in strength and sexual intercourse, and there is no believer except that he is given the power of ten."[156]

In reports provided by Tabarani and Abu Nu'aym, Muhammad's sexed body also demonstrates his privileged station through the specific bodies that he accesses in paradise. The decontextualized narration represents Muhammad as saying, "O A'isha! Don't you know that God married me in paradise to Mary the daughter of Imran, Kalthum the sister of Moses, and the wife of Pharoah?"[157] This polemically potent tradition not only counters A'isha's spousal prestige in paradise by naming three other women from sacred history with whom she must share her status but also presents A'isha as the foil Muhammad personally rebukes.

While Muhammad's sexual performance becomes evidence of his prophethood, sources tend to treat his semen as substantively unremarkable. This means that despite Muhammad engaging in a superhuman amount of sex with his multiple wives, and his bodily substances working in other contexts as transmitters of baraka, the women who regularly access prophetic semen are not represented as seeking unique benefits from contact with the material. Unlike the Companions who access baraka by engaging his sweat and hair, the Companions who directly access his semen do not become sources for imagining these bodily flows as conduits of baraka.

While the corpus at large ignores Muhammad's semen as a potential conductor of baraka for those who directly accessed it, traditions do seem to reflect an anxiety concerning the precise nature of his ejaculations and their relationship to Muhammad's body. Numerous reports attributed to multiple Companions, including A'isha, describe Muhammad waking up in a state of major ritual impurity (*janaba*) during the month of Ramadan, for which he would take a bath and then continue his fast. These narrations, reported in Ibn Hanbal's *Musnad* and Ibn Abi Shayba's *Musannaf*, offer disclaimers that Muhammad's ritual impurity was *not* the result of nocturnal emission.[158] What's exactly at stake in distancing prophetic sexuality from nocturnal emissions does not become self-evident in the reports. However, another tradition found in these same collections represents Muhammad as distinguishing between two types of dream: the *ru'ya* or visionary dream, which comes from God, and the *hulum*, the wet dream, which comes from Satan.[159] In some reports, Muhammad advises those who experience hulum to spit three times to the left and seek refuge in God from the harm of the dream.[160] To experience sexual dreams and ejaculate—a phenomenon that had troubled seekers in Mediterranean antiquity, such as Christian writers and pre-Christian Greek philosophers[161]—signified a loss of bodily control but also the threat of a Satanic intervention. The sources' efforts to distance Muhammad's ritual impurity from the possibility of a wet dream uphold the perfection of his prophetic sexuality. Another narration from Ibn Abi

Shayba's *Musannaf* presents nocturnal emissions as simply an embarrassment, as a houseguest of A'isha attempts to hide the fact of his wet dream from her; A'isha complains that rather than ruin the sheet with water, he could have simply scratched out the semen with his fingernail, as she had done with Muhammad's semen.[162]

As in the earlier musnad and musannaf works, representations of Muhammad's extraordinary sex drive in sources of the later ninth century do not depict prophetic semen as a special substance in itself but still reflect concerns over the character of prophetic ejaculations. These sources, describing Muhammad's ritual purification after waking up in a state of sexual defilement during Ramadan, again emphasize that Muhammad's state of janaba had not been the result of a wet dream.[163] Sahih/Sunan sources follow earlier collections in presenting nocturnal emissions as the result of demonic assaults on the dreamer's body, which require the seeking of refuge with God from Satan's harm.[164] The clarification that Muhammad did not become ritually impure through an involuntary emission thus confirms his security against demonic forces. Just as Satan cannot appear in dreams with the form of Muhammad's body, Satan cannot penetrate Muhammad's mind and master his body by causing him to ejaculate while asleep. Later sources continue to treat prophetic sexuality as exceptional and divinely protected. Tabarani presents Muhammad himself offering an emphatic clarification: "No prophet has had a wet dream. The wet dream is from Satan."[165]

Despite the absence of a report in which Muhammad names a specific benefit of contact with his semen or in which his Companions conceptualize his semen as a source of baraka, Muhammad's body can seemingly transform other bodies through ejaculation into them. These transformed bodies can then operate as transmitters of Muhammad's baraka into other bodies through the corporeal connections achieved by milk kinship. A'isha never treats Muhammad's semen as anything but waste, but her rival co-wife Umm Salama does appear to become an embodied baraka transmitter through her sexual intimacy with the Prophet. In the *Tabaqat*, Ibn Sa'd begins his entry on Hasan al-Basri (d. 728) with a report that Umm Salama's breastmilk facilitated a baraka transmission to Hasan from Muhammad, who had died a decade before Hasan's birth: "They say that his mother was perhaps absent and the child would cry. Umm Salama gave him her breast to keep him busy with it until his mother came. Her breast flowed and he drank from it. They are of the opinion that [Hasan's] wisdom and eloquence are from that baraka."[166]

Early Muslim discourses on breastfeeding share the guiding assumption that a woman's moral character flows into the infant's body with her milk, and also that her milk is not entirely her own. In the logic of *laban al-fahl* ("sire's milk"), a woman's milk production is directed by her husband's (or owner's) semen.[167] By virtue of his semen's involvement, the woman's husband or owner becomes implicated in the familial connections forged by her acts of breastfeeding, which become most relevant in legal discourses concerning marital incest: two babies nursed by the same woman could not marry each other since they shared a "milk father."[168] In the event of Umm Salama rendering Hasan al-Basri a "milk son" of the baraka-transmitting prophetic body, the interface of Umm Salama's breast and Hasan's mouth enables the material flow of a connection to Muhammad from one body into another. Through her sexual relationship with Muhammad, Umm Salama's body retains a trace of the prophetic body's baraka that persists after Muhammad's death; the *Tabaqat* acknowledges Umm Salama's milk as an emission of this baraka directly into Hasan's digestive system that produces observable effects, namely enhanced wisdom and eloquence. Through the mediation of Umm Salama's breast and its gendered flows, Muhammad's gendered flows can reach other bodies, connecting them to his prophetic corporeality and thereby transforming them.

A'isha employs the logic of milk kinship to form connections in a markedly different way. She relies on the logic of milk kinship to solve a legal problem, namely norms of gender segregation that restrict her access to men. As milk kinship changes the status of men to *mahram* (closely related to the point of becoming unmarriageable), A'isha uses milk kinship to circumvent gender segregation; by having adult men drink the milk of her sister Umm Kulthum, she turns these men into close relations and thereby within the limits of her social access. Harald Motzki explains that in this context, "suckling" would have signified that the men consumed a few drops of milk from a dish or in a drink, rather than directly from Umm Kulthum's body. A'isha defends the practice by referencing an incident in which Muhammad had allowed Sahla bint Suhayl to "nurse" her adopted son in order to deregulate their interactions in the home. A'isha's rationale meets with strong disapproval from luminaries among the Companions, including two *rashidun* caliphs ('Umar and 'Ali), early Qur'an exegete Ibn Mas'ud, and A'isha's own cowives, most notably her rival Umm Salama, who regards Sahla's permission as an isolated incident rather than the establishment of a legal norm.[169]

As with other traditions we have observed, the tradition of Hasan al-Basri drinking baraka-infused milk does not achieve inclusion in the most canonically privileged texts of the Sahih/Sunan movement but returns in later sources as the constricted corpus again expands. Abu Nu'aym's *Hilya* also presents milk kinship as a mode of prophetic baraka transmission between two masculine bodies through the mediation of a woman's body: "Hasan al-Basri was the son of the neighbor of Umm Salama, wife of the Prophet. . . . Umm Salama called her neighbor in her poverty, as Hasan was in great need; taking pity on him, she took him in her room and fed her breast to him. It flowed to him and he drank from it, and it is said that Hasan's portion of wisdom [*al-hikma*] was from the milk that he drank from Umm Salama, wife of the Prophet."[170]

Abu Nu'aym's account in his *Hilya* additionally includes a postscript concerning Abu Ja'far Muhammad ibn 'Ali ibn Husayn (Muhammad al-Baqir, the fifth Shi'i Imam), Hasan's contemporary, who reportedly described Hasan as "that one whose speech resembles the speech of the prophets."[171] Suleiman Ali Mourad argues that stories such as the breastfeeding incident privilege Hasan beyond his Follower contemporaries as virtually a Companion.[172] As Mourad calls the historicity of Umm Salama's status as Muhammad's widow into question, the trend of "mythmaking" to intensify connections between Hasan al-Basri and Muhammad would also participate in the cementing of Umm Salama's position as one of the Prophet's wives.[173] In the case of the fifth Shi'i Imam, the great-great-grandson of Muhammad, affirming similarity between Hasan's discourse and the discourse of prophets—reflecting a wisdom and eloquence that Hasan received through the milk of Muhammad's widow—Hasan's status advances beyond a pseudo-Companion level to that of pseudo-*ahl al-bayt*. Hasan's milk kinship with Muhammad does not merely advance his status "metaphorically" but achieves a physical transformation, as the prophetic milk becomes a vehicle for wisdom and eloquence as a material infusion. Umm Salama's breast fulfills a function similar to that of the bottle in which Umm Sulaym kept Muhammad's sweat, or the bowl in which she stored his hair. Umm Salama's body becomes a transmitter of prophetic corporeality and its communicable baraka due to Muhammad's sexual access to her, with her own corporeal flows preserving access to this extended baraka network even after his death.

The Gendered Unseen

If God and the angels exist beyond human categories of gender, the Qur'an and hadith materials depict them as performing drag in order to successfully interact with human communities. Muhammad must himself perform a particular masculinity to take part in his prophetic mediation between these forces and the world. The literature presents a universe of extrahuman agents and interventions in which a masculine God speaks to masculine prophets through masculine angels, who sometimes appear as organized and well-dressed white men to join in battle against polytheists who worship goddesses that take the form of naked, uncontrollable, disruptive Black women. Polytheism is linked to the demonic and the pollutions of animality, and gendered with links to menstrual blood. Polymorphic angels shift between species while remaining consistently gendered, taking the forms of camels and birds but not women. Mary and other women who apparently do the work of prophets remain ostensibly excluded from that category.

These narratives participate in a construction of prophethood that requires the inscription of sex on Muhammad's body. Hadith traditions intensify the gendering of prophethood through representations of God and angels with gendered anthropomorphism, the gendering of access to angels, associations of prophethood with supernaturally enhanced masculine sexuality, attention to the sexed body of Muhammad as evidence of his prophethood, and various traditions that establish an ontological inequality between masculine and feminine bodies. These traditions within the hadith sources construct prophethood as an ultimate performance of masculinity, while also presenting a masculine body as prophethood's prerequisite.

Considering the production of "prophetic sexuality" through these sources' treatments of Muhammad's sexual body, its pleasures and functions, and the ways these pleasures and functions become representative of Muhammad's prophethood, what do the sources yield? Muhammad's sexuality relates him to typical bodies in that it remains under the discipline of ritual purity laws but also positions him as extraordinary in its capacity for performance. Muhammad's sexual vigor is compared to the strength of multitudes of men. Prophetic sexuality benefits from divine protection in that angels defend Muhammad's sexual functions against sorcerers' attacks, and demonstrates its privileged station in his exemption from the demonic phenomenon of wet dreams. Between these traditions, however, the sources also reflect tension as to the precise (in)vulnerability of prophetic sexuality against the demonic. Finally, in the homosociality of prophethood and the transcendent masculinized agents with which prophets interact, prophetic sexuality becomes a route through which privileged women can potentially access those forces. Though entire groups of men enjoy collective witness of Gabriel, women appear to be generally barred from seeing him or incapable of directly interacting with him. A'isha and Umm Salama achieve gendered access to Gabriel through their bodies' being sexually accessible to the prophetic body. Their access to Muhammad's body, meanwhile, is restricted by the fact of their husband's special station; A'isha can engage in penetrative intercourse with the prophetic penis but not see it with her eyes.

Access to Muhammad's penis illustrates both privileged status and limits. He also establishes connections through his access to other masculine bodies. Previous chapters discussed the gendering of intercorporeal baraka transmission as demonstrated in Muhammad's acts of tahnik and saliva transferal for infants, a mode of achieving embodied linkage with Muhammad accessible only to male infants. Examining Muhammad's body for its openings and closings of connection to other bodies, his *sexed* body and performance of prophetic masculinity become significant sites at which these openings and closings find expression. Muhammad forms a desiring-machine in his erotically loaded interactions with a gorgeous youthful god; his sexuality mediates encounters between women and angelic masculinity; and demonic forces seek to assault him at the site of his sexuality, which remains invulnerable to their attack. Finally, Muhammad's prophetic masculinity enables, mediates, and denies access between various beings and his baraka-laden ontology, as well as between these bodies themselves.

CHAPTER FIVE

Secreting Baraka

Muhammad's Body After Muhammad

Even after Muhammad's death, the traces of his body remained operational. As seen in chapter 3, waste traces such as Muhammad's hair and fingernails acted as potent transmitters of baraka. Generations after his death, these echoes of prophetic presence were treated as talismanic by the likes of the caliph Mu'awiya and scholar Ibn Hanbal, both of whom were reportedly buried with their relics of prophetic disjecta. While Muhammad's hair and fingernails were neither his body nor entirely *not* his body, Muhammad's postmortem body forces similar questions of where the prophetic body begins and ends. *Is* Muhammad reducible to his physical matter, or does his Muhammad-ness leave the body with his soul? These questions relate to larger philosophical issues in Islamic interpretive tradition concerning the nature of the soul, its relation to the body, and the afterlife.

Given contemporary debates and conflicts regarding grave visitation, exemplified in the 1920s destruction of raised tombs at the Jannat al-Baqi cemetery in Medina, demolition of shrines in later decades, and the polarizing modern legacies of a figure such as Ibn Taymiyya, we might assume that the hadith corpus—so valorized in a modern Salafism that has become notorious for razing tombs—would absolutely and unambiguously condemn the treatment of anyone's grave, even the grave of Muhammad, as a site for accessing baraka. The sources, however, do not uphold a singular "Sunni" position on prophetic corpses, instead offering multiple ways of thinking about Muhammad's bodily remains.

The prophetic body not only dies but also produces new life, as Muhammad biologically reproduces and thereby extends his corporeality into the future with subsequent generations of descendants. Muhammad is not his children, and his children are not prophets (notwithstanding the hypothetical question of an adult son). Nonetheless, the intercorporeality shared between Muhammad and his children—and by extension, his grandchildren, and their progeny, and so on—could hold implications for the bodies that are materially traceable to him. If merely seeing Muhammad's body with one's own eyes could result in the forgiveness of one's sins, what would it mean to have been materially conceived from this body? This question centers on Fatima, Muhammad's only child to outlive him and the only of his children to continue his biological lineage. At first glance, the issue of whether Fatima, her children, and their descendants retain a special link to the baraka of Muhammad's body makes for an obvious line of demarcation between Sunni and Shi'i traditions. Popular expectations might hold that Shi'i sources treat the inheritance of prophetic DNA (to put it in presentist terms) as something special, and Sunni sources do not. However, our earlier discussion of Muhammad's lineage and physiognomy as they appear in Sunni sources—not to mention the blurring of Sunni-Shi'i boundaries witnessed in chains of transmitters—should encourage caution about what we expect from a "Sunni" treatment of Muhammad's progeny.

This chapter begins with Muhammad's postmortem body, briefly tracing the development of its presentation in the sources from an apparently typical corpse to a conscious, *living* body that remains free of decay and continues to bear witness to the actions of the community. I then turn to the sources' discussions of Fatima, who likewise undergoes a gradual transformation and elaboration as the corpus develops. Over time, Fatima's depiction constructs her as an "Adamic huri" who does not menstruate or otherwise suffer from feminine "defects" but instead appears in the world as a material trace of her father's heavenly ascension—as evidenced by her bodily scent. In the cases of both the postmortem remains of Muhammad and the body of his daughter, we find an intensification of intercorporeal connections and powers as the literary corpus expands.

Muhammad Postmortem

At the end of the prophetic biography, as with every human biography, to think about Muhammad's body means thinking about a corpse. The corpse's relationship to the self—that is, whether a human being was reducible to his or her physical matter or possessed an immaterial soul that existed independently of the body—was not entirely clear in the earliest sources. As Nerina Rustomji discusses in her study of Islamic afterworlds, the Qur'an elaborates on paradise and hellfire in highly material descriptions that focus on the pleasures and torments directed upon bodies.[1] Attempting to convince its audience that God can and will resurrect the dead, the Qur'an does not frame resurrection in terms of an immaterial soul that can continue to exist after the body is gone but instead emphasizes God's power to restore and reanimate bodies that have decomposed and turned to dust and bones (17:49, 17:98, 23:35, 23:82, 37:16, 36:78, 37:53, 56:47). The Qur'an expresses assumptions that Caroline Walker Bynum explores among early and medieval Christians, namely that "formal and material continuity is necessary for survival of body and that the survival of body is necessary for self."[2]

Sarra Tlilli has demonstrated that the words popularly taken to signify the soul in the Qur'an, *nafs* and *ruh*, are not interchangeable synonyms but appear with distinct meanings. *Nafs* refers to a "self" and appears in the Qur'an not only with reference to ensouled humans but also various entities, such as God and even jahiliyya deities. Challenging later interpretive traditions, Tlilli argues that *ruh* (which Tlilli renders as "blown breath") never explicitly appears in the Qur'an as "soul" but more precisely refers to God's acts of breathing life into his creations. The Qur'an shrugs at those who might seek a concrete theory of the soul: "And they ask you about *al-ruh*. Say, 'It is the command of my Lord, and humanity has not been given knowledge except a little'" (17:85).

In contrast with the Qur'an, hadith literature often uses *nafs* and *ruh* interchangeably to describe a soul that may or may not be a physical part of the body. In hadith sources, the soul leaves the body at death and then returns to the grave until resurrection. Though a soul does not typically pass through multiple bodies (apart from consideration of the restored body on the Day as a new creation), a martyr's soul occupies the body of a green bird hanging among the fruit and trees of paradise.[3] In addition to being locatable in space and time (i.e., entering and leaving bodies), souls can theoretically become detectable to the senses, smelling either sweet or foul in relation to the deceased's faith.[4] But the sources also provide traditions in which a human's (or animal's) *nafs* refers to its "life" or "mind" and *ruh* seems to signify a generic "spirit" or life-force possessed by animals that are not ensouled as well as humans. In the early centuries of Islam, Tlilli explains, the concept of *ruh* as a soul that becomes detached from the body at death was not a given; the concept developed over time and gradually exerted force on the meanings found in the Qur'an.[5] Facing challenges similar to those experienced by Christian theologians such as Tertullian regarding the nature of the soul, Muslim theologians debated whether or not this soul was corporeal or entirely distinct from the body. If the soul was entirely immaterial, rather than a substance composed of atoms that occupied physical space, how could it enter, leave, and return to a material body? How could an immaterial soul have a material container? But if the soul is corporeal, what would this mean for the concept of the "torment of the grave," in which the dead are confronted by angel interrogators and punishers—how could a body that has disintegrated into dust undergo torture? Some thinkers, such as Avicenna, conceptualized the afterlife through a soul-body dualism that favored the immortality of the soul over bodily resurrection, while al-Ghazali and others defended the bodily resurrection in part through a corporealized soul. Regarding the soul's ability to experience interrogation and torture in the grave after the body has decomposed, for example, al-Ghazali writes that only comprehension is necessary, which does not require a body that can see or hear but rather a particular "atom" of the heart.[6] Even while defending bodily resurrection against Avicenna, however, al-Ghazali's arguments that one could believe in both a bodily resurrection and incorporeal soul contributed to promoting the incorporeal soul as an Islamic concept. In short, the questions of Muhammad's postmortem condition, the status of his soul in relation to his body, and his sentience in the grave are not entirely isolated to prophetic bodies but collide with broader issues in Muslim theological disputations, including questions of interpretation with immediate stakes for the fate of normal, nonprophetic bodies in their graves.

For imaginaries of Muhammad that prioritize the transcendent beauty and perfection of his body as proof of his prophetic ontology—a body that smells better than musk and feels softer than silk, emanates light, and provides medicinal and metaphysical protection in his urine—what potential challenges arise with rotting flesh that could provoke revulsion? What changes if a prophetic corpse can decay like any other? For Kristeva, abjection toward corporeal waste finds its most intense expression in horror at the corpse, in which the body at large becomes waste and transitory, mixed matter.[7] Our discussion here investigates the problem of Muhammad's corpse potentially becoming Kristeva's "utmost of abjection," "death infecting life," and "the border that has encroached everything."[8] Could Muhammad's body possibly signify what his Companions must "permanently thrust aside in order to live?"[9]

The Qur'an speaks of Muhammad's death as a likely future, reminding believers that messengers had died in the past and asking them whether they would turn away "if he was to die or be killed" (3:144). The earliest sources attribute Muhammad's death to poison; in Ibn Ishaq's narrative, a Jewish woman named Zaynab bint Harith poisons a lamb that she had roasted, making sure to put most of her poison in the shoulder after learning that it is Muhammad's favorite part of the animal. Muhammad takes a bite but before he can swallow, the meat warns him that it was poisoned. Zaynab confesses and tells the Prophet, "You know what you have done to my people." She also reveals that she had poisoned him with the understanding that if he were a mere king, she would rid herself of him; if he were a genuine prophet, he would be alerted of her plot. The account also notes that Bishr, who had swallowed some of the meat, died. By this report alone, it would appear that Muhammad was saved from assassination by a miraculous intervention, which also means that he passed Zaynab's test. However, Ibn Ishaq follows this with a separate account in which Muhammad mentions the incident during his final illness, telling Bishr's sister, "This is the time in which I feel a deadly pain from what I ate with your brother at Khaybar." The latter account also mentions that God honored Muhammad with death as a martyr.[10] As Etan Kohlberg has shown, the link between Muhammad's death and his attempted poisoning appears only in the second report, suggesting that Muhammad's eventual martyrdom reflects a later supplement to what had first been a story of divine protection.[11]

Hadith sources assert that years after the incident, Muhammad died from the poison. In some narrations, Muhammad's physical pain becomes a demonstration of his favored status. A'isha narrates Muhammad's promise that every moment of discomfort, even the prick of a thorn, removes sins;[12] in the same section of Muslim's *Sahih*, she also relates that she had never seen anyone who suffered more in severe illness than her husband.[13] When Muhammad is asked to identify the people who are most severely tested, he answers, "The prophets."[14] Muhammad's pain becomes a miracle that proves his status. The poisoning serves as evidence of Muhammad's station both for his initial survival and the fact that years later, God finally granted him the privilege of a martyr's death. Numerous references to Muhammad's poisoning at Khaybar appear in the developing hadith corpus and enjoy canonical privilege, though details vary between Companions and sources. Depending on the report, hadith texts can reveal that Muhammad felt lingering pains from the poison for the rest of his life, eventually died from the poison, or learned that the meat had been poisoned without even taking a bite. The Six Books canon includes narrations of Muhammad, speaking from his deathbed, attributing his affliction to the poisoned meat and declaring that it has cut his aorta[15] but also a report in which Muhammad receives the meat upon his conquest of Khaybar and immediately gathers the Jews to expose their conspiracy, with no indication that Muhammad ever tasted the meat.[16] Treatments of the incident in Abu Dawud's *Sunan* include an Abu Hurayra narration in which Muhammad suffers from the poison for years until it finally cuts his aorta[17] as well as a Jabir ibn ʿAbd Allah report in which Muhammad is saved by the foreleg talking to him and undergoes cupping as a medical precaution, while multiple Companions die from eating the meat.[18]

The Qur'an speaks on Muhammad's possible or inevitable death but not his postmortem condition or its significance for his community. In early sira/maghazi works, mixed messages emerge concerning the prophetic corpse. In Ma'mar's *Maghazi*, Muhammad's uncle ʿAbbas ibn ʿAbd al-Muttalib answers ʿUmar's refusal to accept Muhammad's death with a statement that would have sparked controversy in a later age: "Indeed, his flesh decays like any other person's."[19] In contrast, Ibn Hisham's recension of Ibn Ishaq reports that Muhammad's postmortem body was unlike ordinary corpses, but the report does not provide further detail on what made his corpse unique.[20]

In early sources, Muhammad's dead body appears as a site of uncertainties. The potential disintegration of boundaries between Muhammad and other bodies threatens an unwanted nearness rather than hope for baraka to seep from one body into another. It seems noteworthy that while sira/maghazi literatures report that Muhammad's bodily by-products displayed miraculous properties, and that Companions desired connection to Muhammad and his bodily baraka through them—even ingesting his blood directly from a wound—these narratives only relate to Muhammad's body while he remains alive. After the life is gone and the fluids dried up, the power of Muhammad's body to transmit baraka appears to have vanished. As far as one can gather from the sources, Companions who possessed hairs of Muhammad had obtained them during his life; traditions do not portray Companions expressing desire for fragments of the prophetic corpse. There is no depiction of Companions attempting to salvage hairs, nails, teeth, or other traces from his dead body, no expression of interest in the heart that had been washed and enhanced by angelic surgery, and no one seeks the ultimate connection of consuming his flesh. While by-products from Muhammad's living body could be cherished after his death, Muhammad's decomposing flesh does not provide his Companions with material access to baraka. Possibilities for Muhammad's baraka to extend from his mortal remains into his community are further denied in the narration found in Ma'mar's *Maghazi*, attributed to A'isha and Ibn 'Abbas, in which Muhammad speaks of curses upon the Christians and Jews for having established their prophets' graves as places of worship.[21]

Early sources also remain unclear as to what this postmortem body can do. While subjected to normal processes of material rot, Muhammad's corpse remains protected when threatened with the exposure of his nakedness; though emptied of its prophetic life, the flesh retains sufficient prophetic ontology to warrant divine intervention on its behalf.[22] Both Abu Bakr and 'Ali show affection for the corpse: Abu Bakr in removing the shroud to kiss Muhammad's face, 'Ali in his remarks on Muhammad's persisting sweetness as he washed the body.[23] Finally, al-Mughira's boast of entering Muhammad's grave and becoming the last person to have touched him complicates the absolute abjection of his corpse. The sira/maghazi literatures produce an unstable relationship of Muhammad's postmortem body to abjection and an unpredictable capacity for connecting with other bodies and transmitting baraka to them.

While Ma'mar's *Maghazi* survives through its inclusion in the *Musannaf* of his student, 'Abd al-Razzaq al-San'ani, the apparently casual attitude toward prophetic decay displayed by Muhammad's uncle 'Abbas (telling 'Umar that Muhammad's "flesh decays like any other person's")[24] remains at odds with the representations of Muhammad's dead body in early hadith collections. Examination of the hadith sources reveals an intensifying stake in the preservation of Muhammad's postmortem remains, which develops in answer to a soteriological crisis. Questions regarding Muhammad's ongoing relationship to his community appear in these sources to provoke Muhammad's promises that his body will remain intact and continue to be operational as a prophetic body.

This change in treatments of Muhammad's postmortem condition is not absolute within the sources considered here, as observed in the archive of Ibn Sa'd. The *Tabaqat* includes reports that Companions had delayed Muhammad's burial until they were certain that he had died (as opposed to having ascended like Jesus or entered into a forty-day occultation like Moses); certainty is attained by the observable signs that Muhammad's body underwent typical human decomposition. These reports mention details of Muhammad's deteriorating corpse that confirmed his death, such as his stomach bloating, an unspecified change in his little finger, and his fingernails turning green.[25] An isolated report in the *Tabaqat* treats the Seal's departure as proof that Muhammad had died. According to this narration, Asma' bint 'Umays places her hand between Muhammad's shoulders, after which she confirms his death because the Seal has disappeared.[26]

Alongside explicit depictions of a corpse that could inspire revulsion and horror, Ibn Sa'd also includes a report in which Muhammad promises that the earth does not hold sway over the bodies of prophets.[27] Ibn Hanbal and Ibn Abi Shayba provide a tradition in which Muhammad promises that the earth has been divinely prohibited from "eating the bodies of prophets."[28] Muhammad attests to the preservation of his corporeal integrity in response to Companions' asking how he can hear their prayers after he has died. According to the operational logic of this tradition, Muhammad requires an intact body to continue bearing witness to the deeds of his community. His body must remain preserved in order to maintain the links upon which his Companions' soteriological welfare depends.

The tradition of a corporeally intact Muhammad who can hear prayers and bear witness to his community's righteousness from his grave, his body remaining intact and alive (or, if not exactly alive, at least sentient) as a resource for connection between Companions and himself, exists within the sources alongside Muhammad's reported condemnation of those who make their prophets' graves into places of worship. Variants of the tradition tend to refer to earlier communities that had been cursed for this transgression, often specifying Jews and Christians; one version includes A'isha's explanation that had it not been for the Jews' and Christians' excesses, Muhammad would have been placed in a grave that surpassed all others, but he had feared that people would treat his grave as a masjid.[29] Muhammad's postmortem body both opens and closes relations, simultaneously enabling continued access to beneficent energies for his community and functioning as a site of prohibition and danger, a boundary marking the limits of proper piety against disobedience. While the sources present detached satellites of Muhammad's body, such as his preserved hairs or bottled sweat, as baraka generators that remain potent long after his death, his buried body's capacity to transmit baraka remains unstable.

Within canonically advantaged sources, Muhammad's protection against decomposition triumphs. The Six Books canon gives multiple affirmations of Muhammad's preservation against decay and the earth's prohibition from consuming prophets' bodies,[30] along with a tradition in which Muhammad witnesses Moses praying in his grave, evidencing a special state for postmortem prophets.[31] In a section of his *Sunan* on visiting graves, Abu Dawud's collection preserves a tradition in which Muhammad proclaims that God temporarily returns his ruh to his body so that he can greet those who greet him.[32] Outside the Six Books, ambiguity persists: al-Darimi's *Sunan* includes reports of both Muhammad's promise that the earth had been forbidden from eating prophets' bodies[33] and ʿAbbas's flippant remark that Muhammad's body would be subjected to normal decomposition.[34]

In another report from al-Darimi that does not appear in the Six Books, A'isha reveals special powers or properties of the postmortem prophetic body. Al-Darimi's A'isha still provides Muhammad's statement that God had cursed Jews and Christians for taking their prophets' graves as houses of worship.[35] However, al-Darimi's introduction to his *Sunan* also includes a subsection, titled "God's Honors upon His Prophet after His Death," that presents A'isha advocating for the prophetic grave as a site at which believers can engage unseen forces. Aws ibn ʿAbd Allah narrates that during an intense drought in Medina, A'isha instructed people to make a window at Muhammad's grave so that there was no obstruction between his grave and the sky. Her plan worked, resulting in abundant rain that restored the grass and caused camels to "burst open from fatness."[36] She additionally narrates Muhammad's statement that whenever a prophet was placed in his grave, 70,000 angels descended upon it.[37] While A'isha reports that communities earn divine curses for worshiping their prophets' graves, she also affirms the postmortem remains of prophets as special sites. In A'isha's corpus, the question is not whether prophets' graves are host to beneficent energies but rather what is the appropriate manner of engaging them.

Muhammad's postmortem corporeality preserves significant coherence in later sources. The possibility for Muhammad's corpse to decay in typical fashion, evidenced in earlier sira/maghazi discussions of his postmortem status and narrations in Ibn Sa'd's *Tabaqat* of Companions observing changes in his body, has been shut down: while in his grave, Muhammad remains conscious. The tradition of Muhammad assuring his Companions that the earth has been prohibited from consuming prophets' bodies consistently receives inclusion.[38] Additionally, the sources emphatically assert Muhammad's continued sentience in the grave as a natural condition of prophetic bodies. Abu Nu'aym provides Anas's report that Muhammad said, "The prophets are praying in their graves" (*Al-anbiya' fi quburihim yusallun*).[39] Abu Ya'la's version in his *Musnad* adds a single word that intensifies Muhammad's assertion: "The prophets are *alive* in their graves, praying" (*Al-anbiya' ahya' fi quburihim yusallun*).[40] Bayhaqi compiled an entire collection devoted to hadiths concerning the lives of prophets in their graves, the straightforwardly titled *Lives of the Prophets in Their Graves* (*Hayat al-Anbiya' fi Quburihim*),[41] that includes the above narrations and another

Anas report in which Muhammad explains that no prophet spends forty days in his grave before arriving in the hands of God until God breathes life into their forms.[42] For Muhammad and other men with whom he shares in prophethood, the grave is not a site of decay. His corporeal integrity fully preserved, Muhammad remains capable not only of bearing witness to the prayers of his community but also of performing his own acts of devotion.

Muhammad's corpse retains its power to connect with other bodies, and through these connections provide greater access to baraka, through their visits to his grave. Bayhaqi and Tabarani both offer reports of Muhammad promising, "Whoever performs hajj and visits my grave after my death is like whoever visited me in my life."[43] Muhammad's grave enables access to baraka, whether baraka should be understood here as a force emanating from the remains of Muhammad's materiality or divinely awarded credits earned for approved devotional acts.

This vision of the prophetic corpse as conscious, alive, and active in worship developed over time. While the Qur'an displays no interest in a postmortem Muhammad and early sources envision a prophetic corpse that can decompose and even elicit disgust, canonical and postcanonical sources affirm Muhammad's body as fully intact and aware of those who greet him. As with other questions of the Prophet's body, however, there is more to consider than a straightforward "A to B" trajectory of change. A closer look at Bayhaqi's *Hayat al-Anbiya'* highlights the variegated transmission networks that inform ideas of Muhammad's body. In the chains of transmission for the book's twenty-one narrations, Anas appears as the source for eight reports, Abu Hurayra provides five, and Ibn 'Abbas and Ibn Mas'ud are each credited with one. A'isha does not tell us that her husband remains conscious or alive in his grave.

While A'isha's narrations tend to normalize her husband's body, however, her archive contains its own heterogeneities. Among her accounts of Muhammad dying in her arms, Ibn Hanbal's *Musnad* offers a unique version with a rare detail: A'isha could smell Muhammad's soul as it left his body. Muhammad "died between my lungs and my throat," she tells her nephew 'Urwa. "When his soul [*nafsihi*] left, I've never found perfume that smelled better than it."[44]

Fatima

Muhammad's only daughter to survive him also changes as the literature takes shape. From the Qur'an, which lacks clear references to Fatima, to the early Sira literature, which mentions Fatima in passing, to narrations of Muhammad's special affection for her in the hadith collections of the ninth century CE, Fatima's significance grows alongside the expansion of hadith literature. As discussed in previous chapters, hadith archives of early ninth-century scholars depict Muhammad assigning special privilege to Fatima: she is a piece of him, and whoever angers her has angered him; she is named the "master of women," often with cautious disclaimers that clarify Fatima's proper relationship to Mary and other great women of sacred history; and during Muhammad's final illness, he gives her advance knowledge that both their deaths are imminent, and informs her that she will be the first from his house to see him again. Beyond these traditions, it can be demonstrated that during the early centuries of the corpus's development, Fatima becomes increasingly salient as a satellite of the baraka-transmitting prophetic body. While a growing body of scholarship has examined Fatima's development into a transcendent mythic character, I resist the narrative that her growing significance and mythologization is purely a Shi'i movement. Fatima's elaboration, while taking place in what has been called the "Shi'i Century,"[45] is not reducible to a Shi'i project or a uniquely Shi'i conception of the body that can be contrasted to Sunni bodies—especially when we recognize the critical impossibility of fully separating proto-Shi'ism from proto-Sunnism within Sunni hadith canon. In this assemblage that has been termed the "Sunni hadith corpus," the intensified transcendence of Fatima's body reflects the significant heterogeneity of that corpus and the multiplicity of voices contributing to it.

While the hadith collections of the ninth century do not explicitly convey investments in special qualities of Fatima's corporeality, reports from tenth-century sources do treat Fatima's body as a powerful signifier. One such narration, appearing in Tabarani's *Mu'jam al-Kabir* and Khatib's *Tarikh*, assigns Fatima an origin that further establishes Muhammad as mediator between paradise and earthly life. The report, presented as Muhammad's recollection of his ascension, asserts that he carried a portion of paradise within his body as he returned to this world, after which the portion left his body and became his daughter. Muhammad's body, therefore, becomes a vehicle by which remnants of paradise can be transferred into this world. Fatima's body becomes significant not only for her being the daughter of the Messenger of God, having originated within his baraka-laden corporeality but also for having origins outside his body, as matter from paradise.

Interestingly, the account of Muhammad revealing Fatima's origin is attributed to her stepmother (and antagonist) A'isha, who appears in the narrative as confused and perhaps jealous of the affection that she witnesses between father and daughter. A'isha's report of Fatima's ontological supremacy becomes provocative not only for its sectarian consequences but also for betraying A'isha's usual treatment of prophetic bodies:

> I saw the Messenger of God, God bless him and give him peace, kissing Fatima. I said, "O Messenger of God! I saw you doing a thing that I had not seen you do before." He said, "O Humayra [Muhammad's pet name for A'isha, diminutive of *hamra'*, in reference to A'isha's fair ("red") complexion],[46] when I ascended to the heavens, I was admitted into paradise. I stopped upon a tree from the trees of paradise of which I had not seen a better tree, or whiter leaves, or more delicious fruit than its fruit. I took one of its fruits and ate it; then it became semen in my sexual organs. When I descended to Earth and had intercourse with Khadija, she became pregnant with Fatima. When I long for smelling paradise, I smell Fatima. O Humayra, Fatima is not like the Adamic women, and she is not defective like they are defective."[47]

Through his journey to paradise and conception of Fatima, Muhammad produces an embodied link between paradise and earthly life. Muhammad's body deposits a remnant of paradise into his wife's body, thereby producing a daughter who exists as a material trace of paradise in this world; as with the superiority of Muhammad's sweat to perfume, Fatima's natural scent displays her exceptional relationship to flows of baraka. She *is* a flow of baraka herself, an extension not only of her prophetic father's corporeality into a new body but also an extension of one plane of existence into another: the presence of Fatima's body in the world complicates the spatial borders of paradise. While Fatima functions as a mode by which Muhammad's body enables connections between his Companions and the realm of the unseen, Fatima's body also maintains a connection for her father, as her bodily scent soothes the pain of his separation from paradise.

Fatima's exceptional corporeality, remaining corporeal, also remains gendered. The sources affirm that believers will see God and prophets in paradise, but Fatima appears to be privileged by a prohibition against witnessing her: Tabarani reports Muhammad stating that on the day of judgment, the people of assembly (*ahl al-jam'a*) will be told to lower their gazes when Fatima passes by, covered in green or red.[48] Muhammad also privileges his daughter as exempt from the "defects" of normal women. Whereas Muhammad's interactions with extrahuman forces and metaphysical realms reconstruct him as an exemplar of performative masculinity (as in the narration of Gabriel empowering Muhammad's sexuality with performance-enhancing supplements),[49] Fatima's paradisiacal origin grants her a degree of separation from typical human bodies. This separation undergoes further articulation in another report, appearing in al-Khatib's *Tarikh Baghdad*, in which Ibn ʿAbbas narrates that Muhammad said, "My daughter Fatima is an Adamic huri. She has never had a period and she has never menstruated, and her name is Fatima because God weaned her [*fatamaha*] and those who love her from the fire."[50] As an Adamic huri, Fatima possesses a unique corporeality that positions her body as liminal between earthly women and the extrahuman maidens of paradise; she has human parents but also originates from paradise and, like the hur, remains exempt from an experience of earthly women.[51] Because she does not menstruate, Fatima also transcends the "deficiency in din" that Muhammad ascribes to women for their loss of prayers and fasting due to ritual impurity.[52]

Reflecting the difference in ways that men's and women's bodily fluids are imagined as polluting and contaminating,[53] Fatima's bodily deabjection brings a different set of gendered consequences than that of her father. While Muhammad's blood is treated in some traditions as a facilitator of baraka's flow, demonstrating his exceptional ontology through the power of his bodily products to achieve special effects, the sources do not imagine Fatima's gendered bleeding as endowed with baraka or any trace of her special origins. Instead of converting menstruation's threat of unwanted connections and violations of bodily boundaries into a desirable linkage to Muhammad's body and material traces of paradise (treating Fatima's menstrual garment, for example, as a point of contact with baraka or glimpse of her transcendent ontology in the same manner as a bowl of Muhammad's blood from his cupping), the sources erase menstruation entirely from Fatima's body. Similarly, the sources do not report Fatima's waste, hair, sweat, saliva, or fingernails as transmitting baraka in the manner of her father's corporeal by-products, despite her paradisiacal origins and status as an earthly huri.

Fatima's sexed body extends her father's corporeality and connects him to other bodies first in her marriage to ʿAli. Tabarani reports Fatima having "guarded her vagina" (*hasanat farjaha*) for which God protected her and kept the fire away from her.[54] In becoming sexually accessible to ʿAli, Fatima intensifies ʿAli's connection to her father. Fatima's body mediates between Muhammad and ʿAli, who are already linked by their shared lineage, and enables them to form a new assemblage. In the *Mu'jam al-Kabir*,

Fatima's function as a point of triangulation between Muhammad and ʿAli positions her not only as a mediator of their relationship but also as subject to extrahuman mediations in the larger homosocial realm of divine, angelic, and prophetic communication. Tabarani includes a narration in which Muhammad announces that Fatima's marriage to ʿAli was a divine order that God had communicated to him via Gabriel.[55] ʿAli's embodied connection to Fatima links him not only to her father's corporeality but also to an extrahuman chain of command into which their marriage enters them as participants.

Muhammad's extension of his prophetic corporeality through the marriage of Fatima and ʿAli reaches future bodies through their acts of reproduction. The complexity and instability of prophetic deabjection finds expression in the paradox of his daughter's body, which becomes pregnant without having a menstrual cycle. In her engagement of Kristevan abjection, Grosz writes of the "cultural horror of menstruation," which signifies not precisely the difference between male and female but rather the difference between men and potential mothers.[56] Fatima's maternal body, which has been exempted from the experience of menstrual bodies, enables future connections to Muhammad's corporeal baraka by giving birth to his grandchildren, but without the menstrual body's threat of unwanted connections and violations of bodily boundaries.

Sources from this period represent familial connections to the prophetic body as enduring into a time at which other such lineages are broken, providing traditions in which Muhammad states that on the day of resurrection, all families and relations will be broken except his own.[57] Prophetic privilege enables connections between Muhammad and Fatima's children beyond typical ways their relationship would have been socially constructed, as Tabarani's *Muʾjam al-Kabir* and al-Khatib al-Baghdadi's *Tarikh Baghdad* include narrations in which Muhammad presents Fatima's children as the exception to conventions of patrilineal genealogy. In this tradition, Muhammad states that while most lineages are traced through fathers, Fatima's children will trace their lineage through her, since Muhammad is their lineage and guardian.[58] Muhammad's prophetic station positions him as a metapatriarch who can overrule ʿAli's paternity and rewrite the ancestral lines for his grandchildren. Tabarani also includes the tradition in which Fatima brings Hasan and Husayn to Muhammad, declares them to be Muhammad's sons, and asks that they inherit from him, to which Muhammad responds by naming his exceptional qualities that they will embody.[59] According to a report that Tabarani attributes to Ibn al-Zubayr's son Mus'ab, Fatima herself was known by a familial honorific that rewrote her lineal relations: Umm Abiha, "Mother of Her Father."[60]

While the valorization of Fatima and her children appears early in the development of the hadith corpus, later sources such as Tabarani's *Mu'jam al-Kabir* demonstrate an amplified investment in the relation of Fatima's corporeality to her father's baraka. Being Muhammad's biological progeny, she appears as a bodily product and also as an extension of his sexed body. The late tradition of Fatima being conceived immediately after the ascension (from paradisiacal fruit that Muhammad's body processed into semen) enhances the powers of Muhammad's body to stretch its network of connections even across the boundary between worlds. Prophetic digestive and reproductive systems mediate between planes of existence, as Muhammad's internal bodily processes convert paradisiacal fruit into reproductive material, and his penis deposits a trace of paradise into this world. The fruit tradition as reflected in this narration from Tabarani stands as an outlier in relation to A'isha's customary treatment of the prophetic body. As demonstrated in earlier chapters, A'isha's corpus often downplays the possibilities for Muhammad's body to be imagined as substantively unique and miraculous. A'isha, after all, reports that her husband "was a human like humans; he removed lice from his garments."[61] She consistently gives Muhammad's semen relevance only as a *fiqh* problem and stain to be cleaned, with no special significance related to its emission from a baraka-transmitting body. The report of Fatima's paradisiacal origin, in profound contrast, portrays A'isha as confirming the power of Muhammad's semen to serve as a point of interdimensional mediation, in large part through the event of his body traveling between worlds (which also stands in tension with A'isha's usual treatment of Muhammad's ascension as strictly a dream or vision rather than a bodily event). The narration of Fatima's otherworldly origins represents an opening of Muhammad's corporeal powers not only due to the content of the tradition itself but also for its attribution to an otherwise skeptical reporter of the prophetic body.

For its powers and limits, Fatima's body highlights the gendering of baraka transactions. Linkages forged by encounters with Muhammad's body and its by-products such as his spit remain gendered: Muhammad executes tahnik as a patriarchal initiation, performing the role of communal father exclusively for the community's newborn sons. Similarly, while examining Muhammad's acts of spitting into men's ailing eyes, open wounds, or corpses for the purposes of healing or blessing, I could not find these traditions paralleled by reports of his spitting into or on the bodies of women. Nor does Fatima appear in the sources as acting upon her privileged biology—whether as a product of Muhammad or paradise—to similarly operate as a public disseminator of baraka. She does not spit into her husband's eye and improve his vision. A'isha does appear to achieve self-authorization through her superior bodily intimacy to Muhammad, but she does not explicitly derive her power from special properties that could be communicable through his bodily products. This is to say not that bodies become meaningless in A'isha's narrations but rather that her intercorporeal linkage to Muhammad materializes by different modes than that of male Companions.

In its work as a baraka-machine, Muhammad's body becomes simultaneously enhanced and constrained by its status as a sexed body. Because Muhammad's socialization in his world is subject to gendered possibilities and limits, routes to his bodily baraka differ in relation to the gendering of bodies with which he interacts. This means that a Companion's degree of contact with Muhammad's bodily baraka depends significantly on whether that Companion is a man, a woman with whom he is in a sexual relationship, a woman whose close familial relation to him deregulates their interactions, or unrelated women from the community, some of whom might still have privileged access (as in Umm Sulaym). Umm Sulaym does not put her hands or mouth to Muhammad's body to obtain his sweat but obtains his sweat from a leather mat on which he had been sleeping. The bottle then becomes an instrument by which Umm Sulaym can loosen the structure of a largely homosocial baraka economy.

Gender qualifies Muhammad's prophethood. To argue that Muhammad's body matters—as a specimen of the perfect human, a proof of his prophetic status, or as a conduit through which beneficent energies flow between worlds—provokes consideration of what it means that his body has been marked as masculine. To ask what the prophetic body can do and how it achieves connections with other bodies, even (perhaps especially) bodies that it has produced, requires attention to the gendered openings and closings of access to that body.

Living Baraka

In this chapter, I turned to two questions of Muhammad's bodily baraka and its continued transmission after his death: first, the capacity of Muhammad's postmortem body to meaningfully link with those who encounter it; second, the body of his daughter Fatima, through whom Muhammad's biological legacy persists in the world.

Speaking on a hypothetical but perhaps inevitable future, the Qur'an asks what Muhammad's followers would do if he died. Muslim biographical materials on Muhammad have always readily acknowledged that his physical life came to an end. Muhammad was not depicted as biologically immortal in the sense that he could forever walk and talk among the living as one of them. The end of his conventional embodied life, however, did not mean the closure of access to his baraka or the end of his corporeal limits, particularly as the hadith corpus developed. The preservation of his body's coherence meant that he could remain alive (in a sense) and sentient in his grave.

Beyond the marvels of dead prophetic bodies, Muhammad's body continued to extend its reach and exist beyond his own life in the rather conventional way to which so many humans aspire: he biologically reproduced, and his grandchildren through Fatima produced children of their own, who in turn continued his corporeal legacy into future generations. Because Muhammad's body was special, however, the bodies that came from him were also special. His body became a vehicle for transporting a remnant of paradise into this world, which manifested with the conception of his daughter Fatima. In turn, Fatima gave birth to Hasan and Husayn, who were designated by their grandfather as masters of the youths of paradise. While modern controversies might lead us to assume that the Sunni hadith corpus resolutely opposes those who seek baraka at graves, many would similarly imagine the significance of Muhammad's progeny to be entirely a Shi'i concern outside the bounds of Sunni hadith sources. Nonetheless, the Sunni hadith corpus valorizes the bodies derived from Muhammad's body. In the cases of both Muhammad's postmortem existence and the continuation of his lineage through Fatima, the notion of a singular "ahl al-sunna" position on prophetic corporeality disintegrates.

Conclusions

The Nabi without Organs (NwO)

This book began with an anecdote shared by Yasir Qadhi at an AlMaghrib weekend seminar, in which Qadhi referred to the drinking of Muhammad's sweat as "baraka." While some students might have been made uncomfortable by the narrative of a pious Muslim and medical doctor consuming another person's sweat—even the sweat of the Prophet within the comparatively safe realm of a dream—the notion of baraka becoming attainable through Muhammad's body resonated with the larger theme of the seminar, which was presented as an introduction to Bukhari's hadith scholarship. In his lectures, Qadhi emphasized the power of what he called the "living isnad," the chain of reporters that continues to grow through oral transmission, as producing an "embodied link" to the Prophet. Qadhi argued that through these intergenerational teacher-student linkages spanning across the centuries to our present, living isnads create the possibility of encountering "somebody in your midst who has only twenty people between himself and the Prophet." That this *somebody* indeed operates with and through a *body* is inseparable from the living isnad's power; prophetic knowledge survives as an exchange between bodies. In the context of the seminar, this corporeal link materialized via Qadhi's own body: Qadhi told the class, "I am connected," due to his having learned prophetic traditions directly from teachers who possessed chains of face-to-face encounters reaching back to the Companions, a privileged class of knowers who had achieved intercorporeity with the Prophet. The development of the hadith corpus, its promises of truth-making power, and the claims of its professional experts to supreme orthodoxy-making authority depended on the construction of this "Companion" category and its claimed relation to Muhammad.

Hadith transmission, Qadhi informed the class, constituted a "nodal system" in which the nodes were scholars, and to link with a well-connected node could instantly plug a student into the entire grid. Qadhi's reception of hadiths as face-to-face transmissions from his teachers entered him into their lineages, attaching him to prominent nodes such as Shawkani (1759–1839), Shah Wali Allah Dihlawi (1703–62), and Sunni hadith tradition's all-time master node, Bukhari, and turning Qadhi himself into a node by which others could enter the system. Qadhi's physical presence in the lecture hall thus placed his seminar's participants into a closer physical relation to the Prophet. As the embodied link standing at the front of the room, he offered an opportunity for attendees of his seminar: students who memorized a hadith and recited it in front of him earned a teaching permission (*ijaza*) from Qadhi for that particular hadith, becoming links in living chains.[1]

Through an investigation of Muhammad's body as depicted in the nodal system's treatment of the Prophet and Companions, ultimately meaning the system's discourses about itself, I have emphasized the explicitly *embodied* dimension of Qadhi's "embodied link." When the hadith corpus constructs Muhammad's body as a powerful conductor of baraka, it also reconstructs the bodies with which this body has formed a web of relations. Through its representation of these bodies as forming a new assemblage, a grid across which baraka circulates, the scholarly compilers of the hadith corpus contribute to their self-authorization. The Companions are more than trustworthy eyewitness reporters: they are body-witnesses, their bodies having been enhanced by their encounters with Muhammad's presence. As illustrated in the episode of Abu Hurayra finding his ability to remember Muhammad's words enhanced after Muhammad rubbed his cloak, the hadith corpus represents more than an archive of rigorously vetted data or arguments for methodological mastery and reliably transmitted discourse. What ends up as "Muhammad's body" reflects a baraka-infused mingling of bodies that have combined their forces. When providing narrations of baraka as a material transmission from Muhammad's body into Companions' bodies, the hadith scholars' nodal system also says something about its own power and the broader network of bodies that comprise it. Narrations of baraka flowing via material vehicles and pathways from Muhammad's body into those of his Companions authorize the hadith partisans' claims of epistemological supremacy and the truth-making power of the isnad. The bodies make a method. Disassembled for consideration of its parts and their possibilities, the prophetic body reveals its most powerful parts to be the bodies into which it enters relations, the machines that plug into Muhammad's baraka-machine and thus multiply its power beyond his boundaries and even their own.

Qadhi's embodied nodal system in fact consists of numerous nodal systems that have become sufficiently entangled to give the impression of a singular voice. The construction of Sunni Islam and its emphasis on the Companions' collective integrity reflect an interpenetration of networks into the retroactive appearance of unity. As the product of these interpenetrative nodal systems, the literary corpus reflects not a singular whole but rather a reterritorialized composition of elements, each containing internal heterogeneity in terms of methodological, sectarian, and geographically centered networks. The assemblage of materials marked as "the hadith corpus" resists a coherent systematization of prophetic bodies and their relationships to baraka. While pointing to a general move in the literature toward representing Muhammad's body as a powerful conduit of baraka, I caution against the assumption of a massive editorial conspiracy and absolute reterritorialization in which one vision of the prophetic body entirely erases another. The hadith sources exhibit a general amplification of the prophetic body's power to transform bodies it encounters, but they do not achieve a unifying logic of the body that operates consistently throughout major and minor canons. Between two hadith scholars' collections, or even between the reports of two Companions such as Anas and A'isha (their names in turn representing assemblages of their student networks, geographic bases, and posthumous branding as much as historical personalities), the prophetic body can be disassembled to reveal an inconsistency among its pieces. What can Muhammad's eyes do? Muhammad's corporeity does not appear as a self-contained, monolithic whole but rather as an ongoing process of movement among thousands of bodies, many of which preexisted a self-regulating field of "hadith science" with professional experts and sophisticated methodologies.

It is to the messiness and instability of these assemblages and their connecting parts that I turn in my concluding remarks. Deleuze and Guattari, Grosz explains, "see the body as elements or fragments of a desiring machine and themselves as composed of a series of desiring machines."[2] In their paradigmatic example, a woman nursing an infant constitutes a desiring-machine forged by the connection of a mouth-machine to a breast-machine. The mouth-machine and breast-machine themselves are composed of relations to other machines. At their point of connection, they facilitate flows between networks of machines, each machine itself defined by flows and relations. Deleuze and Guattari's prime desiring-machine, the nursing interface of mouth-machine to breast-machine, appears in Hasan al-Basri's ingestion of Umm Salama's milk as a facilitator of flows between these machines and a third, the "baraka-machine" of Muhammad's body that connects through Umm Salama's body to Hasan's body and forges a connection of milk kinship. Even years after Muhammad's death, leakages from the Umm Salama breast-machine enable access to his baraka-machine. For Abu Nu'aym's presentation of Hasan al-Basri in his *Hilya*, the linkage of Umm Salama's breast-machine to Hasan's mouth-machine further proliferates the baraka-machine's flows through Hasan's own legacy as an exemplary ascetic and preacher. Hasan's mouth-machine, having sucked wisdom and eloquence from the breast-machine, changes its function and delivers speech "like the speech of prophets," proliferating that wisdom and eloquence to a network of students and ultimately to their students.

Muhammad's body extends itself through countless combinations of desiring-machines. Like Deleuze and Guattari, the Sunni hadith corpus does not provide a systematic account of bodies, specifically Muhammad's body, or a coherent theorization of baraka and the potential routes by which baraka enters bodies and connects them to each other. The untheorized prophetic body becomes characterized not by fixed boundaries, stable unity, or internal consistency but rather by fragments and processes forever in motion and making or severing connections. The literary corpus constructs Muhammad's body as an assemblage of numerous Companions whose names operate as hubs in networks that can overlap, collaborate, and even compete with one another but do not come together as one transcendent hive-mind ordering the textual body with a singular intention.

As the literary corpus develops, Muhammad's body intensifies in its power to spill into other bodies and transmit baraka to them in part through substances and processes that undermine the boundaries between their bodies. Such phenomena, such as digestive waste, blood, and the decaying corpse, might typically provoke discomfort at the breaking down of bodily integrity.[3] In the case of Muhammad, however, these typically abjected substances and processes extend his body's limits in ways that do not render the prophetic body abject but rather connect him to other bodies in this baraka-transmitting power grid. With substances such as Muhammad's blood and urine demonstrating their powers as carriers of contagious prophetic baraka, it becomes seemingly impossible for the prophetic body to achieve an unwanted nearness to other bodies or provoke feelings of disgust or abjection. However, Muhammad's body does not undergo the typical fragmentation of postmortem bodies that would enable his baraka-transmitting flesh to extend its range of power in relics: his body remains intact and alive, denying not only the possibility of corpse abjection but also the potential for a prophetic corpse to be divided into pieces that, when spread out across the map, would expand the range of the body's baraka transmissions. While Muhammad's corporeality extends its reach through shrines devoted to his preserved hairs, contact relics, and footprints, his corpse remains coherent. The prophetic corpse's inability to provoke abjection comes not from the special properties of its fragments but rather from its protection against fragmentation.

While representations of Muhammad's body move toward deabjection, seen in constructions of his blood and urine as baraka-transmitting agents and the preservation of his bodily integrity postmortem, this movement is not absolute: it does not present a new narrative of the prophetic body that censors or purges all resisting narratives. This tension or even contradiction between reports arises from hadith masters' interests in expanding the bounds of the hadith corpus, flexing the comprehensive scope of their own scholarship, and privileging reliable chains of transmission over subjecting the reports to discourse analysis.[4] As the compilers of these collections treated all Companions as unimpeachable authorities—again, even as these Companions fought each other—and (usually) placed a higher premium on methodological than narrative consistency,[5] they produced a massive archive of reports without facing burdens of a systematized body or theory of baraka. In this process, they made a prophetic body that was considerably free from regulatory capture, capable of stripping away the rules inscribed on its parts and unwriting its content, becoming closer to its fullest potential for exceeding corporeal boundaries and achieving limitless new relations.

Instead of adhering to a systematic organization of its parts, Muhammad's body becomes, to draw from Grosz's reading of Deleuze and Guattari, "freely amenable to the flows and intensities of the desiring-machines that compose it."[6] This unorganized prophetic body, placed "in direct relations with the flows or particles of other bodies or things," reads as something akin to Deleuze and Guattari's Body without Organs (BwO).[7] The assortment of parts and processes that can be collectivized and named "Muhammad's body" does not undergo a reliable systemization but remains "permeated by unformed, unstable matters, by flows in all directions, by free intensities or nomadic singularities, by mad or transitory particles."[8] The sources construct Muhammad as a prophetic assemblage of parts through which baraka flows without a singular consistent organizing principle: the Nabi without Organs (NwO).

The Deleuzo-Guattarian Body without Organs does not literally lack organs but rather defies *organization*; it breaks down the reterritorialization of the body in which organs are assigned fixed duties that limit its potential for making connections. The NwO operates as a baraka-machine composed of smaller machines, but these machines will not be organized. Sometimes Muhammad's penis ejects pollutants that break ritual purity (depending on the fluid and the legal school judging it), but on other occasions it produces baraka-loaded fluids that can save one who ingests them from hellfire. His body can transmit a digested trace of paradise into another body, from which it will reemerge as a new body, a half-human, half-huri hybrid who operates in this world and produces new lines of bodies as a living remnant of another dimension. Muhammad's blood does not hold a consistent meaning or value—Ibn al-Zubayr, the small child and future anticaliph who drinks a bowl of prophetic blood, can either personally disturb Muhammad's sensibilities or earn protection from hellfire—and the prophetic anus is neither clearly prophetic nor merely an anus. Muhammad's heart, the locus of his intellect, was washed by angels and injected with material quantities of wisdom and faith but might have once contained a demonic portion that required surgical intervention. Depending on a particular intertextuality of reports, one could read Muhammad's heart prior to the angelic surgery as more capable of abjection than his anus, open wounds, or corpse. The Seal of Prophethood between Muhammad's shoulders could mark the closure of an angelic surgeon's incision or be a divinely ordained birthmark that signals his special destiny to learned men who interpret his body through their scriptures. Muhammad's porous skin, leaking sweat that makes perfume and transmits baraka, also receives and sends knowledge into his heart through the penetrating touch of a youthful god with cool hands, lush hair, a crown of pearls, and a bed of gold. Muhammad's parts comprise the prophetic body in relation to the desires of his Companions and other bodies that act with and upon them: these desires transform Muhammad's body parts into baraka-machines. Muhammad's body in these sources is not his own in the sense of a clearly demarcated entity separate from other bodies but (sometimes literally) bleeds, spits, sweats, and ejaculates into other bodies (or is opened, penetrated, and modified by them) and merges with them, forming a new body that itself lacks self-evident limits or a clear definition of its enhanced powers. "Muhammad's body" as it appears in these sources represents a sum of unstable relations, an assemblage of human and extrahuman bodies, Companions, angels, and even the cool-handed boy god flowing into and through one another, the terms of their exchanges in flux. The assemblage expands exponentially as bodies in this matrix report the prophetic body, and their own relations to it, to other bodies, thereby plugging more bodies into the grid. Those bodies in turn transmit their connections to new bodies that will also link to new bodies, and so on, producing chains of relations that culminate with the master compilers (and their student-transmitters) whose books reimagine this assemblage as a natural and bounded unity.

The extension of Muhammad's corporeality in turn extends the reach of those forces that act upon his body, that is, God and his angels, but also extends the relation-making powers of bodies upon which Muhammad has acted. As Muhammad's body forges linkages with the bodies of his Companions, the Companions in turn find their corporealities enhanced and extended. The development of the early hadith corpus accompanied the ongoing construction of "Companion" as a category, which signified a relationship to the Prophet in physical space. This privileged class then extended its own corporeality with that of Muhammad in its successor class, the Followers, and so on with the Followers of the Followers. Muhammad's body thus appears to merge with Companion bodies, which in turn enable linkages between Muhammad's body and future generations, forming a greater prophetic assemblage with intensified powers that spreads seemingly into infinity through baraka transactions.

Growing into a crystallized network of scholars that could weaponize their methodologies and canonical texts against rival networks, the hadith corpus gives an appearance of what Deleuze and Guattari would term a reterritorialization of Muhammad, a structuring and stratification of heterogeneous elements and the containment of these elements under one governing system.[9] But Muhammad's reterritorialization within a project as stratifying as Bukhari's *Sahih* cannot absolutely suppress the deterritorializing forces found in the latter's pages. The NwO does not depend exclusively on Qadhi's node or method to mingle bodies, since the same hadith corpus that authorizes Qadhi's transmission lineages also presents Muhammad's body as capable of appearing in believers' dreams. The dream visit from Muhammad, protected as conceptually "orthodox" within the hadith archive, can become a deterritorializing line of flight out of the archive's structures and limits. Dreaming's power as a line of flight becomes exemplified in Ibn al-'Arabi's controversial *Fusus al-Hikam*, attributed not to his own pen but rather to his reception of the text directly from Muhammad six centuries after the Prophet's death. Beyond finding support in canonical hadith sources, the *Fusus al-Hikam* becomes a kind of hadith itself, an extension of the corpus. It is not exactly "canonical," but canon signs its permission slip. Just as the reterritorialized assemblage preserves its hidden lines of flight, deterritorializations also carry the potential for reterritorialization, even becoming subject to alternative reterritorializations in new assemblages. Meanwhile, forces of reterritorialization in the assemblage seek to capture and regulate a deterritorializing dream of Muhammad to shut down its lines of flight (Qadhi will tell you that of course dreams cannot become the basis for law), assign the dream fixed duties and limits, and turn it into an *organ*.

Like dreams of Muhammad, baraka's material accessibility can also open and close lines of flight in the prophetic assemblage. Transmissions of baraka between bodies are not governed by any singular human agency, not even that of the Prophet himself. As Dietrich von Denffer explains, "All methods of obtaining baraka can be used without the holder's intention to share, i.e. baraka can be inherited, transferred and stolen."[10] That someone could "steal" prophetic baraka becomes the formula for traditions in which Muhammad's bodily by-products such as sweat, urine, and blood circulate baraka in the community, as Companions take these materials without Muhammad's direction or permission. Muhammad does not tell anyone that drinking his urine or blood can help them until they have already done it.

Baraka's circulation between bodies subjects it to the gendered regulations and limits inscribed upon those bodies, but baraka's material accessibility can also make openings in seemingly homosocial closures. Umm Sulaym bottled the Prophet's sweat as he slept so that she could access its baraka for herself and her children. After Muhammad's death, she maintained her custody over what she had kept of his sweat and hair, which continued to work as satellites of his baraka-transmitting body. Umm Sulaym's custodianship of operational baraka illustrates a deterritorialized prophetic body, a rhizomatic multiplicity with no self-evident center of gravity but rather a multiplicity of centers: shrines housing the graves of holy people, places where they rested, artifacts that had belonged to them, even their footprints, capable of changing both the physical map and maps of power.

The prophetic assemblage, like every assemblage, is about power. As Ian Buchanan writes, assemblage theory does not merely observe the messy heterogeneity within a structure of authority. For Buchanan, assemblage theory asks, "*What* is that structure of authority? How is it constituted?"[11] Baraka's flows remain circulations of power. Shrines thus become the targets of a modern Sunni revivalism (reterritorialization) that marks them for destruction. In one historical setting, access to bodily baraka would have directed negotiations between sultans and saints; in our own world, a modern state that holds Muhammad's body in its custody reconstructs baraka to no longer circulate between bodies as an immanent energy flow but rather descend strictly as transcendent credits earned for obedience to a select archive of textual canons. But even as Muhammad's body undergoes a redrawing of its boundaries and baraka becomes subject to this stabilizing reterritorialization, that same archive preserves its lines of flight.

Notes

INTRODUCTION

1. Qadhi, "Collector's Edition."
2. al-Hilali and Khan, *The Meanings of the Qur'an*.
3. Qadhi, "Collector's Edition."
4. Meri, *The Cult of Saints*, 9.
5. Reinhart, "Juynbolliana, Gradualism, the Big Bang, and Hadith Study."
6. Motzki, *Reconstruction of a Source of Ibn Ishaq's "Life of the Prophet,"* 18.
7. Kister, "'A Bag of Meat.'"
8. Kister, "'And He Was Born Circumcised.'"
9. Rubin, *The Eye of the Beholder*.
10. al-Dārimī, *Sunan*, no. 19.
11. Bukhārī, *Ṣaḥīḥ*, no. 3398.
12. For examples, see Qur'an 7:137, 17:1, 21:71, 21:81, 27:8, 34:18, 37:113, and 41:10.
13. Qur'an 44:3.
14. Qur'an 7:96.
15. Qur'an 6:155.
16. al-Dārimī, *Sunan*, no. 1980.
17. al-Dārimī, no. 1974.
18. Ibn Ḥanbal, *Musnad*, nos. 16150, 16151. The olive tree is most famously designated as *mubarakatin* in the Qur'an's "verse of light," 24:35.
19. Colin, "Baraka."
20. Cited in von Denffer, "Baraka as Basic Concept of Muslim Popular Belief."
21. Amir-Moezzi, *The Spirituality of Shi'i Islam*, chap. 1.
22. Roberts and Roberts, "Mystical Graffiti and the Refabulation of Dakar."
23. Karamustafa, *Sufism*, 130.
24. Meri, "Aspects of Baraka (Blessings) and Ritual Devotion."
25. Safi, "Bargaining with Baraka."
26. Chelhod, "La baraka chez les Arabes."
27. Kugle, *Sufis and Saints' Bodies*, 8–9.
28. Kugle, 181–220.
29. Bashir, *Sufi Bodies*.
30. Bashir, 1–2.
31. Grosz, *Volatile Bodies*, 167.

32. Hughes, "Introduction: Pity the Meat?: Deleuze and the Body."
33. Consider the Deleuze Connections series (Edinburgh: Edinburgh University Press, 2011), which includes titles such as *Deleuze and the Body* (ed. Laura Guillaume and Joe Hughes), *Deleuze and Sex* (ed. Frida Beckman), and *Deleuze and Queer Theory* (ed. Chrysanthi Nigianni and Merl Storr).
34. Grosz, *Volatile Bodies*.
35. Buchanan, "The Problem of the Body in Deleuze and Guattari."
36. Weheliye, *Habeas Viscus*, 47.
37. Deleuze and Guattari, *A Thousand Plateaus*, 127, 380–84.
38. Colebrook, *Deleuze*, 144.
39. Deleuze and Guattari, *A Thousand Plateaus*, 257, 260–61.
40. Juynboll, *Muslim Tradition*, 192–93.
41. Lucas, *Constructive Critics*.
42. Lucas, 191, 217.
43. Lucas, 193–202.
44. Nawas, "The Contribution of the *Mawālī* ."
45. Melchert, "Sectaries in the Six Books."
46. Sayeed, *Women and the Transmission of Religious Knowledge in Islam*, 186–87.
47. Ahmed, *Before Orthodoxy*, 74–76.
48. Ahmed, 74–76.
49. Deleuze and Guattari, *A Thousand Plateaus*, 9.
50. Romanov, "Dreaming Ḥanbalites."
51. At the intersection of Islamic studies and gender studies, one can find a number of significant monographs that examine gender within the Qur'an and *tafsir*. Recent examples include Chaudhry, *Domestic Violence and the Islamic Tradition*, and Bauer, *Gender Hierarchy in the Qur'ān*. The confessionally engaged scholarship of Muslim intellectuals identified with "progressive Islam" have also privileged the Qur'an as the site for reform: major works include monographs such as wadud, *Qur'ān and Woman*, and Kugle, *Homosexuality in Islam*, the latter identifying its project as "liberating" the Qur'an (challenging the Qur'an's interpreters while preserving the text's transcendence and innocence) while "critiquing" hadith (deauthorizing the hadith corpus through recourse to the authenticity question).
52. Shaikh, "Knowledge, Women and Gender in the Ḥadīth"; Hidayatullah, *Feminist Edges of the Qur'an*, 81–86.
53. Sayeed, *Women and the Transmission of Religious Knowledge in Islam*.
54. Spellberg, *Politics, Gender, and the Islamic Past*.
55. Sayeed, *Women and the Transmission of Religious Knowledge in Islam*, 14.
56. Spellberg, *Politics, Gender, and the Islamic Past*, 9–16.
57. Geissinger, "The Exegetical Traditions of A'isha."
58. Geissinger, *Gender and Muslim Construction of Exegetical Authority*.
59. De Sondy, *The Crisis of Islamic Masculinities*.
60. Ayubi, *Gendered Morality*.

61. For an example of how Hammer negotiates these questions in her own work, see Hammer, *Peaceful Families*.
62. Hidayatullah, *Feminist Edges of the Qur'an*.
63. Shaikh, "Knowledge, Women and Gender in the Ḥadīth."
64. Hidayatullah, *Feminist Edges of the Qur'an*, 19.
65. Knight, *Tripping with Allah: Islam, Drugs, and Writing*.
66. Chaudhry, *Domestic Violence and the Islamic Tradition*, 210.
67. Hammer, *Peaceful Families*, 226.
68. Shaikh, *Sufi Narratives of Intimacy*, 29–32, 173–84.
69. Williams, "Tajalli wa-Ru'ya."
70. Donner, *Narratives of Islamic Origins*, 35–61.
71. Donner, *Muhammad and the Believers*.
72. Khoury, *Wahb b. Munabbih*.
73. al-Wāqidī, *The Life of Muhammad*.
74. Zaman, "*Maghāzī* and the *Muḥaddithūn*."
75. Ibn Rāshid, *The Expeditions*.
76. Ibn Rāshid.
77. Donner, *Narratives of Islamic Origins*, 148.
78. Hoyland, "History, Fiction, and Authorship in the First Centuries of Islam."
79. ʿAbd al-Razzāq, *Muṣannaf*.
80. Lucas, *Constructive Critics*, 19–20.
81. Lucas, 19–20.
82. Lucas, 19–20.
83. Brown, *Hadith*, 31.
84. Brown, 31–32.
85. Robson, "al-Bukhārī."
86. Brown, "The Canonization of Ibn Majah."
87. Robson, "The Transmission of Ibn Majah's 'Sunan.'"
88. Brown, "The Canonization of Ibn Majah."
89. Brown.
90. Robson, "The Transmission of Ibn Majah's 'Sunan.'"
91. Lucas, *Constructive Critics*, 80.
92. Juynboll, "al-Tirmidhī."
93. Robson, "al-Dārimī."
94. Brown, "The Rules of Matn Criticism."
95. Melchert, "Bukhārī and Early Ḥadīth Criticism."
96. Safi, *The Politics of Knowledge in Premodern Islam*, 46.
97. Lucas, *Constructive Critics*, 85.
98. Douglas, "Controversy and Its Effects in the Biographical Tradition of al-Khaṭīb al-Baghdādī."
99. Khalidi, *Arabic Historical Thought in the Classical Period*, 73.
100. Bosworth, "al-Ṭabarī."
101. Bosworth.

102. Brown, *Hadith*, 41–42.
103. Lucas, *Constructive Critics*, 99.
104. Brown, *Hadith*, 42.
105. Lucas, *Constructive Critics*, 92.
106. Brown, *Hadith*, 42.
107. al-Kaisi, "Sufi Apologia in the Guise of Biography."

CHAPTER ONE

1. Morimoto, "Keeping the Prophet's Family Alive."
2. Kueny, *Conceiving Identities*, 53.
3. Qur'an 16:4, 18:37, 22:5, 23:13–14, 35:11, 36:77, 40:67, 53:46, 75:37, 76:2, 80:19.
4. Abū Dāwūd, *Sunan*, no. 205; Bukhārī, *Ṣaḥīḥ*, nos. 128, 5653; Nasā'ī, *Sunan al-Sughra*, no. 197.
5. Ibn Māja, *Sunan*, no. 593; Muslim, *Ṣaḥīḥ*, no. 474; Nasā'ī, *Sunan al-Sughra*, no. 200.
6. Kueny, *Conceiving Identities*, 54.
7. Kueny, 55.
8. Kueny, 31, 225.
9. Vorisco, "Metaphors and Sacred History."
10. Vorisco.
11. Ibn Hishām, *The Life of Muhammad*, 3–4.
12. Ibn Hishām, 68–69.
13. Ibn Sa'd, *Ṭabaqāt*, 1:66.
14. Ibn Sa'd, *Ṭabaqāt*, 1:18; Ibn Ḥanbal, *Musnad*, nos. 17111, 17112; Ibn Abī Shayba, *Muṣannaf*, no. 31722.
15. Ibn Abī Shayba, *Muṣannaf*, no. 31630; Ibn Ḥanbal, *Musnad*, no. 17658.
16. Ibn Ḥanbal, *Musnad*, no. 1788.
17. Ibn Sa'd, *Ṭabaqāt*, 1:18.
18. Tirmidhī, *Al-Jāmi'*, no. 3567; Muslim, *Ṣaḥīḥ*, no. 4228.
19. Ibn Sa'd, *Ṭabaqāt*, 1:50–51; Ibn Abī Shayba, *Muṣannaf*, no. 31632.
20. Rubin, "Pre-existence and Light."
21. Rubin.
22. Rubin.
23. Rubin.
24. Ibn Ḥanbal, *Musnad*, no. 8844; Ibn Sa'd, *Ṭabaqāt*, no. 22.
25. Qur'an 26:219.
26. Ibn Sa'd, *Ṭabaqāt*, 1:22. For attention to the tradition's significance in *tafsir*, see Rubin, "More Light on Muhammad's Pre-existence."
27. Ibn Ḥanbal, *Musnad*, nos. 16740, 23599.
28. Ibn Sa'd, *Ṭabaqāt*, 1:118.
29. Ibn Ḥanbal, *Musnad*, nos. 12216, 13870; Muslim, *Ṣaḥīḥ*, nos. 307, 1627; Ibn Ḥibbān, *Ṣaḥīḥ*, no. 584; Bayhaqī, *Dalā'il al-Nubuwwa*, 1:191.

30. Ibn Ḥanbal, *Musnad*, no. 9686; Muslim, *Ṣaḥīḥ*, no. 1627.
31. al-Ḥākim, *Al-Mustadrak*, no. 3422.
32. Husayn, "Treatises on the Salvation of Abu Talib."
33. Ibn al-Jawzī, *Kitāb al-Mawḍuʾāt*, nos. 459, 460.
34. Cox, *Biography in Late Antiquity*, 14–15.
35. Callon, *Reading Bodies*, 15.
36. Obdrzalek, "Socrates on Love."
37. Callon, *Reading Bodies*, 11.
38. Popovic, "Physiognomic Knowledge in Qumran and Babylonia."
39. Lincicum, "Philo and the Physiognomic Tradition."
40. Popovic, *Reading the Human Body*, 277–90.
41. Callon, *Reading Bodies*, 18.
42. Callon, 134–53.
43. Zysk, "Greek and Indian Physiognomics."
44. Zysk.
45. Callon, *Reading Bodies*, 19–20.
46. Bukhārī, *Ṣaḥīḥ*, no. 6300; Muslim, *Ṣaḥīḥ*, no. 2656; Tirmidhī, *Al-Jāmiʾ*, no. 2055; Nasāʾī, *Sunan al-Sughra*, no. 3455; Abū Dāwūd, *Sunan*, no. 1934; Ibn Māja, *Sunan*, no. 2342.
47. Tirmidhī, *Al-Jāmiʾ*, no. 3127.
48. Ibn Ḥanbal, *Musnad*, no. 947; Ibn Abī Shayba, *Muṣannaf*, nos. 31796, 31798.
49. Hoyland, "A New Edition and Translation of the Leiden Polemon."
50. Hoyland, "The Islamic Background to Polemon's Treatise."
51. Hoyland.
52. Hoyland.
53. Ghaly, "Physiognomy."
54. Mālik Ibn Anas, *Al-Muwaṭṭā of Imam Malik Ibn Anas*, xxviii.
55. Ibn al-Jawzī, *Virtues of the Imām Aḥmad Ibn Ḥanbal*, 1:389–91.
56. Ibn Hishām, *The Life of Muhammad*, 96–97.
57. Ibn Hishām, 183–84.
58. Ibn Hishām, 183–84.
59. Ibn Hishām, 183–84, 725–26.
60. Spellberg, *Politics, Gender, and the Islamic Past*, 113.
61. Allam, "A Sociolinguistic Study on the Use of Color Terminology in Egyptian Colloquial and Classical Arabic."
62. Malik Ibn Anas, *Al-Muwaṭṭā of Malik Ibn Anas*, 388.
63. A number of versions appear together in Ibn Saʾd, *Ṭabaqāt*, 1:314–17.
64. Ibn Abī Shayba, *Muṣannaf*, nos. 31796, 31798; Ibn Ḥanbal, *Musnad*, no. 947.
65. Ibn Saʾd, *Ṭabaqāt*, 1:314–17.
66. Ibn Abī Shayba, *Muṣannaf*, nos. 31796, 31798.
67. Ibn Saʾd, *Ṭabaqāt*, 1:324–27.
68. ʿAbd al-Razzāq, *Muṣannaf*, no. 20657.
69. ʿAbd al-Razzāq, no. 20658.

70. Ibn Saʾd, *Ṭabaqāt*, 1:322.
71. Ibn Saʾd, 1:320.
72. Ibn Saʾd, 1:318.
73. Ibn Ḥanbal, *Musnad*, no. 26.
74. Ibn Saʾd, *Ṭabaqāt*, 1:317.
75. Ibn Ḥanbal, *Musnad*, no. 1300; Ibn Saʾd, 1:315.
76. Ibn Saʾd, *Ṭabaqāt*, 1:317.
77. Ibn Saʾd, 1:314–27.
78. Ibn Saʾd, 1:316.
79. Khoury, *Wahb b. Munabbih*, vol. 1, PB 11 (148–49).
80. Ibn Hishām, *The Life of Muhammad*, 80, 709.
81. Ibn Hishām, 96–97.
82. Ibn Abī Shayba, *Muṣannaf*, no. 36594.
83. Ibn Saʾd, *Ṭabaqāt*, 1:129.
84. Ibn Saʾd, 1:328.
85. Ibn Ḥanbal, *Musnad*, no. 1954.
86. Ibn Saʾd, *Ṭabaqāt*, 1:320.
87. Ibn Saʾd, 1:320.
88. Ibn Saʾd, 1:320.
89. Ibn Saʾd, 1:320.
90. G. H. A. Juynboll argues that hadith transmitters in Basra and Kufa, two cities "teeming with very old people who are described as having met their deaths at ages of 120 to 150 years," falsified their ages to claim closer connections to the sacred past, shorten their hadith chains, and thus strengthen their transmissions. *Encyclopedia of Canonical Hadith*, 131–34. See also Juynboll, *Muslim Tradition*, 46–47.
91. Abū Yaʾlā, *Musnad*, no. 3478. Cited in Nur ad-Din al-Haythami, *Majmaʾ al-Zawaʾid*, no. 15800.
92. Ibn Saʾd, *Ṭabaqāt*, 1:322–23.
93. GhaneaBassiri, "Ethics," 241–42.
94. Ibn Saʾd, *Ṭabaqāt*, 1:273–81.
95. Ibn Saʾd, 1:273–81.
96. Ibn Saʾd, 1:273–81.
97. Ibn Saʾd, 1:273–81.
98. Ibn Ḥanbal, *Musnad*, no. 24773.
99. Melchert, "The Early Controversy over whether the Prophet Saw God."
100. ʿAbd al-Razzāq, *Tafsīr*, 3:329.
101. Geissinger, *Gender and Muslim Constructions of Exegetical Authority*.
102. Abū Nuʾaym, *Dalāʾil al-Nubuwwa*, no. 558.
103. al-ʿAsqalani, *Taqrib al-Tahdhib*, 709.
104. Ibn Ḥanbal, *Musnad*, nos. 24896, 25736.
105. Tirmidhī, *Al-Jāmiʾ*, no. 3822.
106. Lindberg, *Theories of Vision*.

107. Stearns, *Infectious Ideas*, 71–72.
108. Melchert, "Sectaries in the Six Books."
109. Melchert.

CHAPTER TWO

1. Ibn Ḥanbal, *Musnad*, nos. 3648, 3802.
2. Ibn Ḥanbal, no. 2181.
3. Bukhārī, *Ṣaḥīḥ*, no. 3006; Muslim, *Ṣaḥīḥ*, no. 3934.
4. Ibn Sulayman, *Tafsir*, 3:496.
5. Ibn Hishām, *The Life of Muhammad*, 71–72.
6. Ibn Hishām, 71–72.
7. Ibn Ḥanbal, *Musnad*, nos. 14115, 12534.
8. Ibn Ḥanbal, nos. 21613, 21453.
9. Ṭayālisī, *Musnad*, no. 1643.
10. Ibn Ḥanbal, *Musnad*, no. 17987.
11. Ibn Sa'd, *Ṭabaqāt*, 1:120.
12. Rubin, *The Eye of the Beholder*, 59.
13. Vuckovic, *Heavenly Journeys, Earthly Concerns*, 18.
14. Muslim, *Ṣaḥīḥ*, no. 240.
15. Ibn Abī ʿĀṣim, *Al-Aḥād wa-l-Mathānī*, no. 1246; al-Dārimī, *Sunan*, no. 13.
16. al-Ḥākim, *Al-Mustadrak*, no. 4161; Bayhaqī, *Dalā'il al-Nubuwwa*, 2:7–8.
17. al-Ḥākim, *Al-Mustadrak*, no. 3878; Bayhaqī, *Dalā'il al-Nubuwwa*, 1:147, 2:7–8; Ibn Ḥibbān, *Ṣaḥīḥ*, nos. 6469, 6471; Abū Ya'lā, *Musnad*, nos. 3320, 3453; Abū Nu'aym, *Dalā'il al-Nubuwwa*, no. 168.
18. Ṭabarānī, *Al-Mu'jam al-Awsaṭ*, no. 5970; Abū Nu'aym, *Dalā'il al-Nubuwwa*, no. 96.
19. Ṭayālisī, *Musnad*, no. 1643.
20. Ahmed, *Before Orthodoxy*, 33.
21. Fahd, "Sakina."
22. Ibn Ḥanbal, *Musnad*, no. 17798.
23. Ibn Ḥanbal, nos. 21453, 21613.
24. Bukhārī, *Ṣaḥīḥ*, nos. 185, 3299, 4335, 5265, 7222; Muslim, *Ṣaḥīḥ*, no. 4335; Tirmidhī, *Al-Jāmi'*, no. 3606.
25. al-Ḥākim, *Al-Mustadrak*, no. 6575.
26. al-Ḥākim, *Al-Mustadrak*, no. 4128; Abū Ya'lā, *Musnad*, no. 7420.
27. Ṭabarānī, *Mu'jam al-Kabīr*, 6:13520.
28. Bayhaqī, *Dalā'il al-Nubuwwa*, 2:7–8.
29. Ibn Ḥibbān, *Ṣaḥīḥ*, no. 6437.
30. van Ess, "Vision and Ascension."
31. Qur'an 7:54, 9:129, 10:3, 11:7, 13:2, 17:42, 20:5, 21:22, 23:86, 23:116, 25:59, 27:26, 32:4, 39:75, 40:7, 40:15, 43:82, 57:4, 69:17, 81:20, 85:15.
32. Sirry, "Muqatil b. Sulayman and Anthropomorphism."

33. Holtzman, "Anthropomorphism."
34. van Ess, "The Youthful God."
35. Shahrastānī, *Muslim Sects and Divisions*, 89.
36. van Ess, "The Youthful God."
37. van Ess.
38. Bukhārī, *Ṣaḥīḥ*, no. 2706.
39. Muslim, *Ṣaḥīḥ*, no. 1458.
40. Melchert, "'God Created Adam in His Image.'"
41. Ibn Māja, *Sunan*, no. 189; Abū Dāwūd, *Sunan*, no. 4102; Tirmidhī, *Al-Jāmi'*, no. 3263.
42. Jackson, "Ibn Taymiyya on Trial in Damascus."
43. Abū Dāwūd, *Sunan*, no. 4767.
44. Ibn Abī 'Āṣim, *Kitāb as-Sunna*, no. 586.
45. al-Dārimī, *Sunan*, no. 2697.
46. van Ess, *The Flowering of Muslim Theology*, 52.
47. Ibn Abī Shayba, *Muṣannaf*, no. 31794; Ibn Ḥanbal, *Musnad*, no. 24731.
48. Melchert, "The Early Controversy over whether the Prophet Saw God."
49. van Ess, "The Youthful God."
50. van Ess.
51. Ibn Ḥanbal, *Musnad*, no. 23597.
52. Ibn Abī Shayba, *Muṣannaf*, no. 31697.
53. Ibn Sa'd, *Ṭabaqāt*, 1:135.
54. Tirmidhī, *Al-Jāmi'*, no. 3176.
55. Tirmidhī, no. 3013.
56. Tirmidhī, no. 3223.
57. Tirmidhī, no. 3220.
58. Muslim, *Ṣaḥīḥ*, no. 267.
59. Muslim, no. 262.
60. Muslim, no. 265.
61. Bukhārī, *Ṣaḥīḥ*, nos. 3013, 4502, 6856.
62. Bukhārī, no. 6986.
63. Melchert, "The Early Controversy over whether the Prophet Saw God." Melchert, "God Created Adam in His Image."
64. Ibn Aḥmad ibn Ḥanbal, *Kitāb as-Sunna*, vol. 1, no. 1121.
65. Ibn Abī 'Āṣim, *Kitāb as-Sunna*, no. 474; al-Dārimī, *Sunan*, no. 2073.
66. Ibn Abī 'Āṣim, *Kitāb as-Sunna*, nos. 470–80.
67. Ibn Abī 'Āṣim, nos. 449–51.
68. Ibn Abī 'Āṣim, nos. 474–80.
69. Ibn Abī 'Āṣim, nos. 433–36.
70. Ibn Abī 'Āṣim, nos. 496–98.
71. Melchert, "God Created Adam in His Image."
72. Ibn Abī 'Āṣim, *Kitāb as-Sunna*, nos. 499–520.
73. Ibn Abī 'Āṣim, nos. 537–39.

74. Ibn Abī ʿĀṣim, nos. 589, 590.
75. al-Wāqidī, *The Life of Muhammad*, 546.
76. Abū Dāwūd, *Sunan*, no. 3379.
77. Daraquṭnī, *Kitāb al-Ruʾyā*, nos. 177, 181, 183, 185, 187, 188, 202; Ṭabarānī, *Muʿjam al-Kabīr*, 8:16640.
78. Bayhaqī, *Dalāʾil al-Nubuwwa*, 2:370–71; Abū Yaʿlā, *Musnad*, no. 4835.
79. Melchert, "The Early Controversy over whether the Prophet Saw God."
80. Bukhārī, *Al-Adab al-Mufrad*, no. 544.
81. Ritter, *The Ocean of the Soul*, 459.
82. Melchert, "The Early Controversy over whether the Prophet Saw God."
83. Tirmidhī, *Al-Jāmiʿ*, no. 3222.
84. Bukhārī, *Ṣaḥīḥ*, nos. 1883, 3326; Muslim, *Ṣaḥīḥ*, no. 1225; Tirmidhī, *Al-Jāmiʿ*, no. 403; Nasāʾī, *Sunan al-Sughra*, no. 391.
85. Katz, *Body of Text*, 71.
86. Katz, 71–73.
87. Bukhārī, *Ṣaḥīḥ*, nos. 3327, 6986.
88. Bukhārī, no. 6765.
89. Halperin, "The Sayyād Traditions."
90. Ghaly, "Physiognomy."
91. Tirmidhī, *Al-Jāmiʿ*, no. 2179.
92. Tirmidhī, *Al-Jāmiʿ*, no. 3278; Ibn Māja, *Sunan*, no. 4242.
93. Malik, *Muwata*, no. 1795.
94. Muslim, *Ṣaḥīḥ*, no. 211.
95. Lange, "'On That Day When Faces Will Be White or Black.'"
96. Grosz, "The Body of Signification."
97. Grosz, *Sexual Subversions*, 72.
98. Kristeva, *Powers of Horror*, 3.

CHAPTER THREE

1. al-Wāqidī, *The Life of Muhammad*, 509–10.
2. al-Wāqidī, 509–10.
3. Ibn Ḥanbal, *Musnad*, nos. 13277, 12373, 14565, 14921; Ṭayālisī, *Musnad*, no. 1935; Ibn Abī Shayba, *Muṣannaf*, no. 31713.
4. Ibn Ḥanbal, *Muṣannaf*, nos. 3808, 4392; Ibn Abī Shayba, *Muṣannaf*, no. 31713.
5. Bukhārī, *Ṣaḥīḥ*, nos. 195, 3329; Muslim, *Ṣaḥīḥ*, no. 4231; Tirmidhī, *Al-Jāmiʿ*, no. 3595; Nasāʾī, *Sunan al-Sughra*, no. 75.
6. Bukhārī, *Ṣaḥīḥ*, no. 5235.
7. Ibn Rāshid, *The Expeditions*, 33.
8. Ibn Rāshid, 272–79.
9. al-Wāqidī, *The Life of Muhammad*, 48.
10. al-Wāqidī, 518.
11. al-Wāqidī, 95, 120, 171, 268.

12. al-Wāqidī, 14.
13. Ibn Hishām, *The Life of Muhammad*, 451.
14. Ibn Hishām, 117.
15. Gil'adi, "Some Notes on *Tahnik* in Medieval Islam."
16. Qur'an 33:40.
17. Ibn Sa'd, *Ṭabaqāt*, 8:318–19; Ibn Abī Shayba, *Muṣannaf*, no. 23471; Ibn Ḥanbal, *Musnad*, nos. 12826, 13242.
18. Ibn Abī Shayba, *Muṣannaf*, no. 36611; Ibn Ḥanbal, *Musnad*, no. 27477.
19. Ibn Abī Shayba, *Muṣannaf*, no. 36611.
20. Bukhārī, *Ṣaḥīḥ*, no. 3645; Muslim, *Ṣaḥīḥ*, no. 4006.
21. Ibn Abī Shayba, *Muṣannaf*, nos. 23473, 23474.
22. Bayhaqī, *Dalā'il al-Nubuwwa*, 6:225.
23. Gibb, "ʿAbd Allāh b. al-Zubayr."
24. Shaddel, "ʿAbd Allah Ibn al-Zubayr and the Mahdi."
25. Amir-Moezzi, *The Spirituality of Shi'i Islam*, 38–39.
26. Ibn Ḥanbal, *Musnad*, no. 16972.
27. Ibn Abī Shayba, *Muṣannaf*, nos. 32071, 36872.
28. Ibn Ḥanbal, *Musnad*, no. 579.
29. Ibn Sa'd, *Ṭabaqāt*, 1:390–93.
30. Ibn Sa'd, 1:391.
31. Ibn Sa'd, 1:391.
32. Ibn Sa'd, 1:392.
33. Ibn Sa'd, 8:315.
34. Ibn Sa'd, 2:202.
35. Ibn Sa'd, 2:202.
36. Ibn Sa'd, 2:201.
37. Bukhārī, *Ṣaḥīḥ*, nos. 1197, 3909; Muslim, *Ṣaḥīḥ*, no. 4982; Nasā'ī, *Sunan al-Kubra*, no. 2131; *Sunan al-Sughra*, no. 1885; Ibn Māja, *Sunan*, no. 1513; Abū Dāwūd, *Sunan*, no. 3398.
38. Ṭabarānī, *Mu'jam al-Kabīr*, 2:2592. Ṭabarānī provides an identical isnad with slightly different wording in 6:12449; Bayhaqī, *Sunan al-Kubra*, no. 591; al-Khaṭīb al-Baghdādī, *Tārikh Madīnat al-Salām*, no. 1089.
39. al-Khaṭīb al-Baghdādī, *Tārikh Madīnat al-Salām*, no. 1089.
40. Bukhārī, *Ṣaḥīḥ*, nos. 2885, 3645; Muslim, *Ṣaḥīḥ*, no. 3645.
41. Bukhārī, *Ṣaḥīḥ*, nos. 2885, 4842.
42. Bukhārī, *Ṣaḥīḥ*, nos. 5331, 5332; Muslim, *Ṣaḥīḥ*, no. 4076; Ibn Māja, *Sunan*, no. 3520; Abū Dāwūd, *Sunan*, no. 3399.
43. Bukhārī, *Ṣaḥīḥ*, no. 4648; Muslim, *Ṣaḥīḥ*, no. 4088; Tirmidhī, *Al-Jāmi'*, no. 1989; Abū Dāwūd, *Sunan*, no. 2968; Ibn Māja, no. 2147; Nasā'ī, *Sunan al-Kubra*, no. 10367.
44. Ibn Hishām, *The Life of Muhammad*, 497.
45. al-Wāqidī, *The Life of Muhammad*, 212.
46. al-Wāqidī, 161.

47. Ibn Sa'd, *Ṭabaqāt*, 1:316; Ibn Ḥanbal, *Musnad*, no. 1300.
48. Ibn Sa'd, *Ṭabaqāt*, 1:317.
49. Ibn Sa'd, *Ṭabaqāt*, 8:315; Ibn Ḥanbal, *Musnad*, nos. 12423, 14105.
50. Fahd, "Ibn Sīrīn."
51. Ibn Sa'd, *Ṭabaqāt*, 8:314.
52. Ibn Sa'd, 8:315.
53. Ibn Sa'd, *Ṭabaqāt*, 1:350; Ibn Ḥanbal, *Musnad*, nos. 25517, 26364.
54. Bukhārī, *Ṣaḥīḥ*, no. 3319.
55. Bukhārī, no. 5836.
56. Abū Dāwūd, *Sunan*, no. 3554; Nasā'ī, *Sunan al-Kubra*, nos. 9182, 9280.
57. Tirmidhī, *Al-Jāmi'*, no. 3596; Nasā'ī, *Sunan al-Kubra*, no. 994; Nasā'ī, *Sunan al-Sughra*, no. 10615; Bukhārī, *Ṣaḥīḥ*, no. 2.
58. Bukhārī, no. 2518; Muslim, *Ṣaḥīḥ*, no. 2770.
59. al-Wāqidī, *The Life of Muhammad*, 542.
60. al-Wāqidī, 300.
61. al-Wāqidī, 300.
62. al-Wāqidī, 300.
63. Ibn Ḥanbal, *Musnad*, nos. 12390, 12427; Ibn Sa'd, *Ṭabaqāt*, 2:139.
64. Ibn Ḥanbal, *Musnad*, no. 13542.
65. Bukhārī, *Ṣaḥīḥ*, no. 168.
66. Abū Dāwūd, *Sunan*, no. 1693.
67. Muslim, *Ṣaḥīḥ*, no. 2308.
68. Ibn Ḥanbal, *Musnad*, no. 13542; Ibn Sa'd, *Ṭabaqāt*, 1:336.
69. Ibn Sa'd, *Ṭabaqāt* ('Umar edition), 6:30.
70. Lecker, "The Bewitching of the Prophet Muḥammad by the Jews."
71. Bukhārī, *Ṣaḥīḥ*, no. 5836.
72. Bukhārī, no. 5473.
73. Bukhārī, no. 5473.
74. Katz, *Body of Text*, 135–40.
75. al-Wāqidī, *The Life of Muhammad*, 121–22.
76. Ibn Hishām, *The Life of Muhammad*, 754.
77. Ibn Hishām, 754.
78. The present study generally uses the 2012 Dar al-Kotob al-Ilmiyah edition, though this edition suffers from an exclusion of material, including the above tradition. The narration of Malik Ibn Sinan drinking Muhammad's blood is included, however, in the critical edition of 'Ali Muhammad 'Umar (Cairo: Maktaba al-Khanji, 2001), 4:363. For discussion of the *Ṭabaqāt*'s complex publishing history, see Lucas, *Constructive Critics*, 206.
79. Lucas, 342–47.
80. Ibn Abī 'Āṣim, *Al-Aḥād wa-l-Mathānī*, no. 538.
81. Muslim, *Ṣaḥīḥ*, nos. 4006, 4008; Bukhārī, *Ṣaḥīḥ*, nos. 3644, 3645, 5072.
82. Gibb, "'Abd Allāh b. al-Zubayr."
83. al-Ḥākim, *Al-Mustadrak*, no. 6364.

84. Abū Nu'aym, *Hilyat al-Awlīyā'*, no. 1199.
85. Ṭabarānī, *Al-Mu'jam al-Awsaṭ*, no. 9331.
86. Bayhaqī, *Sunan al-Kubra*, no. 12412.
87. Bayhaqī, no. 12412.
88. Ibn Sa'd, *Ṭabaqāt*, 1:336.
89. Ibn Sa'd, 1:336.
90. Tirmidhī, *Shamā'il*, no. 374.
91. Ibn Sa'd, *Ṭabaqāt*, 2:200; Nasā'ī, *Sunan al-Sughra*, no. 33; Nasā'ī, *Sunan al-Kubra*, no. 6223; Tirmidhī, *Shamā'il*, no. 374.
92. While traditions differ as to how Muhammad urinated, A'isha condemns those who report that Muhammad stood while relieving himself. Tirmidhī, *Al-Jāmi'*, no. 12; Nasā'ī, *Sunan al-Sughra*, no. 29; Nasā'ī, *Sunan al-Kubra*, no. 25.
93. Jabir, for example, reports that Muhammad had prohibited urinating while facing in the direction of Mecca but adds that he witnessed Muhammad doing so in the final year of his life. Tirmidhī, *Al-Jāmi'*, no. 9; Abū Dāwūd, *Sunan*, no. 12.
94. For learning their toilet practices from Muhammad, polytheists reportedly mocked the Companions. Muslim, *Ṣaḥīḥ*, no. 391.
95. Abū Dāwūd, *Sunan*, no. 22; Nasā'ī, *Sunan al-Sughra*, no. 32; Nasā'ī, *Sunan al-Kubra*, no. 31.
96. Ibn Abī Shayba provides a tradition stating that angels will not enter a house in which there is urine. *Muṣannaf*, no. 1845.
97. Ibn Abī 'Āṣim, *Al-Aḥād wa-l-Mathānī*, no. 2983.
98. Ibn Abī 'Āṣim, no. 2983.
99. Bayhaqī, *Sunan al-Kubra*, no. 12410.
100. Ṭabarānī, *Mu'jam al-Kabīr*, 10:20748.
101. al-Ḥākim, *Al-Mustadrak*, no. 6964; Abū Nu'aym, *Dalā'il al-Nubuwwa*, no. 366.
102. Sayeed, *Women and the Transmission of Religious Knowledge in Islam*, 55.
103. Ibn Sa'd, *Ṭabaqāt*, 8:179.
104. Sayeed, *Women and the Transmission of Religious Knowledge in Islam*, 55.
105. Ibn Sa'd, *Ṭabaqāt*, 8:179.
106. Ṭabarānī, *Mu'jam al-Kabīr*, 10:19998.
107. Abū Nu'aym, *Dalā'il al-Nubuwwa*, nos. 365, 366.
108. Abū Nu'aym, no. 367.
109. Ibn Sa'd, *Ṭabaqāt*, 1:390–92.
110. al-Khaṭīb al-Baghdādī, *Ruwat Malik*; cited in Ṣuyūṭī, *Khasā'is al-Kubra*, 2:50–51.
111. Ibn Sa'd, *Ṭabaqāt*, 3:9.
112. El Cheikh, *Women, Islam, and Abbasid Identity*, 27.
113. Hawting, "'A Plaything for Kings.'"
114. Nadvi, "'Abd Allāh Ibn al-Zubayr and the Caliphate," 42.
115. Ibn Ḥanbal, *Musnad*, nos. 680, 681, 14688, 14998.
116. Ibn Ḥanbal, no. 813.
117. Ibn Ḥanbal, no. 16212.

118. Bukhārī, *Ṣaḥīḥ*, no. 3645.
119. Ibn Ḥanbal, *Musnad*, no. 26299; Ibn Sa'd, *Ṭabaqāt*, 8:52; Ibn Māja, *Sunan*, no. 3737.
120. Ibn Ḥanbal, *Musnad*, no. 25696.
121. Bukhārī, *Al-Adab al-Mufrad*, nos. 848, 849.
122. Campbell, "Telling Memories."

CHAPTER FOUR

1. Sanders, "Gendering the Ungendered Body."
2. Sanders.
3. Bashir, *Sufi Bodies*, 1–2.
4. Bukhārī, *Ṣaḥīḥ*, no. 4983; Muslim, *Ṣaḥīḥ*, no. 1866; Tirmidhī, *Al-Jāmi'*, no. 3306; Ibn Māja, *Sunan*, no. 2875.
5. Ayubi, *Gendered Morality*, 251.
6. Ayubi, 251.
7. Hidayatullah surveys these arguments in *Feminist Edges of the Qur'an*, 112–16.
8. Chaudhry, *Domestic Violence and the Islamic Tradition*, 12.
9. Ṭabarī, *Tafsīr*, vol. 4, nos. 10441, 10447.
10. al-Azmeh, *Arabic Thought and Islamic Societies*, 70.
11. Shahrastānī, *Muslim Sects and Divisions*, 89.
12. Ibn Māja, *Sunan*, no. 101.
13. Ibn Ḥanbal, *Musnad*, no. 16738.
14. Ibn Qutabya, *Ta'wīl Mukhtalif al-Ḥadīth*, no. 66.
15. al-Khaṭīb al-Baghdādī, *Tārikh Madīnat al-Salām*, no. 3347.
16. al-Khaṭīb al-Baghdādī, no. 3735.
17. Ṭabarānī, *Mu'jam al-Kabīr*, 10:20854.
18. Daraquṭnī, *Kitāb al-Ru'yā*, nos. 231, 232.
19. Bayhaqī, *Al-Asmā' wa al-Ṣifāt*, no. 921.
20. van Ess, *Theology and Society*, 427.
21. Ritter, *The Ocean of the Soul*, 460.
22. van Ess, *Theology and Society*, 426.
23. Cokayne, *Experiencing Old Age in Ancient Rome*, 15.
24. van Ess, *Theology and Society*, 426.
25. Bembry, *Yahweh's Coming of Age*.
26. Callon, *Reading Bodies*, 149–54.
27. Ghaemmaghami, "Numinous Vision, Messianic Encounters."
28. al-Khaṭīb al-Baghdādī, *Tārikh Madīnat al-Salām*, no. 3347.
29. el-Rouayheb, *Before Homosexuality in the Arab-Islamic World*, 12–37.
30. el-Rouayheb, 113.
31. Bayhaqī, *Al-Sunan al-Kubra*, no. 12569.
32. Bayhaqī, *Al-Asmā' wa al-Ṣifāt*, no. 658.
33. Ayubi, *Gendered Morality*, 112.

34. Kueny, *Conceiving Identities*, 32.
35. Grosz, *Volatile Bodies*, 198.
36. De Sondy, *The Crisis of Islamic Masculinities*, 98.
37. Ibn Hishām, *The Life of Muhammad*, 134, 137.
38. Qur'an 53:27–28, also 17:40, 37:149–53, 43:16–19, 52:39.
39. Muqatil Ibn Sulayman, *Tafsīr*, 2:309.
40. Geissinger, *Gender and Muslim Construction of Exegetical Authority*, 143–49.
41. al-Wāqidī, *The Life of Muhammad*, 39–41, 116, 200, 445; Ibn Rāshid, *The Expeditions*, 87; Ibn Hishām, *The Life of Muhammad*, 303.
42. Ibn Hishām, *The Life of Muhammad*, 39.
43. Ibn Hishām, 461; Bashear, "The Mission of Dihya al-Kalbi."
44. al-Wāqidī, *The Life of Muhammad*, 115–16.
45. al-Wāqidī, 115–16.
46. Bashear, "The Mission of Dihya al-Kalbi."
47. Ibn Hishām, *The Life of Muhammad*, 135.
48. Ibn Hishām, 107.
49. Khoury, *Wahb b. Munabbih*, vol. 1, PB 5.
50. Ibn Rāshid, *The Expeditions*, 30–31.
51. Ibn Rāshid, 96–97.
52. al-Wāqidī, *The Life of Muhammad*, 429.
53. al-Wāqidī, 429. al-Wāqidī provides a short chain of 'Abdullah b. Yazid < Sa'id ibn 'Amr al-Hudhali. Ibn Hishām's account does not include an isnad; Ibn Hishām, *The Life of Muhammad*, 565.
54. Grosz, *Volatile Bodies*, 203.
55. Halevi, *Muhammad's Grave*, 127–35.
56. Ibn Hishām, *The Life of Muhammad*, 10–11.
57. Ibn Hishām, 2, 12–13.
58. Kristeva, *Powers of Horror*, 71.
59. Ibn Ḥanbal, *Musnad*, no. 25766.
60. Ibn Sa'd, *Ṭabaqāt*, 4:189.
61. Sachiko Murata and William C. Chittick use the "hadith of Gabriel" to frame their introduction to Islam in *The Vision of Islam*.
62. Ibn Abī Shayba, *Muṣannaf*, no. 37547.
63. Ibn Ḥanbal, *Musnad*, no. 367.
64. Ibn Ḥanbal, no. 5857.
65. al-Ḥākim, *Al-Mustadrak*, no. 6345.
66. Ibn Ḥanbal, *Musnad*, no. 24077.
67. Bayhaqī, *Dalā'il al-Nubuwwa*, 7:66; Abū Nu'aym, *Dalā'il al-Nubuwwa*, no. 1450.
68. Ṭabarānī, *Mu'jam al-Kabīr*, 1:757.
69. Spellberg, *Politics, Gender, and the Islamic Past*, 44.
70. Ibn Hishām, *The Life of Muhammad*, 71–72.
71. Ibn Hishām, 46.

72. Spellberg, *Politics, Gender, and the Islamic Past*, 41–44.
73. Ibn Ḥanbal, *Musnad*, nos. 25081, 25369; Ibn Abī Shayba, *Muṣannaf*, nos. 25685, 32276.
74. Spellberg, *Politics, Gender, and the Islamic Past*, 41–44.
75. Bukhārī, *Ṣaḥīḥ*, nos. 2615, 3833; Muslim, *Ṣaḥīḥ*, no. 3321; Ṭabarānī, *Mu'jam al-Kabīr*, no. 18626.
76. Ṭabarānī, *Mu'jam al-Kabīr*, no. 18626.
77. Ṭabarānī, no. 18626; Melchert, "The Early Controversy over whether the Prophet Saw God."
78. Bukhārī, *Ṣaḥīḥ*, nos. 2996, 3508, 3720, 3760, 5810, 5760, 5807; Tirmidhī, *Al-Jami'*, no. 2636; Nasā'ī, *Sunan al-Kubra*, nos. 3915, 8580, 9782, 9783; Nasā'ī, *Sunan al-Sughra*, no. 3915; al-Dārimī, *Sunan*, no. 2557.
79. Bukhārī, *Ṣaḥīḥ*, no. 5807.
80. Bukhārī, no. 3385, 4622; Muslim, *Ṣaḥīḥ*, 2451, 4496.
81. al-Ḥākim, *Al-Mustadrak*, no. 6754.
82. Ṭabarānī, *Mu'jam al-Kabīr*, 9:18614–27; Ibn Ḥibbān, *Ṣaḥīḥ*, no. 7255.
83. Ṭabarānī, *Mu'jam al-Kabīr*, 10:19240; Abū Ya'lā, *Musnad*, no. 6866.
84. Bayhaqī, *Dalā'il al-Nubuwwa*, 7:66.
85. Bayhaqī, 7:66.
86. Ibn Māja, *Sunan*, no. 62; Tirmidhī, *Al-Jāmi'*, no. 2552; Nasā'ī, *Sunan al-Sughra*, no. 498.
87. Sayeed, *Women and the Transmission of Religious Authority in Islam*, 38.
88. Ibn Ḥanbal, *Musnad*, no. 25914.
89. The Qur'an's wording in 6:130, addressing both humans and jinns as having received messengers "from among you," allows for some ambiguity on this point.
90. Ibn Hishām, *The Life of Muhammad*, 106.
91. Ibn Hishām, 497; al-Wāqidī, *The Life of Muhammad*, 212.
92. Ibn Ḥanbal, *Musnad*, no. 2822.
93. Muslim, *Ṣaḥīḥ*, no. 4502.
94. Bukhārī, *Ṣaḥīḥ*, no. 3426.
95. Stowasser, *Women in the Qur'an, Traditions, and Interpretation*, 77.
96. Shaikh, *Sufi Narratives of Intimacy*, 89.
97. Ibn Hishām, *The Life of Muhammad*, 290.
98. Jones, "Ibn Isḥāq and al-Wāqidī."
99. Mirza, "Dreaming the Truth in the Sīra of Ibn Hishām."
100. Guillaume, *New Light on the Life of Muhammad*, 7–8.
101. Ibn Hishām, *The Life of Muhammad*, 290–91.
102. Ibn Ḥanbal, *Musnad*, nos. 757, 1149, 27412, 27416.
103. Ibn Ḥanbal, nos. 3241, 12920, 20848, 21754.
104. Juynboll, "Some *Isnād*-Analytical Methods."
105. Katz, *Body of Text*, 196.
106. Ibn Hishām, *The Life of Muhammad*, 3–4.
107. Ibn Hishām, 68.

108. Ibn Hishām, 68–69.
109. Qur'an 11:78, 15:71.
110. David S. Powers makes a revisionist argument regarding 33:40 and the significance of Muhammad's adopted son Zayd. Powers, *Muhammad Is Not the Father of Any of Your Men*.
111. Ibn Ḥanbal, *Musnad*, no. 12383; Ibn Sa'd, *Ṭabaqāt*, 1:112.
112. Bukhārī, *Ṣaḥīḥ*, no. 5753; Ibn Māja, *Sunan*, no. 1499. Rubin has taken Powers's contentious argument as a provocation to make a "fresh attempt" at the questions of 33:40, which includes consideration of the prophetic traditions concerning Ibrahim. Rubin links these traditions to issues of paternity, arguing that the narrations' purpose is to counter suspicions and establish Muhammad as the baby's biological father. Rubin, "The Seal of the Prophets and the Finality of Prophecy."
113. Ṭayālisī, *Musnad*, no. 1470; Ibn Abī Shayba, *Muṣannaf*, nos. 32167, 32168, 32170; Ibn Ḥanbal, *Musnad*, nos. 11546, 22718.
114. Bukhārī, *Ṣaḥīḥ*, nos. 3460, 3473, 3507; Muslim, *Ṣaḥīḥ*, no. 4490; Tirmidhī, *Al-Jāmi'*, no. 3833; Nasā'ī, *Sunan al-Kubra*, no. 8049.
115. Bukhārī, *Ṣaḥīḥ*, nos. 3377, 3461; Muslim, *Ṣaḥīḥ*, no. 4493.
116. Bukhārī, *Ṣaḥīḥ*, no. 5839; Muslim, *Ṣaḥīḥ*, nos. 4494, 4495; Ibn Māja, *Sunan*, no. 1610; Nasā'ī, *Sunan al-Kubra*, no. 6810.
117. Ibn Rāshid, *The Expeditions*, 43.
118. Kister, "'And He Was Born Circumcised,'" 10–30.
119. Ibn Hishām, *The Life of Muhammad*, 654–55.
120. Ibn Sa'd, *Ṭabaqāt*, 1:82.
121. Bayhaqī, *Dalā'il al-Nubuwwa*, 1:114; Abū Nu'aym, *Dalā'il al-Nubuwwa*, nos. 94, 95; Ṭabarānī, *Al-Mu'jam al-Awsaṭ*, no. 6314; al-Khaṭīb al-Baghdādī, *Tārikh Madīnat al-Salām*, no. 232; Ṭabarānī, *Mu'jam al-Sughra*, no. 936.
122. Abū Nu'aym, *Dalā'il al-Nubuwwa*, no. 94; Ṭabarānī, *Al-Mu'jam al-Awsaṭ*, no. 6314; al-Khaṭīb al-Baghdādī, no. 232; Ṭabarānī, *Mu'jam al-Sughra*, no. 936.
123. Ṭabarānī, *Al-Mu'jam al-Awsaṭ*, no. 5970; Abū Nu'aym, *Dalā'il al-Nubuwwa*, no. 96.
124. Ibn Hishām, *The Life of Muhammad*, 81.
125. Ibn Hishām, 687–88.
126. Ibn Hishām, 687–88.
127. Ibn Hishām, 687–88.
128. al-Wāqidī, *The Life of Muhammad*, 278, 550.
129. 'Abd al-Razzāq, *Muṣannaf*, no. 1105; Ibn Ḥanbal, *Musnad*, no. 24210.
130. Ibn Sa'd, *Ṭabaqāt*, 1:124–25.
131. Ibn Ḥanbal, *Musnad*, no. 24848.
132. Ibn Māja, *Sunan*, no. 654.
133. Ibn Māja, no. 1912.
134. Ibn Sa'd, *Ṭabaqāt*, 1:124–25.
135. Tirmidhī, *Shamā'il*, no. 349.

136. Ibn Sa'd, *Ṭabaqāt*, 1:124–25.
137. Ibn Sa'd, 1:124–25.
138. Ibn Sa'd, 2:213.
139. Bukhārī, *Ṣaḥīḥ*, no. 354; Muslim, *Ṣaḥīḥ*, no. 520.
140. Tirmidhī, *Al-Jāmi'*, no. 2675.
141. Abū Dāwūd, *Sunan*, no. 2735.
142. Abū Nu'aym, *Hilyat al-Awlīyā'*, nos. 9953, 12462.
143. Bayhaqī, *Dalā'il al-Nubuwwa*, 2:54–55; al-Ḥākim, *Al-Mustadrak*, no. 7420.
144. Ibn Sa'd, *Ṭabaqāt*, 1:282; Ibn Ḥanbal, *Musnad*, no. 14155; 'Abd al-Razzāq, *Muṣannaf*, no. 14129.
145. 'Abd al-Razzāq, *Muṣannaf*, nos. 14126, 14127, 14128.
146. Ibn Sa'd, *Ṭabaqāt*, 1:282.
147. Ibn Sa'd, 1:282.
148. Hoffman, *Sufism*, 253. Cited in Shaikh, "Knowledge, Women and Gender in the Ḥadīth."
149. Bukhārī, *Ṣaḥīḥ*, nos. 3046, 5939; Muslim, *Ṣaḥīḥ*, no. 4066; Ibn Māja, *Sunan*, no. 3543; Nasā'ī, *Sunan al-Kubra*, no. 7312.
150. Bukhārī, *Ṣaḥīḥ*, no. 262; Nasā'ī, no. 8698.
151. Bayhaqī, *Sunan al-Kubra*, no. 12356.
152. Ibn Ḥibbān, *Ṣaḥīḥ*, no. 1230.
153. Ibn Khuzayma, *Ṣaḥīḥ*, no. 238.
154. Abū Ya'lā, *Musnad*, nos. 2911, 3133, 3160.
155. Ṭabarānī, *Musnad al-Shāmīyīn*, no. 2546.
156. Ṭabarānī, *Al-Mu'jam al-Awsaṭ*, no. 583.
157. Ṭabarānī, *Mu'jam al-Kabīr*, 3:5353; Abū Nu'aym, *Akhbār Aṣbān*, no. 2250.
158. Ibn Ḥanbal, *Musnad*, nos. 26016, 27165, 27184, 27201; Ibn Abī Shayba, *Muṣannaf*, nos. 9070, 9077.
159. Ibn Ḥanbal, *Musnad*, nos. 22892, 22932, 22964, 22970; Ibn Abī Shayba, *Muṣannaf*, no. 29535.
160. Ibn Ḥanbal, *Musnad*, nos. 22932, 22970, 22964, 22892.
161. Ringrose, "The Byzantine Body."
162. Ibn Abī Shayba, *Muṣannaf*, no. 920.
163. Bukhārī, *Ṣaḥīḥ*, no. 1874.
164. Bukhārī, nos. 3069, 5333, 6497, 6499, 6508, 6515; Muslim, *Ṣaḥīḥ*, nos. 4202, 4203; Abū Dāwūd, *Sunan*, no. 4369; Ibn Māja, *Sunan*, no. 3907; Tirmidhī, *Al-Jāmi'*, no. 2208; Nasā'ī, *Sunan al-Kubra*, no. 10253.
165. Ṭabarānī, *Mu'jam al-Kabīr*, 5:11398.
166. Ibn Sa'd, *Ṭabaqāt*, 7:114.
167. Gil'adi, *Infants, Parents and Wet Nurse*, 79–81.
168. Gil'adi, 79–81.
169. Motzki, Boekhoff-van der Voort, and Anthony, *Analysing Muslim Traditions*, 39. Also Sayeed, *Women and the Transmission of Religious Knowledge in Islam*, 30–31.
170. Abū Nu'aym, *Hilyat al-Awlīyā'*, 2:147.

171. Abū Nu'aym, 2:147.
172. Mourad, *Early Islam between Myth and History*, 27.
173. Mourad, 25–28.

CHAPTER FIVE

1. Rustomji, *The Garden and the Fire*.
2. Bynum, *The Resurrection of the Body in Western Christianity*, 13.
3. Tirmidhī, *Al-Jāmi'*, no. 1641.
4. Nasā'ī, *Sunan al-Sughra*, no. 1833.
5. Tlilli, "From Breath to Soul."
6. Gianotti, *Al-Ghazālī's Unspeakable Doctrine of the Soul*, 75.
7. Kristeva, *Powers of Horror*, 2–4.
8. Kristeva, 3–4.
9. Kristeva, 3–4.
10. Ibn Hishām, *The Life of Muhammad*, 516–17.
11. Kohlberg, "Shi'i Views of the Death of the Prophet Muhammad."
12. Muslim, *Ṣaḥīḥ*, no. 2572.
13. Muslim, no. 2570.
14. Bukhārī, *Ṣaḥīḥ*, no. 8440.
15. Abū Dāwūd, *Sunan*, no. 4512.
16. Bukhārī, *Ṣaḥīḥ*, no. 2949.
17. Abū Dāwūd, *Sunan*, no. 3914.
18. Abū Dāwūd, no. 3913.
19. Ibn Rāshid, *The Expeditions*, 185.
20. Ibn Hishām, *The Life of Muhammad*, 688.
21. Ibn Rāshid, *The Expeditions*, 178–79.
22. Ibn Hishām, *The Life of Muhammad*, 688.
23. Ibn Hishām, 688.
24. Ibn Rāshid, *The Expeditions*, 185.
25. Ibn Sa'd, *Ṭabaqāt*, 2:210.
26. Ibn Sa'd, 2:208.
27. Ibn Sa'd, 2:229.
28. Ibn Abī Shayba, *Muṣannaf*, no. 8697; Ibn Ḥanbal, *Musnad*, no. 16262.
29. Ibn Ḥanbal, *Musnad*, nos. 1884, 10727, 22117, 24561, 25018, 25407, 26708.
30. Abū Dāwūd, *Sunan*, no. 885; Nasā'ī, *Sunan al-Sughra*, no. 1359; Ibn Māja, *Sunan*, nos. 1075, 1626, 1627.
31. Muslim, *Ṣaḥīḥ*, no. 4387; Nasā'ī, *Sunan al-Sughra*, nos. 1623–27; Nasā'ī, *Sunan al-Kubra*, nos. 1310–12.
32. Abū Dāwūd, *Sunan*, no. 2041.
33. al-Dārimī, *Sunan*, no. 1535.
34. al-Dārimī, no. 83.
35. al-Dārimī, no. 1375.

36. al-Dārimī, no. 92.
37. al-Dārimī, no. 94.
38. Ṭabarānī, *Mu'jam al-Kabīr*. 1:588; Bayhaqī, *Sunan al-Kubra*, no. 5530; Bayhaqī, *Sunan al-Sughra*, no. 299; Bayhaqī, *Ḥayāt al-Anbiyā' fī Qubūrihim*, no. 10; al-Ḥākim, *Al-Mustadrak*, nos. 967, 8786; Abū Nu'aym, *Dalā'il al-Nubuwwa*, no. 508; Ibn Khuzayma, *Ṣaḥīḥ*, no. 1642.
39. Abū Nu'aym, *Dalā'il al-Nubuwwa*, no. 1576.
40. Abū Ya'lā, *Musnad*, no. 3371.
41. Bayhaqī, *Ḥayāt al-Anbiyā' fī Qubūrihim*.
42. Bayhaqī, nos. 1, 2, 4.
43. Bayhaqī, *Sunan al-Kubra*, no. 9523; Ṭabarānī, *Al-Mu'jam al-Awsaṭ*, no. 3487.
44. Ibn Ḥanbal, *Musnad*, no. 25417.
45. Hodgson, *The Expansion of Islam in the Middle Periods*, 36.
46. Spellberg, *Politics, Gender, and the Islamic Past*, 113.
47. Ṭabarānī, *Mu'jam al-Kabīr*, 9:18433; al-Khatib al-Baghdadi, *Tārikh Madīnat al-Salām*, no. 1739.
48. Ṭabarānī, *Mu'jam al-Kabīr*, 9:18432.
49. Ibn Sa'd, *Ṭabaqāt*, no. 866.
50. al-Khaṭīb al-Baghdādī, *Tārikh Madīnat al-Salām*, no. 1739.
51. Rustomji, *The Garden and the Fire*, 96.
52. In this tradition, Muhammad states that women are deficient in both din and intellect (*'aql*). The deficiency in the former derives from women missing prayers and fasting due to the ritual impurity of menstruation; in the latter, their deficiency is evidenced by the inferiority of their testimony. In her discussion of what she calls "the most notoriously misogynistic hadith in the established corpus," Marion Holmes Katz calls attention to the relationship drawn in this hadith between gender, uncontrolled bodies, and corporeal pollution. In particular, she notes the *'a-q-l* root's construction of a link between intellect and restraint, which informed premodern exegesis that linked women's uncontrollable bodies to their deficient mental capacities. Katz, *Body of Text*, 196.
53. Grosz, *Volatile Bodies*, 197.
54. Ṭabarānī, *Mu'jam al-Kabīr*, 9:18451.
55. Ṭabarānī, 5:10152.
56. Grosz, "Body of Signification."
57. Ṭabarānī, *Mu'jam al-Kabīr*, 8:16459; Bayhaqī, *Sunan al-Kubra*, no. 12401. al-Ḥākim, *Al-Mustadrak*, no. 4628.
58. Ṭabarānī, *Mu'jam al-Kabīr*, 2:2566, 9:18475. al-Khaṭīb al-Baghdādī, *Tārikh Madīnat al-Salām*, no. 3800.
59. Ṭabarānī, *Mu'jam al-Kabīr*, 9:18474.
60. Ṭabarānī, 9:18418.
61. A'isha goes on to say that Muhammad milked his goats and served himself. Ibn Ḥanbal, *Musnad*, no. 26724. While A'isha's narration of lice removal depicts Muhammad's body as one subject to typical human phenomena, this represen-

tation of a lice-ridden prophetic body does not have the same consequences for all readers. "In contrast to popular opinion today," explains Ian C. Beavis, lice in the ancient Mediterranean milieu "were not regarded as having any particular association with uncleanliness: infestation by them was considered as a perfectly normal and inevitable, if undesirable, fact of life in all sections of society." Beavis, *Insects and Other Invertebrates in Classical Antiquity*, 112.

CONCLUSION

1. Qadhi, "Collector's Edition."
2. Grosz, *Volatile Bodies*, 168.
3. Kristeva, *Powers of Horror*, 109.
4. Zaman, "*Maghāzī* and the *Muḥaddithūn*."
5. Hoyland, "History, Fiction, and Authorship in the First Centuries of Islam."
6. Grosz, *Volatile Bodies*, 168.
7. Grosz, 169.
8. Deleuze and Guattari, *A Thousand Plateaus*, 40.
9. Deleuze and Guattari, 9–10.
10. von Denffer, "Baraka as Basic Concept of Muslim Popular Belief."
11. Buchanan, "Assemblage Theory and Its Discontents."

Bibliography

ʿAbd al-Razzāq al-Sanʾānī. *Muṣannaf*. Beirut: Dar al-Kotob al-Ilmiyah, 2000.

———. *Tafsīr*. Beirut: Dar al-Kotob al-Ilmiyah, 1999.

Abū Dāwūd al-Sijistānī. *Sunan*. IslamWeb. http://library.islamweb.net/hadith/display_hbook.php?bk_no=184&pid=113467.

Abū Nuʿaym al-Isfaḥānī. *Akhbār Aṣhān*. IslamWeb. http://library.islamweb.net/hadith/display_hbook.php?bk_no=621&pid=319035.

———. *Dalāʾil al-Nubuwwa*. IslamWeb. http://library.islamweb.net/hadith/display_hbook.php?bk_no=629&pid=324273.

———. *Hilyat al-Awlīyāʾ*. IslamWeb. http://library.islamweb.net/hadith/display_hbook.php?bk_no=621&pid=319035.

Abū Yaʿlā. *Musnad*. IslamWeb. http://library.islamweb.net/hadith/display_hbook.php?bk_no=327&pid=155201.

Ahmed, Shahab. *Before Orthodoxy: The Satanic Verses in Early Islam*. Cambridge, Mass.: Harvard University Press, 2017.

Al-ʿAsqalānī, Ibn Ḥajar. *Taqrib al-Tahdhīb*. Medina: Darul Minhaj and Darul Yusr, 2012.

al-Ḥākim Naysābūrī. *Al-Mustadrak ʿala al-Ṣaḥīḥayn*. IslamWeb. http://library.islamweb.net/hadith/display_hbook.php?bk_no=594&hid=4161&pid=0.

Allam, Jehan. "A Sociolinguistic Study on the Use of Color Terminology in Egyptian Colloquial and Classical Arabic." In *Diversity in Language: Contrastive Studies in English and Arabic Theoretical and Applied Linguistics*, edited by Zeinab Ibrahim, Nagwa Kassabgy, and Sabiha Aydelott, 7–92. Cairo: American University of Cairo Press, 2000.

Amir-Moezzi, Mohammad Ali. *The Spirituality of Shiʾi Islam: Belief and Practices*. London: I. B. Tauris, 2011.

Ayubi, Zahra. *Gendered Morality: Classical Islamic Ethics of the Self, Family, and Society*. Columbia: New York University Press, 2019.

Al-Azmeh, Aziz. *Arabic Thought and Islamic Societies*. New York: Routledge, 2015.

Bashear, Suliman. "The Mission of Diḥya al-Kalbī and the Situation in Syria." *Jerusalem Studies in Arabic and Islam* 14 (1991): 173–207.

Bashir, Shahzad. *Sufi Bodies: Religion and Society in Medieval Islam*. New York: Columbia University Press, 2011.

Bauer, Karen. *Gender Hierarchy in the Qur'ān*. Cambridge: Cambridge University Press, 2015.

Bayhaqī, Aḥmad ibn al-Ḥusayn. *Al-Asmā' wa al-Ṣifāt*. IslamWeb. http://library.islamweb.net/hadith/display_hbook.php?bk_no=666&pid=329491.

———. *Dalā'il al-Nubuwwa*. Edited by 'Abdul-Mu'ṭi Qal'aji. Beirut: Dar al-Kotob al-Ilmiyah, 2008.

———. *Ḥayāt al-Anbiyā' fī Qubūrihim*. Al-Mansura: Maktabat al-Iman, 1993.

———. *Ḥayāt al-Anbiyā' fī Qubūrihim*. http://library.islamweb.net/hadith/display_hbook.php?bk_no=680&hid=10&pid=0.

———. *Sunan al-Kubra*. IslamWeb. http://library.islamweb.net/hadith/display_hbook.php?bk_no=673&pid=331361.

———. *Sunan al-Sughra*. IslamWeb. http://library.islamweb.net/hadith/display_hbook.php?bk_no=672&hid=299&pid=330203.

Bayless, Martha. *Sin and Filth in Medieval Culture: The Devil in the Latrine*. New York: Routledge, 2012.

Beavis, Ian C. *Insects and Other Invertebrates in Classical Antiquity*. Exeter, UK: University of Exeter Press, 1988.

Beckman, Frida, ed. *Deleuze and Sex*. Edinburgh: Edinburgh University Press, 2011.

Bembry, Jason. *Yahweh's Coming of Age*. Winona Lake, Ind.: Eisenbrauns, 2011.

Bildhauer, Bettina. *Medieval Blood*. Cardiff: University of Wales Press, 2006.

Bosworth, C. E. "al-Ṭabarī." In *Encyclopedia of Islam*, 2nd ed., edited by P. Bearman, Th. Bianquis, et al. Brill Online, 2016.

Brown, Jonathan A. C. *The Canonization of al-Bukhārī and Muslim: The Formation and Function of Sunnī Ḥadīth Canon*. Leiden, the Netherlands: Brill, 2007.

———. "The Canonization of Ibn Majah: Authenticity vs. Utility in the Formation of the Sunni Hadith Canon." *Revue des Mondes Musulmans et de la Méditerranée* 129 (2012): 169–81.

———. *Hadith*. Oxford, UK: Oneworld, 2011.

———. "Even if It's Not True: Using Unreliable Ḥadīths in Sunni Islam." *Islamic Law and Society* 18, no. 1 (2011): 1–52.

———. "The Rules of Matn Criticism: There Are No Rules." *Islamic Law and Society* 19, no. 4 (2012): 356–96.

Buchanan, Ian. "Assemblage Theory and Its Discontents." *Deleuze Studies* 9, no. 3 (2015): 382–92.

———. "The Problem of the Body in Deleuze and Guattari, Or, What Can a Body Do?" *Body and Society* 3, no. 3 (1997): 73–91.

Bukhārī, Muḥammad ibn Ismā'īl. *Ṣaḥīḥ al-Bukhārī*. IslamWeb. http://library.islamweb.net/hadith/display_hbook.php?bk_no=146&pid=97661.

———. *Al-Adab al-Mufrad*. IslamWeb. http://library.islamweb.net/hadith/display_hbook.php?bk_no=141&pid=96875&hid=569.

Butler, Judith. *Gender Trouble: Feminism and the Subversion of Identity*. New York: Routledge, 2006.

Bynum, Caroline Walker. *The Resurrection of the Body in Western Christianity, 200–1336*. New York: Columbia University Press, 1995.

Callon, Callie. *Reading Bodies: Physiognomy as a Strategy of Persuasion in Early Christian Discourse*. New York: Bloomsbury, 2019.

Campbell, Sandra Sue. "Telling Memories: The Zubayrids in Islamic Historical Memory." PhD diss., University of California, Los Angeles, 2003.

Chaudhry, Ayesha S. *Domestic Violence and the Islamic Tradition*. Oxford: Oxford University Press, 2013.

El Cheikh, Nadia Maria. *Women, Islam, and Abbasid Identity*. Cambridge, Mass.: Harvard University Press, 2015.

Chelhod, Joseph. "La baraka chez les Arabes ou l'influence bienfaisante du sacré." *Revue de l'Histoire des Religions* 148, no. 1 (1955): 68–88.

Cokayne, Karen. *Experiencing Old Age in Ancient Rome*. London: Routledge, 2003.

Colebrook, Claire. *Deleuze: A Guide for the Perplexed*. London: Continuum, 2008.

Colin, G. S. "Baraka." In *Encyclopedia of Islam*, 2nd ed., edited by P. Bearman, Th. Bianquis, et al. Brill Online, 2016.

Cooperson, Michael. *Classical Arabic Biography: The Heirs of the Prophets in the Age of al-Ma'mun*. Cambridge: Cambridge University Press, 2000.

Cox, Patricia. *Biography in Late Antiquity: A Quest for the Holy Man*. Berkeley: University of California Press, 1983.

Cuffel, Alexandra. *Gendering Disgust in Medieval Religious Polemic*. Notre Dame, Ind.: University of Notre Dame Press, 2007.

Dakake, Maria. *The Charismatic Community: Shi'ite Identity in Early Islam*. Albany: State University of New York Press, 2007.

Daraquṭnī, Abū al-Ḥasan ʿAlī. *Kitāb al-Ruʾyā*. IslamWeb. http://library.islamweb.net/hadith/display_hbook.php?bk_no=534&pid=305713.

al-Dārimī, Abū Muḥammad Abd ʿAllāh. *Sunan al-Dārimī*. Edited by Mustafa Dib al-Bugha. Beirut: Dar al-Musṭafā, 2011.

Deleuze, Gilles, and Félix Guattari. *A Thousand Plateaus: Capitalism and Schizophrenia*. Minneapolis: University of Minnesota Press, 1988.

De Sondy, Amanullah. *The Crisis of Islamic Masculinities*. London: Bloomsbury Academic, 2014.

Donner, Fred. *Muhammad and the Believers: At the Origins of Islam*. Cambridge, Mass.: Belknap Press of Harvard University Press, 2010.

———. *Narratives of Islamic Origins: The Beginnings of Islamic Historical Writing*. Princeton, N.J.: Darwin, 1998.

Douglas, Fedwa Malti. "Controversy and Its Effects in the Biographical Tradition of al-Khaṭīb al-Baghdādī." *Studia Islamica*, no. 46 (1977): 115–31.

Ed., "Liwāṭ." In *Encyclopedia of Islam*, 2nd ed., edited by P. Bearman, Th. Bianquis, et al. Brill Online, 2016.

Fahd, T. "Ibn Sīrīn." In *Encyclopedia of Islam*, 2nd ed., edited by P. Bearman, Th. Bianquis, et al. Brill Online, 2016.

———. "Sakīna." In *Encyclopedia of Islam*, 2nd ed., edited by P. Bearman, Th. Bianquis, et al. Brill Online, 2016.

Fierro, Maribel. "Al-Ṭabarānī." In *Encyclopedia of Islam*, 2nd ed., edited by P. Bearman, Th. Bianquis, et al. Brill Online, 2016.

Geissinger, Aisha. "The Exegetical Traditions of A'isha: Notes on Their Impact and Significance." *Journal of Qur'anic Studies* 6, no. 1 (2004): 1–20.

———. *Gender and Muslim Construction of Exegetical Authority: A Rereading of the Classical Genre of Qur'ān Commentary*. Leiden, the Netherlands: Brill, 2015.

GhaneaBassiri, Kambiz. "Ethics." In *Medieval Islamic Civilization: An Encyclopedia*, edited by Josef W. Meri, 241–42. New York: Routledge, 2006.

Ghaemmaghami, Omid. "Numinous Vision, Messianic Encounters: Typological Representations in a Version of the Prophet's *Hadith al-Ru'ya* and in Visions and Dreams of the Hidden Imam." In *Dreams and Visions in Islamic Societies*, edited by Özgen Felek and Alexander D. Knysh, 51–76. Albany: State University of New York, 2012.

Ghaly, Mohammed M. "Physiognomy: A Forgotten Chapter of Disability in Islam." *Bibliotecha Orientalis* 66, no. 3–4 (May–August 2009): 162–98.

Gianotti, Timothy J. *Al-Ghazālī's Unspeakable Doctrine of the Soul: Unveiling the Esoteric Psychology and Eschatology of the Iḥyā'*. Leiden, the Netherlands: Brill, 2001.

Gibb, H. A. R. "'Abd Allāh b. al-Zubayr." In *Encyclopedia of Islam*, 2nd ed., edited by P. Bearman, Th. Bianquis, et al. Brill Online, 2016.

Gil'adi, Avner. *Infants, Parents and Wet Nurses: Medieval Islamic Views on Breastfeeding and Their Social Implications*. Leiden, the Netherlands: Brill, 1999.

———. "Some Notes on *Taḥnīk* in Medieval Islam." *Journal of Near Eastern Studies* 47 (1988): 175–79.

Görke, Andreas, and Gregor Schoeler. "Reconstructing the Earliest Sīra Texts: The Hiğra in the Corpus of 'Urwa b. al-Zubayr." *Der Islam* 82, no. 2 (2005): 209–20.

Gil'adi, Avner, and Harald Motzki, "First Century Sources for the Life of Muḥammad? A Debate." *Der Islam* 89, no. 1/2 (2012): 2–59.

Grosz, Elizabeth. "The Body of Signification." In *Abjection, Melancholia and Love: The Works of Julia Kristeva*, edited by John Fletcher and Andrew Benjamin, 80–103. New York: Routledge, 1990.

———. *Sexual Subversions: Three French Feminists*. Sydney: Allen and Unwin, 1989.

———. *Volatile Bodies: Toward a Corporeal Feminism*. Bloomington: Indiana University Press, 1994.

Guillaume, A. *New Light on the Life of Muhammad*. Manchester: Manchester University Press, 1960.

Guillaume, Laura, and Joe Hughes, eds. *Deleuze and the Body*. Edinburgh: Edinburgh University Press, 2011.

Halevi, Leor. *Muhammad's Grave: Death Rites and the Making of Islamic Society*. New York: Columbia University Press, 2007.

Halperin, David J. "The Ibn Sayyād Traditions and the Legend of al-Dajjāl." *Journal of the American Oriental Society* 96, no. 2 (April–June 1976): 213–25.

Hammer, Juliane. *Peaceful Families: American Muslim Efforts against Domestic Violence*. Princeton, N.J.: Princeton University Press, 2019.

Harvey, Susan Ashbrook. *Scenting Salvation: Ancient Christianity and the Olfactory Imagination*. Berkeley: University of California Press, 2006.

Hawting, G. R. "'A Plaything for Kings': A'isha's Hadith, Ibn al-Zubayr, and Rebuilding the Ka'ba." In *Islamic Studies Today: Essays in Honor of Andrew Rippin*, edited by Majid Daneshgar and Walid Saleh, 1–21. Leiden, the Netherlands: Brill, 2016.

al-Hilali, Muhammad Taqi-ud-Din, and Muhammad Muhsin Khan. *The Meanings of the Qur'an: English Translation of the Meanings and Commentary*. Medina: King Fahd Complex for the Printing of the Holy Qur'an, 1998.

Hidayatullah, Aysha. *Feminist Edges of the Qur'an*. Oxford: Oxford University Press, 2014.

Hodgson, Marshall G. S. *The Expansion of Islam in the Middle Periods*. Vol. 2 of *The Venture of Islam*. Chicago: University of Chicago Press, 1974.

Hoffman, Valerie J. *Sufism, Mystics, and Saints in Modern Egypt*. Columbia: University of South Carolina Press, 2009.

Holtzman, Livnat. "Anthropomorphism." In *The Encyclopedia of Islam*, edited by Gudrun Kramer, Denis Matringe, John Nawas, and Everett Rowson, 46–53. Leiden, the Netherlands: Brill, 2011.

Hoyland, Robert G. "History, Fiction, and Authorship in the First Centuries of Islam." In *Writing and Representation in Early Islam*, edited by Julia Bray, 16–46. New York: Routledge, 2006.

———. "The Islamic Background to Polemon's Treatise." In *Seeing the Face, Seeing the Soul: Polemon's "Physignomy" from Classical Antiquity to Medieval Islam*, edited by Simon Swain, 227–80. Oxford: Oxford University Press, 2007.

———. "A New Edition and Translation of the Leiden Polemon." In *Seeing the Face, Seeing the Soul: Polemon's "Physignomy" from Classical Antiquity to Medieval Islam*, edited by Simon Swain, 329–464. Oxford: Oxford University Press, 2007.

Hughes, Joe. "Introduction: Pity the Meat?: Deleuze and the Body." In *Deleuze and the Body*, edited by Laura Guillaume and Joe Hughes, 1–6. Edinburgh: Edinburgh University Press, 2011.

Husayn, Nebil A. "Treatises on the Salvation of Abu Talib." *Shii Studies Review* 1, no. 1–2 (2017): 3–41.

Ibn Aḥmad ibn Ḥanbal, ʿAbd Allāh. *Kitāb as-Sunna*. Riyadh: Dar Alim Kutub, 1996.

Ibn Abī ʿĀṣim. *Al-Aḥād wa-l-Mathānī*. IslamWeb. https://library.islamweb.net/hadith/display_hbook.php?bk_no=277&pid=129843.

———. *Kitāb as-Sunna*. IslamWeb. http://library.islamweb.net/hadith/display_hbook.php?bk_no=282&pid=133155.

Ibn Abī Shayba. *Muṣannaf Ibn Abī Shayba fī al-Aḥādīth wa'l-Āthār*. Beirut: Dar al-Kotob al-Ilmiyah, 2005.

Ibn Ḥanbal, Aḥmad ibn Muḥammad. *Musnad al-Imām Aḥmad Ibn Ḥanbal*. Beirut: ʿĀlam al-Kutub, 1998.

Ibn Ḥibbān, Abū Ḥātim Muḥammad. *Ṣaḥīḥ*. IslamWeb. https://library.islamweb.net/hadith/display_hbook.php?bk_no=454&pid=263537.

Ibn Hishām, ʿAbd al-Mālik. *The Life of Muhammad*. Translated by A. Guillaume. Oxford: Oxford University Press, 2012.

Ibn al-Jawzī. *Virtues of the Imām Aḥmad Ibn Ḥanbal*. Translated by Michael Cooperson. New York: New York University Press, 2015.

———. *Kitāb al-Mawḍūʿāt*. IslamWeb. https://islamweb.net/ar/library/index.php

?page=bookcontents&ID=85&idfrom=181&idto=182&flag=0&bk_no=88&ayano=0&surano=0&bookhad=0.

Ibn Khuzayma. *Ṣaḥīḥ*. IslamWeb. http://library.islamweb.net/hadith/display_hbook.php?bk_no=345&pid=178557.

Ibn Māja. *Sunan*. IslamWeb. http://library.islamweb.net/hadith/display_hbook.php?bk_no=173&pid=109011.

Ibn Qutabya. *Ta'wīl Mukhtalif al-Ḥadīth*. Translated by Che Amnah Bahari. Perpustakaan Negara: International Islamic University Malaysia Press, 2009.

Ibn Rāshid, Ma'mar. *The Expeditions: An Early Biography of Muḥammad*. Translated by Sean W. Anthony. New York: New York University Press, 2014.

Ibn Sa'd. *Ṭabaqāt al-Kubra*. Edited by Dr. 'Alī Muḥammad 'Umar. Cairo: Maktaba al-Khānjī, 2001.

———. *Ṭabaqāt al-Kubra*. Edited by Muhammed Abd al-Qader 'Ata. Beirut: Dar al-Kutub al-Ilmiyah, 2012.

Jackson, Sherman. "Ibn Taymiyya on Trial in Damascus." *Journal of Semitic Studies* 39, no. 1 (1994): 41–85.

Jones, J. M. B. "Ibn Isḥāq and al-Wāqidī: The Dream of 'Ātika and the Raid to Nakhla in Relation to the Charge of Plagiarism." *Bulletin of the School of Oriental and African Studies, University of London* 22, no. 1/3 (1959): 41–51.

Juynboll, G. H. A. "al-Tirmidhī." In *Encyclopedia of Islam*, 2nd ed., edited by P. Bearman, Th. Bianquis, et al. Brill Online, 2016.

———. *Muslim Tradition*. Cambridge: Cambridge University Press, 2008.

———. "Some *Isnād*-Analytical Methods Illustrated on the Basis of Several Woman-Demeaning Sayings from *Ḥadīth* Literature." *Al-Qantara* 10, no. 2 (1989): 343–84.

———. *Encyclopedia of Canonical Hadith*. Leiden, the Netherlands: Brill, 2007.

al-Kaisi, Meis. "Sufi Apologia in the Guise of Biography: The Case of Abū Nu'aym al-Iṣfahānī's *Ḥilyat al-Awliyā' wa-ṭabaqāt al-aṣfiyā'*." *British Journal of Middle Eastern Studies*, 43, no. 1 (2015): 115–34.

Karamustafa, Ahmet T. *Sufism: The Formative Period*. Berkeley: University of California Press, 2007.

Katz, Marion Holmes. *Body of Text: The Emergence of the Sunni Law of Ritual Purity*. Albany: State University of New York Press, 2002.

Khalidi, Tarif. *Arabic Historical Thought in the Classical Period*. Cambridge: Cambridge University Press, 1994.

al-Khaṭīb al-Baghdādī. *Tārikh Madīnat al-Salām*. IslamWeb. https://library.islamweb.net/hadith/display_hbook.php?bk_no=717&pid=351023.

Khoury, Raif Georges. *Wahb b. Munabbih*. Wiesbaden, Germany: Otto Harrassowitz, 1972.

Kister, M. J. "'A Bag of Meat': A Study of an Early Ḥadīth." *Bulletin of the School of Oriental and African Studies* 33, no. 2 (1970): 267–75.

———. "'And He Was Born Circumcised . . . ': Some Notes on Circumcision in Ḥadīth." *Oriens* 34 (1994): 10–30.

Klemm, Verena. "Formation of an Islamic Legend: Fāṭima, the Daughter of the Prophet Muḥammad." In *Ideas, Images, and Methods of Portrayal: Insights into Ara-*

bic Literature and Islam, edited by Sebastian Günther, 181–207. Leiden, the Netherlands: Brill, 2005.

Knight, Michael Muhammad. *Tripping with Allah: Islam, Drugs, and Writing*. Berkeley: Soft Skull Press, 2013.

Kohlberg, Etan. "Shi'i Views of the Death of the Prophet Muhammad." In *Medieval Arabic Thought: Essays in Honour of Fritz Zimmermann*, 77–86. London: Warburg Institute, 2012.

Kristeva, Julia. *Powers of Horror: An Essay on Abjection*. New York: Columbia University Press, 1982.

Kueny, Kathryn M. *Conceiving Identities: Maternity in Medieval Muslim Discourse and Practice*. Albany: State University of New York Press, 2013.

Kugle, Scott. *Homosexuality in Islam*. Oxford: Oxford University Press, 2010.

———. *Sufis and Saints' Bodies: Mysticism, Corporeality, and Sacred Power in Islam*. Chapel Hill: University of North Carolina Press, 2007.

Lange, Christian. "'On That Day When Faces Will Be White or Black' (Q3:106): Towards a Semiology of the Face in the Arabo-Islamic Tradition." *Journal of the American Oriental Society* 127, no. 4 (October–December 2007): 429–45.

Laqueur, Thomas. *Making Sex: Body and Gender from the Greeks to Freud*. Cambridge, Mass.: Harvard University Press, 1990.

Lecker, Michael. "The Bewitching of the Prophet Muḥammad by the Jews: A Note à Propos ʿAbd al-Malik b. Ḥabīb's Mukhtaṣar fī l-Ṭibb." *Al-Qantara* 13, no. 2 (1992): 561–69.

Lincicum, David. "Philo and the Physiognomic Tradition." *Journal for the Study of Judaism* 44, no. 1 (2013): 57–86.

Lindberg, David C. *Theories of Vision: From al-Kindi to Kepler*. Chicago: University of Chicago Press, 1976.

Lucas, Scott C. *Constructive Critics, Ḥadīth Literature, and the Articulation of Sunnī Islam: The Legacy of the Generation of Ibn Sa'd, Ibn Ma'īn, and Ibn Ḥanbal*. Leiden, the Netherlands: Brill, 2004.

———. "Where Are the Legal Ḥadīth? A Study of the Musannaf of Ibn Abī Shayba." *Islamic Law and Society* 15, no. 3 (2008): 283–314.

Mālik ibn Anas. *Al-Muwaṭṭā*. IslamWeb. http://library.islamweb.net/hadith/display_hbook.php?bk_no=19&pid=2353.

———. *Al-Muwatta of Imam Malik Ibn Anas: The First Formulation of Islamic Law*. Translated by A. A. Bewley. London: Kegan Paul, 1989.

Melchert, Christopher. "Bukhārī and Early Ḥadīth Criticism." *Journal of the American Oriental Society* 121, no. 1 (2001): 7–19.

———. "The Early Controversy over whether the Prophet Saw God." *Arabica* 62 (2015): 459–76.

———. "God Created Adam in His Image." *Journal of Qur'anic Studies* 13, no. 1 (2011): 113–24.

———. "The Life and Works of al-Nasā'ī." *Journal of Semitic Studies* 59 (2014): 377–407.

———. "Sectaries in the Six Books: Evidence for Their Exclusion from the Sunni Community." *Muslim World* 82 (1992): 287–95.

Meri, Josef W. "Aspects of Baraka (Blessings) and Ritual Devotion among Medieval Muslims and Jews." *Medieval Encounters* 5, no. 1 (1999): 46–49.

———. *The Cult of Saints among Muslims and Jews in Medieval Syria*. Oxford: Oxford University Press, 2002.

Mirza, Sarah. "Dreaming the Truth in the Sīra of Ibn Hishām." In *Dreams and Visions in Islamic Societies*, edited by Özgen Felek and Alexander D. Knysh, 15–30. Albany: State University of New York Press, 2012.

Morimoto, Kazuo. "Keeping the Prophet's Family Alive: Profile of a Genealogical Discipline." In *Genealogy and Knowledge in Muslim Societies*, edited by Sarah Bowen Savant, 11–23. Edinburgh: Edinburgh University Press. 2014.

Morrison, Susan Signe. *Excrement in the Late Middle Ages: Sacred Filth and Chaucer's Fecopoetics*. New York: Palgrave Macmillan, 2008.

Motzki, Harald. *Reconstruction of a Source of Ibn Ishaq's "Life of the Prophet" and Early Qur'an Exegesis: A Study of Early Ibn 'Abbas Traditions*. Piscataway, N.J.: Gorgias, 2017.

Motzki, Harald, with Nicholet Boekhoff-van der Voort and Sean W. Anthony. *Analysing Muslim Traditions: Studies in Legal, Exegetical, and Maghāzī Ḥadīth*. Leiden, the Netherlands: Brill, 2010.

Mourad, Suleiman Ali. *Early Islam between Myth and History: Al-Ḥasan al-Baṣrī (d.110 H/728 CE) and the Formation of His Legacy in Classical Islamic Scholarship*. Leiden, the Netherlands: Brill, 2006.

Muqātil ibn Sulaymān. *Tafsīr*. Beirut: Dar Al-Kotob Ilmiyah, 2003.

Murata, Sachiko, and William C. Chittick. *The Vision of Islam*. St. Paul, Minn.: Paragon House, 1994.

Muslim ibn Ḥajjāj. *Ṣaḥīḥ Muslim*. IslamWeb. http://library.islamweb.net/hadith/display_hbook.php?bk_no=158&hid=4203&pid=0.

Nadvi, Syed Salman. "'Abd Allāh Ibn al-Zubayr and the Caliphate." PhD diss., University of Chicago, 1972.

Nasā'ī, Aḥmad ibn Shu'ayb. *Sunan al-Kubra*. IslamWeb. http://library.islamweb.net/hadith/display_hbook.php?bk_no=315&pid=137573.

———. *Sunan al-Sughra*. IslamWeb. http://library.islamweb.net/hadith/display_hbook.php?bk_no=319&pid=146831.

Nawas, John. "The Contribution of the *Mawālī* to the Six Sunnite Canonical Ḥadīth Collections." In *Ideas, Images, and Methods of Portrayal: Insights into Classical Arabic Literature and Islam*, edited by Sebastian Günther, 141–51. Leiden, the Netherlands: Brill, 2005.

Nigianni, Chrystanthi, and Merl Storr, eds. *Deleuze and Queer Theory*. Edinburgh: Edinburgh University Press, 2011.

Obdrzalek, Suzanne. "Socrates on Love." In *Bloomsbury Companion to Socrates*, edited by John Bussanich and Nicholas D. Smith, 210–32. London: Bloomsbury Academic, 2013.

Popovic, Mladen. "Physiognomic Knowledge in Qumran and Babylonia: Form, Interdisciplinarity, and Secrecy." *Dead Sea Discoveries* 13, no. 2 (2006): 150–76.

———. *Reading the Human Body: Physiognomics and Astrology in the Dead Sea Scrolls and Hellenistic-Early Roman Period*. Leiden, the Netherlands: Brill, 2007.

Powers, David S. *Muhammad Is Not the Father of Any of Your Men: The Making of the Last Prophet*. Philadelphia: University of Pennsylvania Press, 2009.

Qadhi, Yasir. "Collector's Edition: An Intro to Ṣaḥīḥ al-Bukhārī." Seminar at University of Calgary, June 5–7, 2015.

Reinhart, A. Kevin. "Juynbolliana, Gradualism, the Big Bang, and Ḥadīth Study in the Twenty-First Century." *Journal of the American Oriental Society* 130, no. 3 (2010): 413–44.

Ringrose, Kathryn. "The Byzantine Body." In *The Oxford Handbook of Women and Gender in Medieval Europe*, edited by Judith Bennett and Ruth Karras, 362–78. Oxford: Oxford University Press, 2013.

Ritter, Helmut. *The Ocean of the Soul: Men, the World and God in the Stories of Farīd al-Dīn ʿAṭṭār*. Translated by John O'Kane with editorial assistance of Bernd Radtke. Leiden, the Netherlands: Brill, 2013.

Roberts, Allen F., and Mary Nooter Roberts. "Mystical Graffiti and the Refabulation of Dakar." *Africa Today* 54, no. 2 (2008): 51–77.

Robson, J. "al-Bukhārī, Muḥammad b. Ismāʾil." In *Encyclopedia of Islam*, 2nd ed., edited by P. Bearman, Th. Bianquis, et al. Brill Online, 2016.

———. "al-Dārimī." In *Encyclopedia of Islam*, 2nd ed., edited by P. Bearman, Th. Bianquis, et al. Brill Online, 2016.

———. "The Transmission of Ibn Majah's 'Sunan.'" *Journal of Semitic Studies* 3, no. 2 (1958): 129–41.

Romanov, Maxim. "Dreaming Ḥanbalites: Dream-Tales in Prosopographical Dictionaries." In *Dreams and Visions in Islamic Societies*, edited by Özgen Felek and Alexander Knysh, 31–50. Albany: State University of New York Press, 2012.

el-Rouayheb, Khaled. *Before Homosexuality in the Arab-Islamic World, 1500–1800*. Chicago: University of Chicago Press, 2005.

Rubin, Uri. *The Eye of the Beholder: The Life of Muḥammad as Viewed by the Early Muslims—A Textual Analysis*. Princeton, N.J.: Darwin, 1995.

———. "More Light on Muhammad's Pre-existence: Qur'ānic and Post-Qur'ānic Perspectives." In *Books and Written Culture of the Islamic World: Studies Presented to Claude Gillot on the Occasion of His 75th Birthday*, edited by Andrew Rippin and Roberto Tottoli, 288–311. Leiden, the Netherlands: Brill, 2015.

———. "Pre-existence and Light: Aspects of the Concept of Nur Muhammad." *Israel Oriental Studies* 5 (1975): 62–119.

———. "The Seal of the Prophets and the Finality of Prophecy: On the Interpretation of the Qur'anic Surat al-Ahzab (33)." *Zeitschrift der Deutschen Morgenlandischen Gesellschaft* 164, no. 1 (2014): 65–96.

Rustomji, Nerina. *The Garden and the Fire: Heaven and Hell in Islamic Culture*. New York: Columbia University Press, 2009.

Safi, Omid. "Bargaining with Baraka: Persian Sufism, 'Mysticism,' and Pre-modern Politics." *Muslim World* 90, no. 3/4 (2000): 259–88.

———. *The Politics of Knowledge in Premodern Islam: Negotiating Ideology and Religious Inquiry*. Chapel Hill: University of North Carolina Press, 2006.

Sanders, Paula. "Gendering the Ungendered Body: Hermaphrodites in Medieval Islamic Law." In *Women in Middle Eastern History: Shifting Boundaries in Sex and Gender*, edited by Nikki R. Keddie and Beth Baron, 74–96. New Haven, Conn.: Yale University Press, 1991.

Sayeed, Asma. *Women and the Transmission of Religious Knowledge in Islam*. Cambridge: Cambridge University Press, 2013.

Schoeler, Gregor. "Urwa b. al-Zubayr." In *Encyclopedia of Islam*, 2nd ed., edited by P. Bearman, Th. Bianquis, et al. Brill Online, 2016.

Sedgwick, Eve Kosofsky. *Between Men: English Literature and Male Homosocial Desire*. New York: Columbia University Press, 1985.

Shaddel, Mehdy. "'Abd Allah Ibn al-Zubayr and the Mahdi: Between Propaganda and Historical Memory in the Second Civil War." *Bulletin of the School of Oriental and African Studies* 80 (2017): 1–19.

Shahrastānī, Muhammad ibn 'Abd al-Karīm. *Muslim Sects and Divisions: The Section on Muslim Sects in Kitāb al-Milal wa 'l-Niḥal*. Translated by A. K. Kazi and J. G. Flynn. New York: Routledge, 1984.

Shaikh, Sa'diyya. "Knowledge, Women and Gender in the Ḥadīth: A Feminist Interpretation." *Islam and Christian-Muslim Relations* 15, no.1 (January 2004): 99–108.

———. *Sufi Narratives of Intimacy: Ibn 'Arabi, Gender, and Sexuality*. Chapel Hill: University of North Carolina Press, 2012.

Shoemaker, Stephen J. "In Search of 'Urwa's *Sīra*: Some Methodological Issues in the Quest for 'Authenticity' in the Life of Muḥammad." *Der Islam* 85, no. 2 (2011): 257–344.

Sirry, Mun'im. "Muqatil b. Sulayman and Anthropomorphism." *Studia Islamica* 107, no. 1 (2012): 38–64.

Spellberg, D. A. *Politics, Gender, and the Islamic Past: The Legacy of 'A'isha Bint Abi Bakr*. New York: Columbia University Press, 1994.

Stearns, Justin K. *Infectious Ideas: Contagion in Premodern Islamic and Christian Thought in the Western Mediterranean*. Baltimore: John Hopkins University Press, 2011.

Stowasser, Barbara Freyer. *Women in the Qur'an, Traditions, and Interpretation*. Oxford: Oxford University Press, 2011.

Ṣuyūṭī, Jalāl ad-Dīn. *Khasā'is al-Kubra*. Beirut: Dar al-Kotob al-Ilmiyah, 2003.

Ṭabarānī, Abū al-Qāsim Sulaymān. *Al-Mu'jam al-Awsaṭ*. IslamWeb. http://library.islamweb.net/hadith/display_hbook.php?bk_no=475&pid=280455.

———. *Mu'jam al-Kabīr*. Beirut: Dar al-Kutub al-Ilmiyah, 2007.

———. *Musnad al-Shāmīyīn*. IslamWeb. https://library.islamweb.net/hadith/display_hbook.php?bk_no=480&pid=291747.

———. *Mu'jam al-Sughra*. IslamWeb. http://library.islamweb.net/hadith/display_hbook.php?bk_no=476&pid=280759.

Ṭabarī, Abū Ja'far Muḥammad ibn Jarīr. *Tafsīr al-Ṭabarī*. Beirut: Dar Al-Kotob Al-Ilmiyah, 2009.

Ṭayālisī, Abū Dāwūd. *Musnad*. Beirut: Dar Ibn Ḥazm, 2013.

Tirmidhī, Muḥammad ibn ʿĪsā. *Al-Jāmiʾ*. IslamWeb. http://library.islamweb.net/hadith/display_hbook.php?bk_no=195&pid=120459.

———. *Shamāʾil*. IslamWeb. http://library.islamweb.net/hadith/display_hbook.php?bk_no=193&pid=119467.

Tlilli, Sarra. "From Breath to Soul: The Quranic Word *Ruh* and Its (Mis)interpretations." In *Arabic Humanities, Islamic Thought: Essays in Honor of Everett K. Rowson*, edited by Joseph E. Lowry and Shawkat M. Toorawa, 1–21. Leiden, the Netherlands: Brill, 2017.

van Ess, Josef. *The Flowering of Muslim Theology*. Translated by Jane Marie Todd. Cambridge, Mass.: Harvard University Press, 2006.

———. *Theology and Society in the Second and Third Centuries of the Hijra*. Vol. 4. Edited by Gwendolin Goldbloom. Leiden, the Netherlands: Brill, 2018.

———. "Vision and Ascension: *Surat al-Najm* and Its Relationship with Muhammad's *Mir'aj*." *Journal of Qur'anic Studies* 1, no. 1 (1999): 47–62.

———. "The Youthful God: Anthropomorphism in Early Islam." University Lecture in Religion at Arizona State University, 1988.

von Denffer, Dietrich. "Baraka as Basic Concept of Muslim Popular Belief." *Islamic Studies* 15, no. 3 (Autumn 1976): 167–86.

Vorisco, Daniel Martin. "Metaphors and Sacred History: The Genealogy of Muhammad and the Arab 'Tribe.'" *Anthropological Quarterly* 68, no. 3 (July 1995): 139–56.

Vuckovic, Brooke Olson. *Heavenly Journeys, Earthly Concerns: The Legacy of the Mi'raj in the Formation of Islam*. New York: Routledge, 2005.

wadud, amina. *Qur'ān and Woman*. Oxford: Oxford University Press, 1999.

al-Wāqidī, Muḥammad ibn ʿUmar. *The Life of Muḥammad: Al-Wāqidī's Kitāb al-Maghāzī*. Edited by Rizwi Faizer. Translated by Rizwi Faizer, Amal Ismail, and Abdulkader Tayob. New York: Routledge, 2011.

Weheliye, Alexander G. *Habeas Viscus: Racializing Assemblages, Biopolitics, and Black Feminist Theories of the Human*. Durham, N.C.: Duke University Press, 2014.

Williams, Wesley. "Tajalli wa-Ru'ya: A Study of Anthropomorphic Theophany and Visio Dei in the Hebrew Bible, the Qur'an and Early Sunni Islam." PhD diss., University of Michigan, 2008.

Zaman, Muhammad Qasim. "*Maghāzī* and the *Muḥaddithūn*: Reconsidering the Treatment of 'Historical' Materials in Early Collections of Hadith." *International Journal of Middle East Studies* 28 (1996): 1–18.

———. *Religion and Politics under the Early ʿAbbāsids: The Emergence of the Proto-Sunnī Elite*. Leiden, the Netherlands: Brill, 1997.

Ze'evi, Dror. *Producing Desire: Changing Sexual Discourse in the Ottoman Middle East, 1500–1900*. Berkeley: University of California Press, 2006.

Zysk, Kenneth. "Greek and Indian Physiognomics." *Journal of the American Oriental Society* 138, no. 2 (April–June 2018): 313–25.

Index

ISLAMIC CIVILIZATION AND MUSLIM NETWORKS

Michael Muhammad Knight, *Muhammad's Body: Baraka Networks and the Prophetic Assemblage* (2020).

Kelly A. Hammond, *China's Muslims and Japan's Empire: Centering Islam in World War II* (2020).

Zachery V. Wright, *Realizing Islam: The Tijaniyya in North Africa and the Eighteenth-Century Muslim World* (2020).

Alex Dika Seggerman, *Modernism on the Nile: Art in Egypt Between the Islamic and the Contemporary* (2019).

Babak Rahimi and Peyman Eshaghi, *Muslim Pilgrimage in the Modern World* (2019).

Simon Wolfgang Fuchs, *In a Pure Muslim Land: Shiʿism between Pakistan and the Middle East* (2019).

Gary R. Bunt, *Hashtag Islam: How Cyber Islamic Environments Are Transforming Religious Authority* (2018).

Ahmad Dallal, *Islam without Europe: Traditions of Reform in Eighteenth-Century Islamic Thought* (2018).

Irfan Ahmad, *Religion as Critique: Islamic Critical Thinking from Mecca to the Marketplace* (2017).

Scott Kugle, *When Sun Meets Moon: Gender, Eros, and Ecstasy in Urdu Poetry* (2016).

Kishwar Rizvi, *The Transnational Mosque: Architecture, Historical Memory, and the Contemporary Middle East* (2015).

Ebrahim Moosa, *What Is a Madrasa?* (2015).

Bruce Lawrence, *Who Is Allah?* (2015).

Edward E. Curtis IV, *The Call of Bilal: Islam in the African Diaspora* (2014).

Sahar Amer, *What Is Veiling?* (2014).

Rudolph T. Ware III, *The Walking Qur'an: Islamic Education, Embodied Knowledge, and History in West Africa* (2014).

Saʿdiyya Shaikh, *Sufi Narratives of Intimacy: Ibn ʿArabī, Gender, and Sexuality* (2012).

Karen G. Ruffle, *Gender, Sainthood, and Everyday Practice in South Asian Shiʿism* (2011).

Jonah Steinberg, *Ismaʿili Modern: Globalization and Identity in a Muslim Community* (2011).

Iftikhar Dadi, *Modernism and the Art of Muslim South Asia* (2010).

Gary R. Bunt, *iMuslims: Rewiring the House of Islam* (2009).

Fatemeh Keshavarz, *Jasmine and Stars: Reading More Than "Lolita" in Tehran* (2007).

Scott Kugle, *Sufis and Saints' Bodies: Mysticism, Corporeality, and Sacred Power in Islam* (2007).

Roxani Eleni Margariti, *Aden and the Indian Ocean Trade: 150 Years in the Life of a Medieval Arabian Port* (2007).

Sufia M. Uddin, *Constructing Bangladesh: Religion, Ethnicity, and Language in an Islamic Nation* (2006).

Omid Safi, *The Politics of Knowledge in Premodern Islam: Negotiating Ideology and Religious Inquiry* (2006).

Ebrahim Moosa, *Ghazālī and the Poetics of Imagination* (2005).

miriam cooke and Bruce B. Lawrence, eds., *Muslim Networks from Hajj to Hip Hop* (2005).

Carl W. Ernst, *Following Muhammad: Rethinking Islam in the Contemporary World* (2003).

CPSIA information can be obtained
at www.ICGtesting.com
Printed in the USA
LVHW110600020920
664772LV00009B/997

9 781469 658919